Praise for Ben Kaplan and
How to Go to College Almost for Free

"College offers the keys to the kingdom, and Ben Kaplan's brilliant book offers the keys to winning college scholarships—and even going to college for free! This is a must-read book."

> —Mark Victor Hansen
> Co-author, *Chicken Soup for the Soul* series

"If winning college scholarships were a sport, Ben Kaplan would surely be in the Hall of Fame. Ben's exceptional book, *How to Go to College Almost for Free*, takes students step by step through the process of finding and winning scholarship money in an informing, entertaining, and inspiring way. Ben made it happen, and he shows how anyone in pursuit of college cash can make it happen too."

> —Stedman Graham
> Author, *You Can Make It Happen*

"Ben Kaplan's practical experience is an invaluable resource for anyone trying to scrape together money for college tuition in the face of skyrocketing prices. Ben demonstrates, through his own personal example, that the proof is literally in the author! His advice really does get results—unleashing the potential not just to attend college, but to attend almost any college practically for free. Anyone seeking higher education in America, young and old, should entertain Kaplan's advice, not only for financial reasons, but also to share in the greater lesson he has to offer—anything is possible if you put your mind to it!"

> —U.S. Senator John F. Kerry

"A talk-show and bookstore favorite."

> —*The New York Times*

"[Ben speaks] with an energy and confidence that might remind an older generation of Dale Carnegie."

> —*Seattle Post-Intelligencer*

"Ben's book provides great advice for students seeking scholarships, especially merit-based scholarships. In fact, several key chapters will not only help students seek money for college, but will also help them to become more successful in other important aspects of their lives."

> —Dr. William C. Nelsen
> President, Citizens' Scholarship Foundation of America

"What Dr. Ruth does for the human libido, Ben aims to do for the tuition subsidy."
—*The Boston Globe*

"A terrific example of a proactive person choosing to make it happen. . . . Great tips for college aspirants."
—Sean Covey
Author, *The 7 Habits of Highly Effective Teens*

"One of the hottest self-help authors on the market today."
—*Heritage Newspapers*

"If you want to win scholarship money, then go with a winner. Ben Kaplan won several of our scholarships, and many others. His book speaks directly to students in their language, with practical tips and interesting insights into the 'winning attitude.'"
—Rocco Marano, Director of Student Activities
National Association of Secondary School Principals

"Ben's the man! Everyone who has a kid to send to college will be hanging on his every word. . . . In mere minutes, Ben will save you thousands of dollars in tuition payments. Ben did it himself, and he'll show you exactly how to do it too. He knows."
—Steve Harmon and Scott Evans
Co-hosts, WXTU-FM radio

"The story of how a kid from Oregon became an Ivy League economics grad and pied piper of cash for class is an epic testament to those time-tested American virtues of hard work [and] persistence."
—*Orlando Sentinel*

"Ben possesses such wonderful information and enthusiasm. . . . He may be the next Tony Robbins."
—Russell Scott
Host, KOAI-FM radio

"If you are looking for something that includes everything you need to know about this [college scholarships] game, you will find this book very useful. . . . It's obvious Kaplan put a lot of hard work into writing this guide."
—*The Richmond Times-Dispatch*

"Benjamin's book is simply outstanding. It's full of so much useful information. . . . Every student and parent should read it cover to cover."
—Ben Davis and Patty Dee
Co-hosts, KMXC-FM radio

"I hadn't been looking forward to all of the reading, writing, and research that I need to do, but once I started reading Ben's book, I became, more or less, fascinated. I couldn't put the book down! . . . It's amazing how much a person can learn from another person's experiences."

— Emily Crawford, High School Student

"Every once in a while, a book comes along that is remarkably insightful, expertly written, and that addresses a pressing need in a bold and innovative way—a book destined to change the lives of everyone who reads it. *How to Go to College Almost for Free* is indeed such a book—a true classic in its field."

— Jerry Jenkins
    Author, *Inside the Bestsellers*

"*How to Go to College Almost for Free* is truly an exceptional book—the 'bible' for anyone who needs help in paying for college."

— Jim Barnes
    Editor, *Independent Publisher* magazine

"Because of Ben's book I was able to help my daughter get a full scholarship to the University of Alaska! Thanks for all the hints and tips! They worked!"

— Janet Bowser, Parent

"I can't even begin to say thank you for this wonderful book."

— Randi Johnson, Student

"Ben's book is awesome. I haven't been able to put it down. Even my daughter who hates to read has started the book and now has hope that she can make it into the college of her dreams."

— Danielle A. Wagner, Parent

"For the sake of your college bound child, don't say that you 'almost' read this book—your young student could be missing an important lifetime opportunity for higher education! Take advantage of Mr. Kaplan's research and personal experience, written in a highly readable format that both you and your child will navigate with confidence."

— Pat Jermov, Parent

HOW TO GO TO
COLLEGE
Almost
FOR
FREE

HOW TO GO TO

COLLEGE

Almost FOR

FREE

The Secrets of Winning
Scholarship Money

BEN
KAPLAN

HarperResource
An Imprint of HarperCollins*Publishers*

SECOND EDITION

Designed by: Stratford Publishing Services, Brattleboro, Vermont
Waggle Dancer Media, Inc., Gleneden Beach, Oregon

Ben Kaplan also conducts seminars, workshops, and other events. For more information visit: **www.BenKaplan.com**

Trademarks and Permissions: All brand names, product names, and services used in this book are trademarks, registered trademarks, service marks, or trade names of their respective holders. *How to Go to College Almost for Free, The Scholarship Scouting Report,* Scholarship Coach, the Scholarship Coach Search Profile Worksheet, Ask the Scholarship Coach, Ask the Coach, and ScholarshipCoach.com along with their associated logos, are all trademarks of Waggle Dancer Media, Inc.

Disclaimers: The author, Ben Kaplan, has no affiliation with Kaplan Educational Centers or Kaplan Books, neither of which has endorsed this publication. Although the author is a graduate of Harvard, the information in this book is not endorsed by Harvard University. *How to Go to College Almost for Free* should not in any way be construed as a representation or warranty that the reader will achieve this result. This book is designed to provide accurate and authoritative information in regard to the subject matter covered. The author and the publisher, however, make no representation or warranties of any kind with regard to the completeness or accuracy of the contents herein and accept no liability of any kind. Furthermore, this book is sold with the understanding that neither the author nor the publisher is engaged in rendering legal, accounting, or other professional service. If legal advice or other expert assistance is required, the services of a competent professional person should be sought. Any advice given about how to win specific scholarship contests is solely the opinion of the author, and is not endorsed by any individuals or organizations affiliated with these programs.

Library of Congress Cataloging-in-Publication Data
Kaplan, Benjamin R.
    How to go to college almost for free : the secrets of winning scholarship money / Ben Kaplan.—2nd ed.
      p. cm.
    Includes index.
    ISBN 0-06-093765-3 (Pbk.)
    1. Scholarships—United States—Handbooks, manuals, etc.   I. Title.

LB2338 .K36 2002

378.3′4′0973—dc21   2001024822

07 RRD 17

Use of Companion Web Resources

Purchasers of this book are granted access to an interactive Coach's Locker Room located at **www.ScholarshipCoach.com** on the World Wide Web. Follow the directions in the Coach's Locker Room box on the ScholarshipCoach.com home page, and when prompted for an access password, enter the following code:

COACH236527526A

To Mom and Dad —

whose recipe for love and encouragement
demonstrates that they are indeed master chefs.

Acknowledgments

If winning scholarships is a game, then writing a book about winning scholarships is a no-holds-barred, in-your-face, full-contact team sport. I'd like to take this opportunity to give a round of applause to the many individuals and organizations who were invaluable members of this team.

First of all, I'd like to thank Laureen "Wonder Agent" Rowland for being such a strong believer in and supporter of this book, and for contributing endless supplies of energy, creativity, optimism, determination, and panache. Thanks, Laureen, for taking my calls at 2:00 A.M. and still doing your best to sound fully awake. You know what kind of genius you are!

I'd also like to thank all of the good folks at HarperCollins Publishers who played such an important role in the success of this new edition:

> Adrian "Phoenix" Zackheim and Megan "Lightning" Newman, for their vision in taking on this project, their belief in the potential of this book to help change lives, and the leap of faith they showed in me.

> Joe "Thunder" Veltre, for shepherding the new edition of this book through to completion, contributing many helpful suggestions, and making sure all the trains ran on time.

> Kate Stark, for her many marketing insights and suggestions. Thanks for all your help, Kate!

> Chin-Yee Lai, for all of her hard work and creativity in developing the new book cover.

> Shelby "High Roller" Meizlik, for being such a strong promoter and advocate of this book.

> Sarah "Nick" Beam, for coordinating many logistical matters facing this project and always being a friendly, cheerful voice on the other end of the phone.

> Kim Burns, Leah Carlson-Stanisic, Kristin Fassler, Jane Friedman, Cathy Hemming, Keith Pfeffer, Maura Raphael, Laurie Rippon, and Suzie Sisoler, for all of their efforts on behalf of this book.

In addition to the people at HarperCollins, many other individuals made key contributions to this book. My thanks goes out to:

Kurt Mueller for the many wonderful drawings, graphics, and illustrations he created. (Did somebody say "gorilla"?)

Arlon Gilliland for his terrific Scholarship Coach drawings. (By now I think you have my cheekbones memorized!)

Roger Swanton for his artistic eye and design expertise. (Let's jam on the guitar sometime, Roger!)

Deborah Klenotic for all of the time and energy she invested and fresh perspective she brought to the design and production of this book.

Luca Pioltelli for his great front cover photo and Colin Park for his fun shots of me and my family, including the back cover photo. Thanks guys for always shooting my "good side!"

Everyone at Waggle Dancer Media for their truly outstanding research and development work. I'd like to especially thank Gary Michaels, Pat Rattan, and Mike Dudley.

Not only am I thankful for the many people who have contributed directly to this book, but I am also eternally grateful to all who have assisted in my scholarship quest:

My heartfelt appreciation goes out to the many organizations, foundations, corporations, and individuals whose scholarship programs helped turn my educational dreams into reality. Your generosity has made all the difference in the world.

I would like to extend special thanks to everyone at South Eugene High School. So many of you have provided me with numerous opportunities, encouraged me to do my best, and always supported me on my scholarship journey. Deserving special mention are Sue Barr, Lynne George, Larry Perry, and Chuck Vaughn, without whom none of this would have been possible.

And, of course, to my friends and family:

High-fives go out to Harvard buddies and roommates Daniel "The Peruvian Prince" Alarco, Sid "Kristen called" Burke, "Cowboy" Clay Cowan, and Greg "G-Force" Lau for constantly harassing me about not having the first edition of this book finished. A special thanks goes out to Greg for allowing me to bounce plenty of book ideas off him.

A big thank you goes out to Uncle Skip and Aunt Ellen for their unending support and encouragement. I always look forward to our visits and conversations!

Much love and gratitude go out to Grandma and Grandpa, who read an early version of this book and provided very helpful comments. How 'bout those Las Vegas editors!

A standing ovation is in order for Grandma E, my beloved book cheerleader, for all of her love, support, and radiant smiles!

No acknowledgments would be complete without thanking Dudley, my very ferocious canine sidekick who scared away countless numbers of evil book saboteurs with his menacing bark and intimidating seven-pound frame.

Most of all, I'd like to thank my parents for all of their support in making this project a success. Everything I have ever done, or will ever do, I owe to them.

What's Inside

"The Game"   xvii
Let the Games Begin!   1

PART I: HOW THE GAME IS PLAYED

CHAPTER 1:   **The Big, Bad World of Financial Aid**   23

Exploding Seven Scholarship Myths   24
Demystifying the Lingo   30
Need Versus Merit   33
Other Forms of Financial Aid   44
The Importance of Merit-Based Awards   55
Chapter 1 Summary and Keywords   56

CHAPTER 2:   **Rules of the Merit Money Game**   59

A Game for Everyone   60
The Scholarship Funders   67
The Scholarship Administrators   72
Application Judges   73
Targeted Scholarship Awards   74
Scholarship Application Components   79
Steer Clear of (Most) Entry Fees   84
Spending Your Merit Scholarships   85
Chapter 2 Summary and Keywords   87

CHAPTER 3:   **What Parents Can Do to Help**   91

Seven Ways Parents Can Help   92
Helping with Scholarship Searching   93
Strategizing with Your Kids   95
Providing Research Assistance   96
Keeping Things Organized   97
Being a Good Sounding Board   97
Reviewing the Application   98
Giving Support and Encouragement   100
Chapter 3 Summary and Keywords   103

CHAPTER 4:   **Finding Your Own Pot of Gold**   **107**

The Scholarship Rainbow   108
Five Principles of Scholarship Searching   108
Ten "Show Me the Money" Action Steps   114
Action Step #1: Assemble Your
    Scholarship Search Tools   115
Action Step #2: Tap Into Your School's
    Resources   116
Action Step #3: Search Scholarship
    Databases   119
Action Step #4: Politely Raid Other
    Schools' Resources   148
Action Step #5: Canvas Your Community   149
Action Step #6: Seek Out Government
    Sources   152
Action Step #7: Pursue All Personal and
    Family Affiliations   154
Action Step #8: Apply Effective Internet
    Search Techniques   156
Action Step #9: Uncover School-
    Specific Awards   161
Action Step #10: Seek Out Related
    Organizations   165
Chapter 4 Summary and Keywords   169

PART III: STRATEGIES THAT GIVE YOU THE EDGE

CHAPTER 5:   **Painting Your Own Portrait**   **175**

Knowing the Person   176
The Painter's Touch   177
Employing Your Theme   181
Nine Winning Themes   185
Finding Your Theme   195
Chapter 5 Summary and Keywords   195

CHAPTER 6: **Positioning Strategies** 197

Scoring Points 198
Considering Your Competitors 205
Ten Universal Judging Criteria 207
Chapter 6 Summary and Keywords 215

CHAPTER 7: **Content Strategies** 217

Scholarship Bodybuilding 218
Analyzing Depth and Width 219
The Essential Content Strategies 220
All About Academics 228
Chapter 7 Summary and Keywords 233

PART IV: WHEN THE WHISTLE BLOWS

CHAPTER 8: **A Winning Game Plan** 237

Eight Principles of Effective Scholarship
    Campaigns 238
Chapter 8 Summary and Keywords 251

CHAPTER 9: **Essay Excellence** 253

Five Principles of Winning Essays 254
Spanning Topics and Recycling Essays 261
Finding Your Own Voice 266
Getting in the Flow 270
Honing Your Essay 273
Advice for Specific Topics 278
Short Answer Questions 281
Chapter 9 Summary and Keywords 283

CHAPTER 10: **Glowing Recommendation Letters** 285

In Search of Perfect Recommendations 286
Star Witnesses 287
Five "Great Recommendation"
    Action Steps 287
Qualities of a Great Letter 299
Chapter 10 Summary and Keywords 303

CHAPTER 11: **Filling in the Blanks** 305

Paperwork Prowess 306
The Stat Sheet 310
Activity Lists 311
Awards and Honors Lists 314
The Transcript 315
Additional Materials 319
Mailing Your Application 320
Chapter 11 Summary and Keywords 321

CHAPTER 12: **Acing the Interview** 323

Interview Mastery 324
Preparing for the Interview 324
The Big Day 332
The Main Event 334
Chapter 12 Summary and Keywords 338

PART V: WHEN THE BUZZER SOUNDS

CHAPTER 13: **Parting Shots** 343

The Home Stretch 344
Keeping Track of Your Winnings 344
Using Testing to Slash College Costs 349
What We've Learned 353

THE APPENDICES

APPENDIX A: **Scholarship Coach Search Profile Worksheet** 355

APPENDIX B: **State Agency Contacts** 357

APPENDIX C: **ScholarshipCoach.com Keyword Master List** 363

INDEX: 367

ASK THE COACH

#1 For the purpose of financial aid how do I "demonstrate need"? **34**

#2 What does "merit" really mean? **35**

#3 How would winning merit scholarships affect the financial aid package a college offers me? **43**

#4 What are prepaid-tuition and college-savings plans? **46**

#5 If I can get an athletic scholarship, should I still pursue merit awards? **51**

#6 Can homeschoolers do anything to become eligible for more college scholarships? **62**

#7 Are there scholarships for distance learning? **67**

#8 Do U.S. government agencies provide scholarship funds? **68**

#9 When do most scholarship deadlines occur? **84**

#10 Is scholarship money taxable? **86**

#11 How can I motivate my child to pursue scholarships? **99**

#12 Should I pay others to help me find scholarships? **130**

#13 Can graduate students find scholarships and fellowships in online databases? **134**

#14 Are there any special scholarship databases for minority students? **139**

#15 What Internet resources are available for Canadian students? **144**

#16 How do I find scholarships for study abroad? **147**

#17 Are there any special ways to find scholarships for students with disabilities? **155**

#18 Are there special search strategies for adult returning students? **160**

#19 What are some top school-specific scholarships for incoming freshmen? **163**

#20 How can international students find scholarships to study in the U.S.? **167**

#21 Do scholarship judges look at college students differently than high school students? **223**

#22 What can younger students do to prepare for winning scholarships?   **227**

#23 Should I still apply for scholarships that are very tough to win?   **242**

#24 How much time must I invest to win scholarships?   **249**

#25 Are word limits for essays strictly enforced?   **259**

#26 Can scholarship recommendation letters be used for college applications?   **290**

#27 How can homeschoolers submit grade transcripts to scholarship contests?   **317**

#28 What should I do differently in a scholarship interview conducted by phone?   **337**

SPECIAL FEATURES

GUERRILLA TACTICS

Work Your School's Scholarship Center   **118**

Search Source Databases First   **125**

Explore a Variety of Scholarship Databases   **126**

Travel the Internet to Scout Other Schools   **149**

Interview Local Bank Managers   **152**

Follow the Internet Bread Crumb Trail   **159**

Tailor Your Materials for a Perfect Fit   **204**

Work to Highlight Key Personal Qualities   **214**

Patch Holes in Your Résumé   **224**

Make Your Homework Count   **247**

Trust Your Ear to Help You Edit   **277**

Collect an Assortment of Recommendation Letters   **290**

Capture Recommendations on Disk   **297**

Expand Activity Descriptions to Fill Blank Space   **308**

Append School Transcripts with Extra Information   **317**

Place Supplementary Materials with Interviewers   **332**

KEY TO ICONS IN THIS BOOK

The following icons appear throughout the book and identify sections of special interest to particular categories of readers.

 Adults going back to school (age 25 or older)

 Students attending graduate school

 Parents of scholarship seekers

 Students from ethnic minority groups

 Students age 15 or younger

 Students studying abroad

 Students participating in sports

 Students from other countries

 Students attending home school

▌ THE GAME

Winning scholarships is a game—

A game with high stakes and huge rewards.

To succeed, you must learn the rules and understand the players.

You must internalize the principles, strategies, and guerrilla tactics that lead to victory.

Then it's a matter of preparing, practicing, and perfecting: Enhancing your record in key areas, strengthening your self-promotional skills, and refining your application materials.

And when the whistle blows you'll be ready.

And when the buzzer sounds you'll have won.

Winning scholarships is a game.

The best way to master the game is to learn from someone who has played it well.

Let the
Games
Begin!

▌ How It All Began

In the twentysomething movie *Reality Bites,* a jobless and penniless college valedictorian named Lelaina Pierce (played by the charming Winona Ryder) discovers, among other things, just how much mini-mart food she can buy on her father's gas card. And several years ago, I found myself in a related predicament. No, it wasn't that I shopped at the corner gas station. Nor did I have a taste for Chevron cuisine.

Rather, it was that reality had just bitten *me*—and bitten me hard. It happened one day during my junior year in high school, as I was leafing through glossy college catalogs with dreams of wild collegiate adventures dancing in my head. Suddenly, I felt the reality of having to *pay* for my undergraduate education sink its ugly teeth.

Growing up, I had always assumed that I would go to college on a tennis scholarship. Then a stress fracture in my lower back took me away from competitive play for nearly 18 months. And although I fully recuperated from the injury, and returned to the junior tennis rankings, I had fallen behind my former tennis rivals. I soon realized that the only tennis scholarships available to me would be at colleges I had absolutely no desire to attend.

What I hoped to do was enroll at a top university, but how would I ever pay the six-figure tab at the school of my choice? Would I have to put my educational dreams on hold? Even if I could somehow cover the cost, was it my destiny to be buried alive beneath a mountain of student debt?

Granted, this wasn't a memorable scene from a slick Hollywood movie, but still, it was *my life.* And unlike Lelaina, I didn't have my father's gas card. Even if I did, the corner Chevron station didn't have any diplomas for sale.

REALITY BITES . . .
BUT IT DOESN'T HAVE TO

One day at my high school's college and career center, however, I came across a stack of colorful applications for a nationwide scholarship program called the Discover Card Tribute Awards. As I held the application in my hands, my mind raced with questions. Were there a lot of scholarship programs like this one? Could I win them? Did a kid from a public high school in Eugene, Oregon, actually have a chance? There was probably some child prodigy out there who had mastered calculus at age 5, won Olympic gold at 9, and discovered a cure for cancer before hitting puberty.

Despite my doubts, I decided to give the scholarship application a try. So I wrote a couple of short essays, diligently filled out the forms, and rounded up a few letters of recommendation. Sending in the application was something like entering the Publishers Clearing House Sweepstakes. Sure, I hoped for the best, but I didn't exactly expect the Prize Patrol to come knocking on my door.

A couple months passed. Then I got a letter in the mail that changed my life: "Congratulations," it said, "you've just won a $2,500 scholarship." The story gets better. A few weeks later, I received a phone call notifying me that in addition to the first award on the state level, I had just won another $15,000 in the national portion of the scholarship contest! You should have seen my parents dancing around the house!

Then I made another life-altering discovery: Plenty of other corporations, associations, organizations, institutions, and community groups can't wait to give away college money. So I filled out more forms, crafted more essays, gathered more recommendation letters, and started expanding my involvement in school and community activities. Through a process of trial and error, I formulated winning strategies, developed step-by-step

Who says "big"
scholarship money
isn't out there?

*I graduated from Harvard
University in 1999 with a
degree, appropriately
enough, in economics.*

procedures, and perfected a set of "guerrilla tactics." The scholarship checks started pouring in . . .

Don't get me wrong—it wasn't as if I just threw together some application materials and money started falling from the sky. (We can wish, can't we?) Applying for these awards took a good bit of work, and I lost my share of scholarship contests, too. But by sticking with the process, staying focused on my goals, and keeping a positive outlook, I ended up reaping enormous rewards.

By the time I headed off to college, I had applied for about three dozen merit scholarships, won more than two dozen of them, and amassed nearly $90,000 in scholarship winnings—funds that I could use at any school I desired. Thanks to these funds and some college credit I had earned in high school, virtually the entire cost of my Harvard education was covered.

BITING BACK

So is applying for scholarships worth the effort? Definitely! I'm living proof of it. Can *you* win money, too? You bet! It does, however, take some acquired knowledge and a bit of old-fashioned elbow grease. What's the best way to get started? Read this book! You will then be well equipped to find among the many thousands of organizations that give away billions of dollars enough college cash awards to help make your educational dreams come true.

Several years ago, when I faced the daunting task of trying to pay for my own college education, there wasn't anyone out there to show me the ropes. Trial and error became my mentor. But it doesn't have to be that way for you, because you are now holding the definitive "how-to-play" book on the scholarship game—the book I wish I had when I stepped out on the field my rookie year.

Now I can't guarantee that you'll pay for *all* of your college expenses by winning college scholarships (doing so also takes some luck), but with your hard work and determination plus my guidance, you can make a significant dent in your financial burden.

Reality may indeed bite, but winning college scholarships can help enterprising students bite back.

▌ HOW I BECAME THE SCHOLARSHIP COACH

Once my scholarship application adventures were over, and I was a sleep-deprived Harvard student, I had a chance to reflect on all that I had learned from my incredible journey. I realized that I had been extremely blessed in every sense of the word: I had discovered merit scholarships accidentally, and that discovery had

Fortunately, by this point I had enough money to virtually cover my entire education. If I hadn't done so, however, there were plenty of scholarships for undergraduates that I could have applied for. Playing the game does not have to stop unless you want it to.

changed my life. I thought about how different my situation would have been if I hadn't stumbled upon that first scholarship application.

So I decided to offer others some pointers based on my own experience. Editors at both the *New York Times* and *U.S. News & World Report* believed I had something important to say, and gave me the opportunity to write articles on the subject for their publications.

A funny thing happened when my articles hit newsstands: I started getting hundreds of e-mails at my college dorm room, with students and parents from all over the world asking for advice on how to win college scholarships and tap into additional sources of financial aid. I began the daunting task of writing back, fitting it in between classes, extracurricular activities, and searching for quarters to do my laundry. Because everyone I wrote to seemed to appreciate the advice I offered, I kept at it—and finally decided to write a book on the subject. In fact, those e-mail responses eventually became the first drafts of some chapters in the first edition of this book.

Wanting the book to be based on more than just my own experiences, I set out to interview dozens of other scholarship winners and distill *their* core secrets, too. I discovered that many of the same strategies and tactics that had worked for me had worked for them as well. I also interviewed numerous scholarship application judges and scholarship program administrators, and pored over countless winning applications—and plenty that were not successful—to learn what to do and what *not* to do. Although no university that I know of offers a Ph.D. in Scholarship Science, I tried my best to merit the make-believe degree. (Unfortunately, you can't hang imaginary degrees on your wall.)

After the first edition of this book was published, I again found myself overwhelmed by an ever increasing stack of e-mail messages and letters that posed questions, contained scholarship essays for review, and thanked me for writing a book that had helped so many students and families earn college cash. I started conducting scholarship workshops at schools and bookstores in several states; produced regular columns, features, and scholarship essay critiques for some of the leading scholarship websites; answered caller questions on radio and television shows; and began work on creating my own website for scholarship advice. Such was my serendipitous, yet fateful, journey from scholarship seeker to scholarship adviser. Before I knew it, I had become, as some on the Internet and in the press started calling me, the "Scholarship Coach."

❘ THE JOURNEY TO A NEW EDITION

In the fall of 2000, my metaphorical scholarship journey became a literal one as I set out on my first annual Scholarship Coach National Tour, a 7-week, 25-city nationwide trek. The goal: Conduct free scholarship workshops from coast to coast, and provide students, parents, and families with a roadmap for financing college, as well as the knowledge, skills, and opportunities to mount their own scholarship campaigns. Thanks to my tour sponsor, I had at my disposal a 40-foot custom motor coach for much of the tour. So I cruised from stop to stop, trying my best to inform, inspire, and not get a speeding ticket!

Before and after many of my tour workshops, I had the opportunity to meet and advise many high school, college, graduate, and adult returning students, as well as a host of interested parents. These interactions gave me an even better

Hey, that's my book on the side of the bus! This cool tour bus was provided by my sponsor, wiredscholar.com.

During the tour, I surveyed parents about their opinions on educational and financial matters. Virtually all of the parents surveyed said they were willing to devote significant time to help their children pursue scholarships. Good job, parents!

sense of the type of information the current crop of scholarship seekers need to know most. Quite frankly, I learned as much from these personal coaching interactions as (I hope) the workshop attendees learned from me.

In addition, I initiated the tour's college scholarship program, which gave me the greatest thrill of all: the opportunity to give away ten $1,000 scholarship awards. Student applications, consisting mostly of short personal essays on key life experiences, started flooding in from all over the country. Along with the program's judges, I scanned them with eager eyes. Reviewing these submissions from the perspective of a scholarship judge helped me better understand the scholarship application areas that most students needed help with and isolate the mis-

Hanging out after a scholarship workshop on Homecoming Day with students from Centennial High School in Circle Pines, Minnesota.

takes that all but the best scholarship applicants repeatedly made.

When the dust settled, I knew that I wanted to incorporate all of the things I had learned and new insights I had gained into a revised edition of the book. I also wanted to uncover more research techniques and application strategies for a perpetually widening range of college and university attendees with an ever more specific list of considerations and concerns. Such individuals included adult returning students, grad students, Canadian students, student-athletes, international students, students with disabilities, minority students, and U.S. students wishing to study abroad. The result has been this spankin' new edition of *How to Go to College Almost for Free,* revised and improved in every way.

■ WHO SHOULD READ THIS BOOK

This book is for *any* student in search of scholarship money for higher education, including students currently enrolled in high school, trade and technical schools, community colleges, four-year colleges and universities, distance learning programs, and graduate school. The book is also ideal for adults wanting to go back to school or change careers, interested parents, and younger students wanting to get an early start. Furthermore, the topics covered in this book are of special importance to families caught in the "middle-income financial aid crunch"—the dilemma families face when they have too much income to qualify for substantial need-based financial aid but not enough money to comfortably pay off mounting college tuition bills. This book will teach all of these individuals how to win unrestricted merit scholarships—funds awarded on the basis of merit that students can use at the institution of their choice—as well as school-specific scholarship awards.

If you're a junior or senior in high school, the material in this book will provide you with a powerful set of tools for winning your fair share of the cornucopia of scholarships available to you in the next year or two. Indeed, a tremendous amount of scholarship money is available to students about to embark on their college careers.

Likewise, if you're already enrolled in college and could benefit from additional funds, this book is for you. I'll show you how to stake your claim to the huge number of scholarships targeted at college freshmen, sophomores, juniors, and seniors. Furthermore, the tactics detailed in this book are essential strategies to use when applying for fellowships, grants, and scholarships for graduate-level work.

If you're an adult returning to school, you'll learn how you can tap into the same scholarships that 18- to 22-year-old undergraduates apply for, how to uncover money awards specifically for older learners, and how to use your years out of school to your advantage. (I'm guessing you probably have some more interesting life experiences to share than your average MTV-reared 18-year-old.)

Finally, if you're a high school freshman or sophomore, or even in middle school, you may reap the most dramatic monetary results from this book. A surprisingly large number of scholarship contests are geared toward younger students. But more important than the immediate scholarship options is the chance for younger students to position themselves early for scholarship winnings (and other exciting opportunities) in later years. I didn't begin my search until late in my junior year of high school, but if I could do it all over again, I would start preparing for scholarships as early as seventh or eighth grade.

This book is also designed to appeal to students with a broad range of backgrounds, achievements, and interests. If you've had a rocky academic history, I'll show you how to distinguish yourself in other ways. If you have particular vocational or career goals, I'll detail creative methods for demonstrating passion and talent in a field. If you've been confronted with significant obstacles in your life, you'll learn how to use these challenges to demonstrate courage and determination, creating a powerfully compelling story in the process. If you attend a high school with fewer opportunities and resources than other schools, you'll find ways to create your own opportunities, and piggyback on outside resources. If you're hoping to attend one of the nation's most competitive colleges (such as an Ivy League school), I'll show you how to round out your résumé and turn your best skills into standout talents.

▌ WHY YOU NEED THIS BOOK

When I immersed myself in my own scholarship quest, I knew that I needed to win numerous scholarships if I were to cover the big-time costs of a well-respected private school. And because, like most students, I lacked a singularly amazing achievement, developing superior application strategies was critical. So I ventured out to libraries and bookstores, looking for anything to give me an edge. What I soon discovered was that the typical scholarship book was not much more than a directory with listings comprised mostly of contact information for specialized scholarships that most students aren't eligible to apply for. It was more like a hefty phonebook than a step-by-step guide—more useful as a doorstop than a financial aid toolbox. What these books did offer in the way of guidance was extremely vague and not much more than common sense.

Unfortunately, the financial climate is becoming even more scorching: College tuition has been increasing at a rate of 5–7 percent per year.

Furthermore, most books were written from the perspective of an educator or college admissions officer. Although such an approach may help readers understand the judge's point of view, it tells them nothing about the winning techniques and behind-the-scenes strategies that successful scholarship applicants have used.

Consequently, books were not a big help in my money quest. None of the many books I read even recognized that success in this venture is not something that you automatically know how to do, but rather an acquired skill. I had to discover this on my own. In light of this fact, it is no wonder that the same schools and communities— the ones in which past scholarship winners have grown up and passed on this critical information—have dominated scholarship awards ceremonies year after year.

This book is the culmination of my attempt to level the playing field by centralizing the critical strategies, tactics, and techniques of winning scholarships into one accessible volume. Of course, you could try to teach yourself through experimentation, like I did. But why reinvent the wheel when you don't have to? You can save yourself plenty of time, energy, and frustration by learning from the high scorers—the students who have played the game well.

By following the advice contained in these pages, you can avoid many of the mistakes some scholarship seekers (including me) have made, and can learn from our

> "To know the road ahead, ask those coming back."
>
> *—Chinese Proverb*

greatest successes. Throughout these pages, I'll be your personal scholarship coach, helping you to build on the things you've already done, identify the strategies that are best for you, and then enhance your applications in key areas to achieve maximum results in minimum time. How do you avoid getting overwhelmed by the size of the task before you? I'll show you how to focus on the small things you need to do *now*, rather than dwell on all the stuff that might come *later*. This is the essence of an action step: A small, achievable goal that gets you quickly moving along the path of success. Throughout the book you'll encounter action steps to get you through each phase of the process.

Winning scholarships may be a game, but it's a game that can be learned—and learned quickly, too.

▮ FEATURES OF THIS BOOK

Several features of this book are designed to make the material especially useful. Because I believe in being as specific as possible, the book is chock-full of examples. I've reprinted many examples from my own scholarship applications—including a lot of winning material from scholarship applications that many of you are likely to fill out yourselves.

Throughout this new edition you'll also find 28 "Ask the Coach" boxes, in which I answer the most frequently asked and thought-provoking questions posed to me during my Scholarship Coach National Tour workshops and on my ScholarshipCoach.com website. (You'll be able to recognize these special sections by looking for the graphic shown left.) You'll undoubtedly find that many of these questions are the very ones you've been asking. A list of the "Ask the Coach" boxes and the pages on which they appear is given in the table of contents and in the index.

I've also taken great pains, in this new edition, to make the sections on searching for scholarships the most up-to-date and comprehensive information on the planet (or any other planet). After logging hundreds of hours on the Web searching for scholarships, I have substantially expanded or entirely revamped sections on Internet scholarship sleuthing. I've profiled the leading scholarship databases and rated each one on key criteria so you'll know what to expect and be able to spend your time where it counts.

Keep in mind that sections not identified by icons (most sections) are important to all types of scholarship seekers.

To avoid the one-size-fits-all approach found in most how-to books, I have included sections outlining custom-tailored resources and strategies for particular groups of applicants. To help you find the material especially relevant to you, I've included icons in the left margins (like the ones shown here) that identify sections of special importance to specific types of scholarship seekers. I've included icons for parents, graduate students, adult returning students, younger students (age 15 or younger), international students, minority students, homeschoolers, student-athletes, and students who wish to study abroad. A depiction of all nine icons can be found in the table of contents.

Sixteen "Guerrilla Tactics" also appear throughout the book. Guerrilla Tactics are unconventional, yet extremely effective, techniques that will give you a competitive edge over other scholarship seekers. You'll find these Guerrilla Tactics alongside one of the many gorilla (pun totally intended!) graphics found in the book, such as the one shown on the right. A list of the Guerrilla Tactics and the pages on which they appear is given in the table of contents and index.

Each chapter concludes with a Chapter Summary that distills its main points. The summaries reinforce, in a compact way, the book's most important concepts and provide a Jiminy Cricket–like reminder checklist that you can repeatedly refer back to.

THE COACH'S LOCKER ROOM

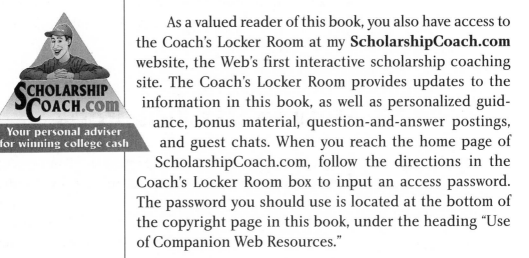

As a valued reader of this book, you also have access to the Coach's Locker Room at my **ScholarshipCoach.com** website, the Web's first interactive scholarship coaching site. The Coach's Locker Room provides updates to the information in this book, as well as personalized guidance, bonus material, question-and-answer postings, and guest chats. When you reach the home page of ScholarshipCoach.com, follow the directions in the Coach's Locker Room box to input an access password. The password you should use is located at the bottom of the copyright page in this book, under the heading "Use of Companion Web Resources."

SCHOLARSHIPCOACH.COM KEYWORDS

As you read each chapter, you'll see references to all sorts of scholarship programs and contests. If a particular scholarship sounds interesting and you want to find out more about it, you'll definitely want to take advantage of the "ScholarshipCoach.com Keywords" I've included in this edition. As part of the chapter summary that concludes each chapter, I list each scholarship mentioned in the chapter and assign it a keyword. (For example, the keyword for the Discover Card Tribute Awards is DISCOVER.)

All you have to do is visit the Coach's Locker Room at ScholarshipCoach.com, and type a keyword into the keyword link box. Seconds later, information about the scholarship, including contact information, will appear. The great thing about this feature is that because I constantly update the website you will always have the latest information at your disposal.

I've also included in this book keywords for a variety of special topics and bonus material that you will definitely want to check out. These subject-specific keywords not only are listed at the end of the chapter, but also are referenced in margin notes. For an alphabetical list of all the ScholarshipCoach.com keywords contained in this book, see Appendix C.

■ How to Use This Book

I recommend first skimming the entire book to get a general sense of where we're headed. You may even want to read all of the chapter summaries first to get an overview of the book's major points and concepts. Then you will want to read the chapters in the order presented, since each chapter builds on the previous ones. If you want to skip to a topic of special interest, use the table of contents or check out the index.

If you're already familiar with how merit scholarship applications work, and you're eager to get going right away, you may want to jump to Chapter 4, which takes you step by step through the process of conducting your own personalized scholarship search. Don't forget to come back to earlier chapters, however, since they will provide you with a good sense of the overall scholarship and financial aid landscape and contain important information for parents.

THE SCHOLARSHIP SCOUTING REPORT

Nearly 90 percent of students and parents surveyed during my first national tour said they were extremely frustrated with those thick, but mostly unusable, scholarship directories—just like I was. Chances are, most of you feel the same way.

In response, I've written, along with this brand new edition of *How to Go to College Almost for Free,* another new book, titled *The Scholarship Scouting Report.* Together, they comprise a two-volume set for determined scholarship seekers. The book you are now reading is the "how-to" part of the process: It contains everything you need to know to locate and research scholarship opportunities perfect for you, position yourself for the best chance of winning them, and manage the entire application process from start to finish.

The Scholarship Scouting Report is my behind-the-scenes guide to America's leading and most financially rewarding scholarship programs—the ones you definitely need to know about! I scoured the scholarship landscape, analyzed thousands of scholarship program "nominations," and narrowed down the list to create an in-depth scouting report of the nation's best, and most widely accessible, scholarship opportunities.

For those of you who want to kick-start the application process, *The Scholarship Scouting Report* is the advance leg-work—a dossier on the scholarship programs that best meet my tough criteria. I analyze them for you and provide insider tips on how to play the game by each organization's rules. In *The Scholarship Scouting Report,* you'll hear from many winners, judges, and administrators of selected scholarships and see some of the past applications that took home the money.

▌ THE OTHER REWARDS

This game we're about to play may sound like a lot of work, but I can't emphasize enough that this relatively small investment of your time can reap you enormous rewards. And these rewards can be measured in more than just dollars. During my senior year, I zigzagged across the nation nearly a dozen times, attending various scholarship award ceremonies and sight-seeing tours (sometimes my parents even got to come along, too). For several scholarships, I was interviewed by local television stations and newspapers. For many others, I got the chance to meet interesting students from across the nation, as well as notables such as Hillary Clinton, Olympic Gold Medalist Scott Hamilton, Grammy winner Trisha Yearwood, Supreme Court Justice Ruth Ginsberg, and Ed Bradley of *60 Minutes* fame. One scholarship program even agreed to pick up the airfare of an extended college visitation tour.

More importantly, the experience of applying for these scholarships affected my life in profound ways. I dramatically enhanced my writing skills, clarified my life and career goals, and began a process of self-analysis that led to dramatic self-improvement. In addition, scholarship contests gave me a tremendous head start when it came time to apply to colleges: I had essays ready to go, a collection of recommendation letters to choose from, well-constructed summaries of my extracurricular activities, and some important award credentials under my belt.

Entering scholarship contests also provided me with valuable feedback about what works (and what doesn't) on an application. This accumulated experience played a major role in helping me gain admittance to my first-choice college, and learning the art of self-promotion—what the scholarship game really trains you to do—

helped me secure several summer internships and job offers once I became a college student. Regardless of the monetary prizes, just entering scholarship contests is a very rewarding endeavor in and of itself.

▎ WHAT IT TAKES

P*ut in one hour every two months and win $50,000! Just fill out a form and college is free! Five easy steps and you're in the money!* If you embark on your scholarship quest believing claims like these—and I hope you don't—you're setting yourself up for failure. But if you're willing to put in the time, effort, and hard work that the process demands, great success is yours for the taking.

Don't make the mistake of thinking that "scholarships are great and everything, but they just aren't for students like me." I'm here to tell you otherwise. Scholarships are within the reach of *all* students, as long as they are willing to put in the time and effort. In fact, judging from the extremely diverse group of scholarship recipients I've met at various award ceremonies, virtually *every* type of student with practically *every* type of interest and background is represented in the scholarship winner's circle.

Go for it! You have nothing to lose, and a better future to gain. A college education is far too important to settle for the cheapest path. Rebel against those who say that financial constraints make it impossible for you to attend this or that school. Fight back against those college budget offices that habitually increase tuition bills, while their financial aid allocations fail to keep up. And above all, have fun making a great future happen.

So make sure your shoes are laced, your mental muscles are stretched, your competitive juices are flowing, and your game face is on. Let's get going!

PART I

How the Game Is Played

The Big, Bad World of Financial Aid

INSIDE THIS CHAPTER

▪ Exploding scholarship myths

▪ The language of financial aid

▪ Need versus merit

▪ Other forms of financial aid

I Exploding Seven Scholarship Myths

Hold your ears and take cover! Before I take you on a tour of the broader financial aid landscape, I'm going to explode seven widespread myths of the scholarship game—myths that have deterred many worthy students from even trying to play the game. By revealing the real story known to scholarship-savvy students, I will expose these tall tales for what they are. Just reading this section can make your chances of winning, well, *dynamite*.

MYTH 1

"Only low-income families get help paying for college."

THE REAL STORY: This myth stems from confusion between need-based and merit-based scholarships, as well as a lack of understanding about how the financial aid process works. Merit scholarships, by definition, do *not* consider financial need. Such scholarships are awarded for all sorts of reasons—including interests, talents, achievements, personal qualities, activities, and skills—but financial need is never one of them. Your last name can be Gates, Rockefeller, or Carnegie, and your financial situation still won't be considered. (Well, maybe that's an exaggeration . . . the funding organization may turn around and hit you up for a donation!) Furthermore, financial aid that does consider need isn't just for low-income families. Plenty of middle-income and upper-middle-income families qualify for significant amounts of need-based aid. And because of how "demonstrated need" is usually defined, the more expensive the college, university, or technical school you attend, the more need-based aid you will likely receive.

The bottom line is that regardless of how much money you and your family have in the bank or stashed under your bed, you *can* win substantial college scholarships. So never rule out a college simply because of its price tag. Paying for college isn't like buying a new toaster; you can get others to help kick in some money—and you don't have to worry about getting the bagels stuck.

"Only students with high GPAs win merit awards."

THE REAL STORY: Don't think you have to be the next Albert Einstein or Doogie Howser, M.D., to win merit awards. Merit scholarships are awarded to students with all sorts of talents and interests. In fact, some of the best scholarship programs are designed for students who devote time to such diverse endeavors as music and performing arts, foreign languages, community service, Web design, science projects, leadership, amateur radio, writing, photography, oratory, and part-time jobs. Many of these programs are entirely "grade blind," meaning that grades are *not* used as a judging criterion. Furthermore, some scholarships that do take into account GPAs use them only as preliminary cutoff points. For instance, if you apply for a scholarship that specifies that "applicants have a minimum 2.5 GPA," once you've cleared this hurdle, your grades don't affect your chances of winning.

Finally, even when GPA is used as an evaluation factor, it's only one aspect out of many that judges consider. Some scholarship programs are, in fact, known for selecting students who do not necessarily have top grades. Others use a broader definition of "academics" that includes areas of interest and study outside the traditional school curriculum. Most scholarship programs aren't myopic: They take into account that applicants have much more to offer than simply the sterile grades that appear on their official transcripts.

"Most scholarships are for athletes or minority students."

THE REAL STORY: If the greatest athletic feat you have accomplished in recent memory has been diving onto the TV room sofa, don't worry. If you have blond hair and blue eyes and sunburn easily, you shouldn't worry, either. Although many scholarships for athletes or minority students do exist, they are only one small portion of the scholarship landscape. To comprehend why so many scholarships exist for every imaginable type of student, you have to understand that each scholarship provider seeks to recognize different types of students—usually students who are like themselves, with the same traits, abilities, interests, or heritage they have. Some want to recognize athletes and minority students; others want to recognize surfers, filmmakers, burger flippers, horse groomers, southpaws, or descendants from the man who invented the machine gun (all real scholarships!).

Now, if you are skilled on the playing field or court, or are part of an ethnic minority group, I will certainly show you how to find the scholarships especially targeted for you. But I will also show you, and everyone else, powerful techniques to find scholarship awards that are a "good fit" no matter what your particular profile is.

"Once you've graduated from high school, it's too late."

THE REAL STORY: Scholarships are *not* the financial aid equivalent of your senior class prom: Even if you missed out in high school, you still have plenty of time to show up at the party. There are suitable scholarships for higher education no matter where you are along your educational path. Students already in college have a veritable bonanza of scholarship programs to apply for—general scholarship programs for *all* college students, as well as programs focused on particular areas of interest and study. Students going on to graduate school in any field have enormous scholarship opportunities as well. If anything, the variety of educational financing options increases when you enter grad school. Adults and "nontraditional students" going back to school also have a variety of options. Most scholarship programs for college students don't specify age requirements, and some colleges and organizations have special programs just for nontraditional or returning students.

"Applying for scholarships is just like applying to college."

THE REAL STORY: Scholarship applications have many of the same components as college applications, but applying for scholarships demands more strategic planning. Most of us approach each college we're applying to in pretty much the same way. We don't have to highlight our great love for sunshine when applying to schools in warm climates, while emphasizing our vast wool sweater collection to schools located in colder regions. Overall, we try to show that we meet the school's general admissions standards and will fit in well with its next class.

In applying for a scholarship, however, it's essential to understand the specific mission of the organization awarding the scholarship, define each scholarship program's "ideal applicant," and implement tailor-made strategies that emphasize personal attributes consistent with the scholarship's goals. To use an obvious example, highlighting your personal perspectives on the importance of military service may be perfect for a scholarship sponsored by a veterans group but will not go over big with judges for a scholarship sponsored by an anti-war organization. Even when an individual college sponsors merit scholarships, the goal of the scholarship program is usually more specific and more targeted toward particular types of students than that of the college's general admissions process.

Despite the differences between college applications and scholarship applications, important synergies do exist, allowing you to adapt the similar material for both applications and incorporate the strategic lessons you learn from applying for scholarships into your college applications.

MYTH 6 — "Past actions and choices predetermine scholarship success."

THE REAL STORY: What you do *after* you decide to apply for scholarships is just as important as the record you have already accumulated. No matter what trouble spots exist in your record or what mistakes you've made in the past, you can turn these weaknesses into strengths in your scholarship applications. If you've had some rocky academic years, you can transform that issue into a character-

building experience. If your participation in extracurricular activities is limited, you can fix the situation. I'll show you what past students in your situation have done to reach scholarship success, so you can do it, too. One individual I've profiled actually won an extremely prestigious scholarship contest from *prison*—winning out over plenty of students with high GPAs and test scores. (Also, he didn't exactly have the best extracurricular activities of the application pool.)

Applying for scholarships is indeed a growth process, so don't think you need to have all of your ducks in a row when you begin. (I know I didn't!) You'll learn as you go and will continue to grow (as a person, that is—not just getting taller) with every action step along the way. So don't fall into the trap of thinking that your die has already been cast. What you do *now* will make all the difference in the world.

There is, in fact, a scholarship sponsored by Tall Clubs International that recognizes unusually tall students.

"Focusing on a few awards maximizes your odds of winning."

THE REAL STORY: Some students think they maximize their chances of winning money by pouring all their energy into just a few scholarship applications. Such a strategy is exactly what you *don't* want to do. Applying for scholarships is partially a numbers game. A variety of factors beyond your control can affect the outcome of any given scholarship program or contest. Only by applying for a large number of scholarships can you minimize such factors.

Besides, applying for a lot of scholarships isn't as much work as you probably think. By recycling old passages and bridging multiple applications with every sentence your write, list you make, recommendation letter you secure, or form you create, you

"If you start out winning a few little scholarships, it directly leads to winning other, bigger awards. It's a totally cumulative process."

–Melissa Gambol
Scholarship Winner
Madison, OH

powerfully leverage your time. Once you've applied for two scholarships, you've done 60 percent of the work to apply for ten—*if you're smart about how you approach the process.*

Don't listen to anyone who tells you to look at the universe of scholarships and choose only a few to apply for. As the saying goes, don't put all your eggs in one basket.

■ DEMYSTIFYING THE LINGO

Now that we've exploded some persistent scholarship myths, let's look at the overall financial aid landscape and see how scholarships fit into the big picture. Trying to make sense of all of the financial aid jargon out there can be like trying to learn Swahili verb conjugation from a stuttering parrot with a short attention span.

> *Even if your EFC on the SAR and ISIR sent out by the CPS, as determined by the FAFSA, is less than the COA, your FAA may require a CSS Profile.*

Yes, this sentence does make sense, but only to a financial aid administrator born before the invention of the No. 2 pencil. And sometimes, even the most zealous financial aid administrators fail to use all of the various mind-numbing financial aid terms in the same way.

According to the College Board, in the past 10 years, tuition has gone up 51 percent at public universities and 34 percent at private schools, even after adjusting for inflation. In the past two decades, tuition has increased 115 percent at public and private schools alike.

So what do you absolutely need to know to play the college scholarships game? Let's start by understanding the various landmarks along the financial aid landscape, and how merit-based scholarships and grants (what I won) fit into the big picture. You'll soon discover that regardless of your background or your family's financial circumstances, you can get substantial help in paying for college.

We can break down the various forms of financial aid for college into two basic categories: (1) money you have to pay back and (2) money you *don't* have to pay back. First, let's examine the money that isn't yours to keep. This type of financial aid is often associated with that infamous four-letter word shouted out by frustrated students and parents when confronted with excessive tuition payments. That word, of course, is **loan**. (What did you think I was going to say?) Loans for higher education can be **subsidized** or **unsubsidized**.

Subsidized loans are usually awarded only to those who demonstrate financial need. The subsidy part of a subsidized loan refers to the fact that the loan has some benefit besides the lent money for the borrower. Usually the benefit is that the borrower pays only a portion of the total interest payment or is exempt from the interest payment for a period of time, with the government (or some other group) picking up the rest of the interest tab. In the case of the Direct Stafford Loan, for instance, the government pays the interest on your loan while you're in college, for the first six months after you leave school, and when you qualify for payment deferments. In contrast, unsubsidized loans don't carry any extra benefit. Unsubsidized loans are available to any student or family, regardless of financial need, but you have to pay the full interest payment on your own, with interest charged from the moment you assume the loan. Ouch!

Now what about that category of financial aid you don't have to pay back? This wonderful type of college funding is referred to as **scholarships** or **grants**. What's the difference between a scholarship and a grant, you ask? Over time, the terms have come to be used somewhat interchangeably, so don't worry too much about the distinction. Scholarships and grants from private groups typically are paid either to the student's institution of higher education or directly to the student. Some scholarship winnings must be paid out in a lump sum, and

Even when paid for by loans, a college education is still a great investment. Over a 40-year career, the difference in income between a high school graduate and a college graduate is said to be about $1 million.

As I show later, having this discretion can be extremely important in minimizing your total out-of-pocket educational cost.

others are paid in equal annual disbursements over four years. The best payment plans let the student decide how and when to receive the money. Scholarships and grants given out by the colleges themselves—sometimes referred to as "institutional" awards—are usually never paid directly to you, but rather are discounts off the school's sticker price.

REPLACING LOANS WITH SCHOLARSHIPS AND GRANTS

By winning scholarships and grants, you and your family can substantially lower your debt burden or even avoid borrowing money altogether. This is especially important in a debt-ridden era when increasing numbers of parents resist taking out new loans for college expenses, opting instead for less expensive schools. Scholarships and grants allow students to take the reins of their educational destinies, choosing the right college regardless of their family's financial limitations.

Replacing a $1,000 loan with $1,000 in scholarships and grants benefits your pocketbook even more than it might at first seem. This is because the loan interest accumulates relentlessly over time: The $1,000 in scholarship and grant money saves you not only the face value of the loan, but also the ever increasing cost of *holding* the loan. Therefore, each dollar of scholarship and grant money you earn now pays out even bigger dividends in the future.

■ NEED VERSUS MERIT

Now you have the inside scoop on how loans compare to scholarships and grants. The next step in our wondrous journey of inner financial aid enlightenment (sounds more impressive when you call it that) is to understand that not all scholarships and grants are the same. In fact, scholarships and grants come primarily in two tasty flavors: **need based** and **merit based**.

Need-based awards—the "vanilla" of the scholarships and grants world—are awarded on the basis of demonstrated financial need. The "demonstrated" part means that interested parties don't take your word for how much financial aid you truly need (too bad!), and require that you submit personal and family financial information (see Ask the Coach #1).

The "lower income" determination is based on each calendar year. This means that if one year your mom or dad happened to be laid off from work for a long time, and your family's income substantially dropped that year, you might be eligible for one year of Pell money.

The largest need-based grant program is the Pell Grant, sponsored by the U.S. government, which awards money to students from lower-income families. Colleges and universities dole out their own need-based scholarships and grants as part of their financial aid packages. State governments and private organizations also provide need-based awards.

ASK THE COACH #1

For the purpose of financial aid how do I "demonstrate need"?

You demonstrate your need generally by answering one simple question: How does your family's financial resources compare to the cost of attending your desired school? To answer this question, each student, or the student's parents, completes the Free Application for Federal Student Aid (FAFSA). On the basis of the financial information you supply, Uncle  Sam (the federal government, not your wacky relative) takes a percentage of your parents' income and assets, divides it by the number of members of your family currently attending college, and adds in a percentage of your own income and assets. What you get back is an assessment of how much you are expected to contribute to college (referred to as your Expected Family Contribution, or EFC). If the cost of the college (referred to as the Cost of Attendance, or COA) is greater than what you are expected to contribute, then voilá: you have demonstrated financial need. Therefore, *the more expensive the college you attend, the greater the amount of financial aid you are likely to receive.* Colleges may also require that you submit a CSS PROFILE, or college-specific financial aid application. These forms basically take the same approach as the FAFSA, using slightly different financial indicators. ∎

The National "Make It Yourself With Wool" contest asks students to sew and model a garment made of at least 60 percent wool fabric. (No polyester leisure suits allowed here!)

Conversely, merit-based funds—the "chocolate" of scholarships and grants—are awarded on some measure of individual achievement, ability, or potential. What constitutes merit depends on who is awarding the money, but you'll soon discover that merit-based scholarships and grants are targeted at virtually *every* type of student. The

The "Stuck at Prom" scholarship contest awards two $2,500 scholarships to one couple attending their high school prom in the most creative outfit made from or accessorized with duct tape. (I kid you not!) The question I have is, will the winning couple "stick together" after high school?

criteria used to evaluate achievement vary substantially among scholarship and grant programs—taking into account the full spectrum of student talents, abilities, and interests. Merit-based awards are provided not only by the government and individual schools, but also by corporations, nonprofit groups, foundations, service clubs, associations, and other organizations.

ASK THE COACH #2

What does "merit" really mean?

Unlike need-based scholarships and grants, merit awards are based on an endless and ever changing list of criteria—there is no set formula. For some scholarships, merit means overcoming obstacles in life or learning from past mistakes. For other applications, merit involves showcasing a talent, such as artistic ability, Web page design, or oratorical skill. Other pro-

grams base merit on an interest or curiosity an individual has exhibited in a particular field, career, or hobby. Still others determine merit by having applicants demonstrate personal qualities such as creativity, character, determination, or compassion for others. Merit can mean grades and test scores, too, but as I explain later, this is only one small portion of the total merit scholarship landscape. I discuss the many types of merit scholarship programs, as well as the various components of merit scholarship applications, in detail in Chapter 2. ■

The Elks "Most Valuable Student" Scholarship awards college funds to 500 high school seniors based on both merit and need. In their weighting system, need accounts for 20 percent of the overall judging criteria.

Finally, some scholarship and grant programs are "vanilla and chocolate swirls," basing awards on both merit and need criteria. A swirl type of program may require that students have a certain level of financial need before judges consider merit criteria, or it may factor in both types of criteria as weighted components of the judging process.

LIMITATIONS OF NEED-BASED AWARDS

Need-based financial aid represents a huge pile of college cash to which you most definitely want to stake your claim. In general, be sure you know the need-based application process, and in particular the FAFSA form, inside out. Fill out the form carefully, don't forget to sign it, and make sure you start the process early enough that you don't miss each school's financial aid deadline. *Never make the mistake of assuming that your family makes too much money to qualify.* Plenty of middle- and upper-middle-income families receive need-based financial aid (loans as well as scholarships and grants), especially at more expensive colleges.

You should try to file the FAFSA form as soon after January 1 as possible, since some schools give out need-based aid on a first-come, first-served basis.

There are several problems, however, for students and families who rely solely on need-based aid to finance an education. First, there just aren't enough need-based funds to go around. Most colleges have strict financial aid budgets, limiting the amount of need-based scholarships and grants they can award. I have yet to find a student who thought that a financial aid office *overestimated* his or her family's financial need. On the contrary, most students soon discover that a financial aid office's estimate of their "demonstrated need" is very different from the reality of their family's cash flow and bank accounts.

Second, students from middle-income families often find themselves caught between the proverbial rock and a hard place. Such families aren't wealthy enough to cover

According to a survey conducted by Gallup and Robinson, most parents of college-bound students have saved only 25 percent or less of college costs by the time their children are ready to enroll.

Don't get me wrong, student loans are a good thing and a wise investment: Obtaining a quality education is one of the most important things you'll ever do, and loans help make it possible. But why take on more debt if you don't have to?

On average, the typical undergraduate leaves college $15,000 to $20,000 in debt.

all the costs on their own, but they don't have a low enough income to qualify for large levels of need-based scholarships and grants. Having to send more than one child to college can aggravate the situation.

Some colleges advertise that they "meet 100 percent of need" or that "a high percentage of the student body receives financial aid," but such statements can be misleading. Many colleges can make such claims because loans are classified as "financial aid" when they carry an interest rate below the current market level, don't have to be paid back until after graduation, or carry some other benefit. Unfortunately, many college students and their families soon discover that these low-interest loans make up the bulk of the financial aid that schools offer them. In fact, the College Board reports that since 1980, loans have jumped from 41 percent to 59 percent of the average financial aid package. Although such loans are helpful in delaying payment, they still have one overwhelmingly undesirable feature: *They eventually have to be paid back.*

Other colleges don't even attempt to meet your full demonstrated financial need. Instead, they practice "need-gapping"—awarding students only part of the financial aid they need, so the college can spread aid money among more students. You're on your own to fill the gap between the college's limited financial aid package and the rest of your bill. As a result, many students and parents are forced to commit themselves to a string of postcollege debt payments. This financial burden can negatively affect a variety of life decisions for years to come:

▌ Students interested in attending graduate school may have to delay or forego such plans because of this excessive debt.

▌ Students entering the workforce may have to pass up more satisfying but lower paying career opportunities in favor of better paying, less interesting jobs.

Unfortunately, some of my friends from college with large debt burdens ended up taking jobs they weren't interested in and didn't enjoy, instead of having the flexibility to travel, go on to more school, or do something entrepreneurial.

▮ Students and parents alike may have to substantially reduce their quality of life or take on even more debt to maintain their lifestyle.

Finally, you should be aware that colleges distribute need-based aid on a year-to-year basis. You may receive a sizable financial aid package in your first year, but that doesn't mean you'll be awarded the same level of aid in later years. Unfortunately, some colleges engage in "front-loading," awarding highly attractive aid packages to prospective college freshmen to entice them to enroll and then reducing aid in subsequent years, when the odds of a student's transferring to another school are low.

Although students should apply for and fight for every last penny of need-based financial aid (especially need-based scholarships and grants), no student should rely solely on need-based aid.

THE POWER OF LEVERAGE

An additional aspect of need-based financial aid that troubles me is the student's lack of **leverage** in the application process: The actions you take at any given time in the process don't seem to have a huge impact on the amount of need-based awards you can ultimately receive. This is because need-based awards are determined mostly by factors outside your control, namely, your family's income and assets.

Sure, your family can shift assets around a bit and take on a few strategic expenditures, all for the express purpose of maximizing aid. But for most families' financial situations, the allocation of income and assets really isn't that flexible. You can negotiate with financial aid officers and do your best to persuade them to offer you more need-based scholarships and grants, but, again, this strategy alone is not likely to change your financial aid package dramatically. You could even try to fill out your FAFSA form with extra-careful penmanship, and write sweetly in the margin that you "have deep affection and respect for financial aid officers who believe in random acts of scholarship kindness," but this won't produce the desired results, either.

In general, once you've dutifully and properly filled out financial aid application forms in a timely manner (a straightforward task once you get the hang of it), your influence over the process of awarding need-based aid is extremely limited. The process just isn't designed to leverage your time and effort.

Unlike scholarships based on need, the merit-based scholarship application process does offer tremendous leverage: **Enterprising, determined students and parents can exert enormous influence over the amount of merit-based grants they receive**. What you do today and tomorrow (and the day after) makes all the difference in the world. If you do nothing, you won't receive any merit-based awards. If you read this book but don't follow through and actually *apply* for the scholarships, you won't receive merit-based awards, either. (Sorry, can't help you there.) But if you take the small action steps and embrace the strategic principles I outline in this book, you can't help but be successful.

That's what's great about merit-based scholarships and grants: Because they are by definition based on the notion of individual achievement, the relatively modest amount of time and energy you need to invest in this process can reap you enormous rewards. This is the essence of leverage. And this is what playing the scholarship game is all about.

THE HIDDEN BENEFITS OF MERIT SCHOLARSHIP STRATEGIES

We've discussed many reasons why it's important to apply for merit-based scholarships and grants. But there's more. By cultivating your skill in applying for merit-based scholarships, you also gain two important advantages that can affect your ratio of loans to grants and help you get into the college of your choice.

Preferential Packaging

In practice, need-based scholarships and grants are not given out solely on the basis of your and your family's financial need.

How can this be, you ask? *The truth is, merit-based factors often infiltrate the need-based application process.* To understand this, we first must examine the differences between need-based awards given out by government programs and need-based awards that come straight from a college's coffers.

Whereas the government distributes its aid solely on the basis of a strict need-based formula, a college can give away its own aid according to its own rules—so long as the total package does not exceed a student's demonstrated need. Because financial aid packages include loans as well as scholarships and grants, schools use their discretion when determining how much of each student's total package is made up of repayable loans and how much is made up of nonrepayable scholarships and grants. Thus, two students with the same level of demonstrated financial need (and thus receiving the same amount of "financial aid") could actually end up with two very different aid-component allocations—one with mostly loans and the other with mostly scholarships and grants. And here's a secret: *Students who can demonstrate more merit are much more likely to get the better financial aid deals.*

This scenario is sometimes referred to as **preferential packaging** or **merit within need**. Why do colleges do this? They do it because they have a powerful incentive to encourage strong applicants to enroll. As part of their "enrollment management" practices, schools know that inducing preferred students to attend raises the reputation and ultimately the overall well-being of the institution.

A high-quality student body induces better faculty to take up shop at the school, which in turn attracts more research dollars and increases the reputation of the school, which can then attract even better faculty and students. Furthermore, stronger students are more likely to have higher incomes after college, proudly promote their alma mater, and make larger alumni contributions later in life. All of this positions the school to be highly regarded by future applicants, further boosting its reputation and level of alumni donations. The bottom line is a healthy swelling of the school's precious endowment. At the end of the day, preferred applicants end up getting better need-based as well as merit-based aid.

How does preferential packaging actually work? At Johns Hopkins University, for example, admissions officers review piles and piles of applications, sorting each applicant into one of three categories based on the merits of the application. They then send to the financial aid office the names of students being considered for admission. The financial aid office, in turn, awards more scholarship and grant money and fewer loans to the students who demonstrate the most merit. In this way, preferred students get preferred packages.

Although the ability to get high grades and test scores certainly is a desirable skill, it's only one of many skills, abilities, and interests that can convince a college that it needs to persuade you to attend.

This, of course, has dramatic implications for students who aren't yet enrolled in their desired institution of higher education. *Embracing the strategies, techniques, and Guerrilla Tactics outlined in this book not only will help you stake your claim to merit-based scholarships and grants, but also will make you a much stronger applicant in the eyes of those who make the admissions and financial aid decisions.*

Furthermore, actually winning a scholarship award (and including this credential on your application) signals to admissions and financial aid officers that you are indeed one of those special applicants who deserve the best financial aid package the school can offer. It's like proclaiming to the school's admissions and financial aid officers, "Hey guys, ABC scholarship organization thinks I'm pretty darn cool, shouldn't you too?" You're in a great position to receive preferential financial aid treatment from that college. Bring on the scholarships and grants, baby, and hold back the loans!

The College Admissions Advantage

If you are a student who hasn't yet applied to college, the process of strategically becoming a more meritorious applicant—something you'll master with help from this book—dramatically improves your chances of getting admitted to the college of your choice. Here's why: The scholarship application game encourages you to enhance both your record and your application skills in creative and strategic ways that otherwise wouldn't have occurred to you. Because each scholarship organization seeks to reward specific types of student achievement (as opposed to college admissions officers, who typically focus on finding students that match a well-defined standard), the process of continually positioning yourself and communicating who you are (so as to have the best chance of collecting these awards) provides you with a leg up on your college applications. You'll have more opportunities than a lone dog at a fire hydrant convention.

When it comes time to apply to college, you'll be able to draw on a suite of fine-tuned essays and summaries of extracurricular activities. You'll have developed a menu of recommendation letters and will able to choose the most appropriate ones for your college applications. More importantly, you will have been through an application process numerous times, will have honed your skills, and will know exactly what works (and what doesn't) on a written application.

If you happen to be on the borderline of getting admitted to a particular school, real-world application experience could make all the difference. This is especially true because many of the schools that for the most part don't consider your finances in the general admissions process do consider your need for college-sponsored financial aid *if* you're "on the margin" of getting admitted. To use Johns Hopkins again as an example, about 200–400 students per year are not admitted in part because of their inability to pay full tuition and their resulting need for financial aid. By getting off the admissions borderline, you take your family's financial need out of the *admissions* equation and will likely be able to take your place in the pool of admitted students.

ASK THE COACH #3

How would winning merit scholarships affect the financial aid package a college offers me?

Winning merit-based scholarships can indeed affect the amount of need-based aid you qualify for, by suddenly increasing the financial resources at your disposal. In the language of financial aid, winning merit scholarships causes your Expected Family Contribution (see Ask the Coach #1) to increase. As a result, you could have unintentionally reduced the amount of need-based aid you would have otherwise received from individual colleges (assuming you would have received need-based aid to begin with).

There are several reasons, however, why any potential reductions in need-based aid are somewhat limited. First, many colleges, following a nationwide trend, have adopted a policy with regard to outside merit scholarships whereby they first reduce subsidized loan packages before reducing any need-based grants. Remember, the majority of need-based financial aid comes in the form of loans. In this way, what you're actually losing out on is the "opportunity" to assume more debt. Not a bad loss.

Second, colleges that don't subscribe to the aforementioned policy sometimes have other policies in which only a fraction of the merit scholarships you win are factored into their need-based aid equations: For every dollar you win from merit awards, perhaps only 40 cents will affect your need-based aid.

Third, as I mentioned earlier, winning outside merit scholarships can actually increase the amount of need-based grants you receive (at the expense of need-based loans), as a result of "preferential packaging" policies. This can occur because students who have won outside merit scholarships are more attractive admissions candidates and therefore more likely to receive need-based aid packages that have a higher percentage of grants to loans. Although you would qualify for less overall financial aid, you could still be awarded more grant money from the school. In addition, an increasing number of schools have created "matching scholarships" in which they provide an additional scholarship to each student who brings in an outside award.

Finally, winning merit-based scholarships gives you an added bargaining chip when you're negotiating with colleges for better aid packages. Financial aid officers have the authority to use professional judgment to determine financial aid on a case-by-case basis, and the fact that you took the initiative to earn merit scholarships may persuade them to make an exception and improve your aid package. ∎

▌ OTHER FORMS OF FINANCIAL AID

Although loans, scholarships, and grants are the most prevalent forms of financial aid for college, several others are available. So that you understand how all the puzzle pieces of financial aid eventually fit together, let's briefly look at these components.

TAX CREDITS

In 1997, Congress enacted two separate tax credits— the "HOPE Scholarship" and "Lifetime Learning" tax credits—to help students, parents, and families afford higher education. Unlike a tax deduction, which lowers the amount of income subject to taxation, these tax credits directly reduce the full tax you pay.

HOPE Scholarship tax credit

It's called a "scholarship," but the HOPE Scholarship is actually a federal income tax credit for some of a student's educational expenses. This means that you are required to pay less money than you otherwise would have to pay on your tax return, and thus can use the extra money in your bank account to pay college costs.

Here's how it works: Students in their first two years of college or vocational school—or their parents, if the students are dependents—can claim a tax credit equal to 100 percent of their first $1,000 of tuition expenses and 50 percent of the second $1,000 of such expenses; this assumes that the students are pursuing a degree and attending school at least half-time. The bottom line is that students and parents can claim, at most, a $1,500 tax credit.

Eligibility for the tax credit is limited to taxpayers with a modified adjusted gross income of less than $50,000 ($100,000 if you file a joint return). Those earning between $40,000 and $50,000 (between $80,000 and $100,000 if a joint return) are eligible for a smaller tax credit. The IRS permits you to claim a HOPE credit only for two taxable years per student, but if a family has more than one student, it may claim more than one HOPE tax credit. Every little bit helps!

Lifetime Learning tax credit

The Lifetime Learning tax credit targets adults who want to go back to school, change careers, or take a course or two to upgrade their skills, as well as college juniors, college seniors, and graduate-degree seekers. The Lifetime Learning tax credit is equal to 20 percent of the first $10,000 in educational expenses, resulting in a

You cannot claim both the HOPE Scholarship and the Lifetime Learning tax credit in the same year. You can, however, claim the HOPE credit for the first two years of college and then claim the Lifetime Learning credit for later years.

For more information on these tax credits, see IRS Publication 970, "Tax Benefits for Higher Education" (which you can download at www.irs.gov). Because rules on tax matters are subject to change, consult a certified tax adviser.

maximum tax credit of $2,000. Until 2003, however, the IRS will limit the Lifetime Learning tax credit to 20 percent of the first $5,000 in educational expenses, for a maximum tax credit of $1,000.

Like HOPE Scholarship recipients, Lifetime Learning recipients must have a modified adjusted gross income of less than $50,000 for individual returns ($100,000 for joint returns); smaller tax credits go to individuals who grossed more than $40,000 ($80,000 for those filing joint returns) but less than $50,000. A key distinction, however, between the HOPE credit and the Lifetime Learning credit is that whereas one HOPE credit can be claimed for each *student*, only one Lifetime Learning credit can be claimed for each *family's* tax return. Furthermore, whereas the HOPE credit requires that you attend college at least half-time, to receive the Lifetime Learning credit you need to be taking only one course at an institution of higher education and need not be pursuing a degree. Another great aspect of the Lifetime Learning credit is that you can claim it each year for an unlimited number of years.

ASK THE COACH #4

What are prepaid-tuition and college-savings plans?

Often referred to as "529 investment plans" (named after a section of the tax code by investment plan–naming geniuses), prepaid-tuition plans and college-savings plans are run by the states in response to authorization by Congress in 1996.

Prepaid-tuition plans allow parents to lock in tomorrow's tuition rates at today's prices, with the money they save today guaranteed to increase in value at the same rate that tuition costs at state-run colleges increase. The plans vary from state to state, with different restrictions regarding, for example, whether the money can be used at private as well as public schools and whether it can be applied to out-of-state colleges.

In a **college-savings plan**, on the other hand, you contribute to a fund that's managed by the state treasurer or an outside investment adviser. Many such plans lean toward stocks when the child is young and shift toward bonds and cash as college appears on the horizon. You can generally use the money at any accredited school for tuition, books, and room and board. And many states don't even require you to be a state resident to participate in their college-savings plans.

Both prepaid-tuition and college-savings plans offer tax benefits. Gains on your money are tax deferred, and then taxed at the student's tax bracket when the money is withdrawn to cover college costs. One drawback of these plans, however, is that your money is tied up. If you use the funds for something other than college, or if tax laws change and other investment opportunities present themselves, you may face a 10 percent penalty. Furthermore, stowing away money in such a plan could ultimately reduce the amount of college-sponsored need-based aid you receive. In general, the desirability of such plans depends on the particulars of your situation. ■

WORK-STUDY

When your school's financial aid office helps arrange or administer on-campus or certain off-campus employment for you, your wages count as a type of financial aid called **work-study**. Work-study is an additional component of many students' need-based financial aid package, albeit usually a much smaller component than allocations for loans or scholarships and grants.

The largest source of work-study funding is the Federal Work-Study (FWS) program. Students are automatically considered for the FWS program when they complete a FAFSA form and qualify for the program on

An added benefit of the FWS program is that the wages you earn from your current FWS job are not treated as income on your next application for need-based aid.

the basis of demonstrated financial need. Most students work at on-campus jobs, although off-campus jobs at nonprofit or community agencies also qualify. The federal government pays a portion of the salary at such jobs, lowering the cost for businesses and organizations to hire a student and thus making it easier for the student to get a part-time job. Individual colleges administer the program, and students generally work 10–15 hours per week. About 700,000 students receive FWS funds each year.

Some states, as well as individual colleges, fund their own work-study programs. For instance, Grinnell College, a small liberal arts college in Iowa, administers work-study aid from three separate sources: the federal government, the state of Iowa, and the college. Each work-study program at Grinnell is based on financial need and pays not less than $6.40 per hour.

Work-study can be a good financial aid option, especially if it's difficult to get part-time jobs around your campus. If you're an enterprising individual, however, and can locate your own job, you may be able to find more interesting work that pays a higher wage.

Proactive student-athletes send prospective coaches an athletic portfolio that includes key statistics, a list of athletic awards, competition videotapes, newspaper clippings, recommendation letters from high school coaches, and an academic summary.

ATHLETIC SCHOLARSHIPS

You don't have to be the next Shaquille O'Neal or Mia Hamm to get an athletic scholarship to college. Plenty of better than average high school athletes capitalize on their athletic skills to get help paying for college. The key for the vast majority of student-athletes who aren't the top national prospects is that they don't wait for college coaches to contact them: *They take appropriate steps to initiate contact with the coaches and make themselves known.*

College athletic programs are classified according to size, competitiveness, and the extent to which they can award scholarships based on athletic ability. National Collegiate Athletic Association (NCAA) Division I schools award a lot of athletic scholarships, and include college and universities with the most competitive athletic programs. NCAA Division II schools also award athletic scholarships, but in fewer numbers than their generally larger, more competitive Division I counterparts. NCAA Division III schools do *not* award athletic scholarships and are smaller, less athletically competitive schools. Finally, National Association of Intercollegiate Athletics (NAIA) member schools tend to be smaller, but frequently have solid sports programs. Many of them offer some form of athletic scholarships.

What separates this type of scholarship from others I've discussed is that the college's obligation to provide you with funding runs only as deep as your obligation to actively participate in your sport. Participating in college athletics is a wonderful opportunity and potentially life-changing experience, but it is *not* a commitment that should be entered into lightly. If you haven't yet been exposed to athletics at the collegiate level, you should be aware that participating in college sports is not the same as playing in high school—the demands on your time are far greater, and sports training and practice can quickly become the focal point of your life in college.

Moreover, there is no such thing as a guaranteed four-year athletic scholarship. Under NCAA rules, scholarships are awarded only one academic year at a time. A college can tell a prospective athlete that its athletic department *plans* to recommend renewal of his or her scholarship each year for four years, but the renewal is *not* automatic. If the institution decides not to renew a scholarship or to reduce the amount of the scholarship in future years, the student-athlete does have certain protections: The NCAA mandates that each student has the right to demand that the college hold a hearing on the issue. But the actual decision to renew or not renew an athletic scholarship—even in the case of a career-ending injury—is left up to the college alone.

That said, many colleges and universities do afford students additional scholarship protections. Villanova University, for example, stipulates that the university will continue to renew a student's athletic scholarship if the student is injured during practice, competition, or university-sponsored travel. An athletic grant may be withdrawn, however, if the student-athlete fails to make the team.

At the University of Nebraska, as mandated by state law, renewal of athletic scholarships cannot be withheld solely because of an injury. Renewal is customary at the University of Nebraska, although it can be withheld if the student-athlete does not reach reasonable athletic performance goals, has problems related to motivation, or is incompatible with the coaching staff. The bottom line is that prospective student-athletes should ask potential coaches about their college's commitment to renew athletic scholarships in subsequent years, especially in the case of injury or lower than expected athletic performance.

Finally, note that most college athletes *don't* get "full-ride" athletic scholarships. Unless you regularly make city, state, and even national headlines, you're more likely to receive a partial scholarship. College coaches often prefer to award partial scholarships, because this allows them to recruit a greater number of skilled players and ultimately field stronger teams. In fact, on some national championship teams there isn't a single player receiving a full-ride scholarship!

ASK THE COACH #5

If I can get an athletic scholarship, should I still pursue merit awards?

Although athletic scholarships are a great way to help pay for college, it is not a good idea to rely on them exclusively. You are more likely to receive partial athletic scholarships—meaning that the scholarship covers a fraction of tuition or covers costs such as books or room and board—so you'll still want to accumulate additional funds. In addition, since athletic scholarships are awarded only one year at a time, there's no guarantee that you'll get the same amount of scholarship money each year of college. Many schools have policies in place that protect the rights of student-athletes to scholarship money in subsequent years, especially in the event of injury, but such policies aren't universal. Merit scholarships are always a good insurance policy to have in your back pocket.

In addition, some college athletes discover that the importance of athletics in their lives changes. One student-athlete I know devoted himself to a rigorous NCAA Division I tennis program for two years but realized that the time he spent training for tennis was getting in the way of some of his other career and life goals. He decided to depart the team his junior year, had to give up his athletic scholarship as a result, and ended up working two part-time jobs to help cover tuition costs. Had he also pursued merit scholarships, he would have had far greater financial flexibility.

Furthermore, many student-athletes who haven't yet applied to college discover that the schools that offer them athletic scholarships are not the ones they really want to attend. If you have merit scholarships to draw on, you don't have to sacrifice school choice just to get an athletic scholarship. This also gives you financial flexibility to pursue an NCAA Division III or Ivy League school—institutions that don't award athletic scholarships. Even though these schools have no sports scholarships, many do offer academic prestige and terrific learning and social environments. Being recruited by one of these schools' athletic departments helps you get accepted into a more selective college than might be possible otherwise. This can lead to higher earnings and more opportunities after college.

Finally, note that the personal qualities you demonstrate through athletic participation make great material for merit-based scholarship applications (see Chapter 5). In fact, some merit scholarship programs specifically look for students with strong athletic participation, as well as a devotion to school, extracurricular, and community activities. As a competitive tennis player, I was able to take advantage of this. ∎

MILITARY SCHOLARSHIPS AND BENEFITS

Do you have a desire to serve your country as well as an inexplicable love for camouflage and movies like *Top Gun*? Do you also look great in dog tags? If so, a military scholarship could be just right for you. The military offers a number of excellent ways to get all or a big chunk of your college education paid for. Yes, that's right—in return for military service, you can obtain a bachelor's degree that costs you nothing. Programs are available for college students on active duty, students who are veterans or dependents of veterans, or students who will enter the military after college.

For students interested in nursing, there are several ROTC nursing scholarship programs.

The Reserve Officers' Training Corps (ROTC) allows students to get scholarship money for college now and pay it back later in the form of service to the country. An ROTC scholarship can cover as much as the total cost of tuition, books, and fees, plus a monthly stipend to help cover living expenses. As a rule of thumb, for every year of college that ROTC finances, you can expect to serve roughly 12–18 months of active duty. Each branch of the military offers its own ROTC program, and there is a competitive selection process for the limited number of ROTC scholarships each year.

Admission to a military service academy—the U.S. Military Academy, the U.S. Naval Academy, the U.S. Air Force Academy, or the U.S. Coast Guard Academy—is considerably more competitive than the ROTC scholarship selection process. Those who do get admitted, however, can expect a top-quality education (especially in technical fields) and absolutely free tuition, room, and board. After completing the four-year program, graduates receive a bachelor's of science degree and a commission in the military. Service academy graduates have a minimum five-year service obligation, but many academy graduates choose to make the military their career.

Another avenue of military funding is available through state National Guard programs. Each state maintains both an Army and Air Force National Guard, and some states pay a substantial portion of members' tuition at state colleges. In exchange, you are required to devote some weekend hours each month and some additional time over the course of the year to performing your National Guard duties.

If you're the dependent of a veteran who is disabled because of a service-related condition, or who died as a result of active duty, additional educational benefits are available.

In addition, if you are or were on active duty, you can get help from the military in paying for college costs. If you wish to study a subject during your off-duty hours, the U.S. Department of Veteran Affairs, as part of the Montgomery GI Bill, will pay for your coursework. The Department of Defense also pays tuition for on-duty coursework designed to upgrade skills in your area of specialty, but you probably won't be able to choose the training you get. The Montgomery GI Bill generally pays benefits for 10 years after your release from active duty. Many states also award qualified veterans reduced or even free tuition at state-run public institutions. Some colleges may have an Office of Veteran Affairs that provides additional resources and benefits for veterans. If you are a member of the Selected Reserve—which includes the Army Reserve, Navy Reserve, Air Force Reserve, Marine Corps Reserve, Coast Guard Reserve, Army National

Guard, and Air National Guard—you may also be eligible for certain educational funding.

The key point to consider in evaluating such options is that the decision to pursue a military scholarship should *not* be primarily a financial aid decision. Instead, it should be based on a careful examination of whether serving in America's armed forces is right for *you*. If you think you would enjoy and benefit from military life, the military's financial aid programs may be an excellent way to pay for your education.

AMERICORPS

More than 40,000 Americans participate in AmeriCorps and serve their communities in programs such as Habitat for Humanity, the American Red Cross, Boys and Girls Clubs, and other local and national organizations. AmeriCorps members teach children to read, mentor at-risk young people, clean up the environment, help seniors live better lives, and provide assistance to victims of natural disasters, among other projects. If you serve full-time in the AmeriCorps, you'll earn an educational award of close to $5,000 and a modest living allowance, and you may be eligible for special loan deferments. If you serve part-time, you'll earn a smaller educational award. In general, the benefits of AmeriCorps as a means of paying for college are fairly modest, but that's not the program's main objective: If you're looking for a great way to help others, make a meaningful contribution to society, and earn some college funding on the side, AmeriCorps may be right for you.

■ THE IMPORTANCE OF MERIT-BASED AWARDS

As we've seen, merit-based scholarships and grants are unique among the various types of financial aid. Unlike loans, merit money doesn't have to be paid back. Unlike work-study, athletic scholarships, military scholarships, and the AmeriCorps, merit scholarships have few strings attached. Unlike need-based aid and tax credits, merit-based scholarships are highly leverageable—the small action steps you take now have enormous impact on your college cash flow. That's why in this book I focus on the key strategies and techniques that prepare you to win merit-based scholarships and grants. If you apply the principles I present in the following chapters, you'll leverage the power of merit-based scholarships to your greatest advantage.

These principles are becoming more important than ever, given the well-documented trend toward *increased availability of merit-based scholarship money*. A variety of studies have reported that U.S. college and universities have dramatically increased their funding of merit-based scholarships and grants in the past decade. According to a congressional advisory panel, funding by individual states for merit-based financial aid programs has increased 336 percent since 1993. More private organizations than ever offer merit scholarships, and many organizations with longtime merit programs are substantially increasing the number of awards and amount of money they offer.

CHAPTER 1 SUMMARY AND KEYWORDS

The Real Story: Students and families from every income bracket can get help in paying for college—merit scholarship programs do not even consider financial need. Being an academic whiz, star athlete, or member of a minority group is not a prerequisite, either.

It is never too late to apply for scholarships; a bounty of funds exists for students in college or grad school and adults returning to school. Although scholarship applications have many of the same components that college applications have, applying for scholarships is inherently more strategic in nature.

Applying for as many scholarships as you can tilts the odds in your favor. Past actions and choices don't predetermine scholarship success; what you do now makes all the difference. ■

Loans: Funds that have to be paid back are called loans. Loans for college are either subsidized or unsubsidized. Subsidized loans are awarded to those who demonstrate financial need and have added benefits, such as low interest payments or an interest exemption while the borrower is enrolled in college. Unsubsidized loans do not carry any such benefit. ■

Scholarships and Grants: Money that you don't have to pay back is referred to as scholarships or grants. Scholarships and grants from private groups are usually paid to the student's institution of higher education, but they are sometimes paid directly to the student. Scholarships and grants awarded by the colleges themselves, referred to as institutional aid, are not paid out and are actually discounts off the school's "sticker price." Each dollar of a loan that is replaced with a dollar of scholarship and grant money results in even bigger savings, because of the interest cost of holding a loan. ■

Need versus Merit: Need-based scholarships are awarded on the basis of demonstrated financial need as determined by strict formulas; merit-based scholarships are doled out on the basis of some measure of achievement. A wide variety of merit scholarships exist, recognizing virtually every type of student with every type of interest or background. ■

Limitations of Need-Based Funds: Be sure to apply for need-based financial aid, but don't rely exclusively on it. Many families believe that financial aid offices underestimate their true need or don't meet it at all. Colleges consider loans to be financial aid, and loans have become the largest component of the typical need-based financial aid package. Just because you have received a sizable amount of need-based aid in your first year of college doesn't mean that you will receive the same amount in later years. ■

Leverage: Whereas the amount of need-based aid you receive is determined primarily by factors outside your control, you can exert enormous influence over the amount of the merit-based scholarships and grants you receive. ■

Preferential Packaging: The strongest applicants to a college often get the best need-based financial aid packages—the ones with more scholarships and grants and fewer loans. Because of this, pursuing merit-based scholarship strategies can actually help you procure a higher percentage of need-based grant money. ■

College Admissions: If you haven't yet applied to college, using the strategies for applying for merit scholarships outlined in this book will help you get into the college of your choice. ■

How Merit Affects Need: Winning merit scholarships can unintentionally lower need-based aid awards from colleges , since you have more financial resources available. But the effect of this is limited, because many colleges first deduct loan amounts or factor in only a fraction of the merit funding. Practices like preferential packaging and college-sponsored matching scholarships further benefit the merit scholarship winner who also seeks need-based aid. ■

Other Types of Aid: Additional types of aid for college include tax credits, work-study, athletic scholarships, military scholarships and benefits, and AmeriCorps educational awards. Even if you are pursuing these other types of aid, you should still apply for merit scholarships. Merit scholarships are unique in that they aren't accompanied by future obligations and have few strings attached. ■

ScholarshipCoach.com Keywords

For more information on a scholarship or topic mentioned in this chapter, enter the associated keyword in the keyword link box located in the Coach's Locker Room section of ScholarshipCoach.com.

Scholarship/Topic	Keyword
Elks "Most Valuable Student" Scholarship	ELKS
National "Make It Yourself With Wool" Contest	WOOL
"Stuck at Prom" Scholarship Contest	PROM
Tall Clubs International Scholarship	TALL

Rules of the Merit Money Game

INSIDE THIS CHAPTER

▮ A game for all ages

▮ Meet the money people

▮ Getting to know the judges

▮ How awards are targeted

▮ Components of the application

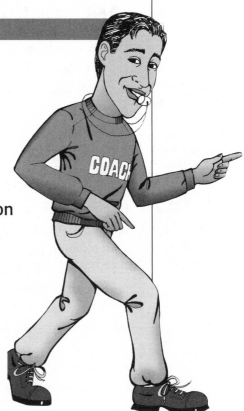

■ A GAME FOR EVERYONE

Now that you understand, on a broad level, how college financial aid works, let's get down and dirty into the specifics of merit-based scholarship awards. As I mentioned in Chapter 1, there are a wide variety of merit scholarships for students with all sorts of talents, interests, backgrounds, affiliations, and higher education goals. Although estimates vary, the general consensus is that *billions of dollars in scholarship money are awarded every year!* And there's even better news: No matter where you now are along your educational path, and no matter where you're headed in the future, you'll encounter plenty of scholarship spandex—college cash opportunities that fit your personal profile, skin tight.

HIGH SCHOOL STUDENTS (AND YOUNGER KIDS, TOO)

It should be no surprise that of the vast array of eclectic scholarships created for high school students, the majority are targeted at high school seniors, whose proud parents will soon have the distinct pleasure of receiving their progeny's first college tuition bill. It's a mistake, however, to think that students must wait until their final year of high school to apply for any scholarship awards. There are plenty of merit scholarships out there for high school juniors, sophomores, and freshmen, too. And you can apply for scholarships even if your voice hasn't changed or you haven't found that one stray hair yet. A surprising number of scholarship programs are also geared toward middle school and even elementary school students!

To give you a sense of the wide range of scholarship awards available to high school students and their younger siblings, peruse this sampler of scholarship programs. Notice that even in this short list, the fields, interests, and activities that are recognized for meritorious

Scholarship contests for younger kids are often project oriented and team driven, and have a strong learning component. Many programs use adult mentors as well.

Some of these scholarships are described in depth (with insider strategies and sample winning entries) in my companion book, The Scholarship Scouting Report.

awards include oratory, jazz performance, environmental reporting, government service, inventions, visual arts, sports, creative writing, essay writing, science research, community service, history appreciation, computer programming, and graphic design.

A SCHOLARSHIP SAMPLER FOR STUDENTS AGE 19 OR YOUNGER

American Legion High School Oratorical Contest (grades 9–12)

Canon Envirothon (grades 9–12)

Coca-Cola Scholars Program (grade 12)

Discover Card Tribute Awards (grade 11)

DuPont Challenge (grades 7–12)

Duracell/NSTA Invention Challenge (grades 6–12)

ESPN SportsFigures Scholarship (grade 12)

Executive Women International Scholarship Program (grade 11)

Imation Computer Arts Scholarship (grades 9–12)

Jazz Club of Sarasota Scholarship Program (grades 9–12)

Miss Active Teen Across America (ages 13–19)

National History Day Contest (grades 6–12)

Optimist International Essay Contest (grades 10–12)

Optimist International Oratorical Contest (under age 16)

President's Student Service Scholarships (grades 11–12)

Prudential Spirit of Community Awards (grades 5–12)

Scholastic Art and Writing Awards (grades 7–12)

ThinkQuest Internet Challenge (ages 12–19)

Toshiba/NSTA ExploraVision Awards (grades K–12)

U.S. Senate Youth Program (grades 11–12)

Voice of Democracy Program (grades 10–12)

Washington Crossing Foundation Scholarship (grade 12)

Young American Creative Patriotic Art Awards (grades 9–12)

Young Naturalist Awards (grades 7–12)

Home School

ASK THE COACH #6

Can homeschoolers do anything to become eligible for more college scholarships?

College scholarship programs that don't require proof of high school enrollment are certainly open to home-schooled students. Other programs, however, frequently specify that recipients attend or have graduated from an accredited high school, thereby placing homeschooled students out of the running. Even in such cases, you should always ask the scholarship administrators whether any exceptions are made for homeschooled students.

If you are a homeschooled student, or a parent of a homeschooled student, and wish to increase your scholarship paths, there are two different paths you could pursue. First, you could consider enrolling in a public distance education high school. One such institution is the North Dakota Division of Independent Study (www.dis.dpi.state.nd.us). Second, you could enroll in a "credential management" program designed specifically for homeschooled students, such as the one offered by the North Atlantic Regional Schools (www.narsonline.com). In such programs, you choose your own curriculum, and program administrators at an accredited school monitor your progress. After you provide adequate documentation of your coursework, the school grants high school credits, prepares official transcripts, and eventually awards a diploma. For both of these options, you must give up some flexibility, but you gain a more traditional structure that can make you eligible for additional scholarship awards and help you in the college admissions process. ■

UNDERGRADUATE COLLEGE STUDENTS

If you are already in college, you're also in the money—a broad range of scholarship programs are out there for you, too. There are general scholarship programs for all types of undergraduate study, as well as a seemingly endless supply of programs targeted at students pursuing particular majors or career goals. These programs are as wide and varied as those for high school students, and you can win scholarship awards during your freshman, sophomore, junior, and senior years of college. For students nearing completion of their undergraduate degree, the scholarship award is sometimes earmarked for graduate school.

Check out this sampler of scholarships for you and your peers. Once again, diversity rules: Even this short list includes awards based on interest or participation in student government; journalism; visual and literary arts; essay writing; performing arts; musical composition; technical innovation; community service; film production; careers in math, engineering, and natural science; and majors in political science, history, business, or government.

A SCHOLARSHIP SAMPLER FOR COLLEGE UNDERGRADUATES

Barry M. Goldwater Scholarship

BMI Student Composer Awards

Dore Schary Awards

Elie Wiesel Prize in Ethics

First Nationwide Network Scholarship Program

FTE Undergraduate Fellows

Golden Key Art Competition/Literary Contest/Performing Arts Showcase

Harry S. Truman Scholarship Program

Hearst Journalism Awards Program (writing, broadcast, photojournalism)

John Lennon Scholarship

Karla Scherer Foundation Scholarship

Kemper Scholars Grant Program

Kodak Scholarship Program

Morris K. Udall Scholarship

NACA Regional Council Student Leader Scholarships

National Alliance for Excellence Scholarships

State Farm Companies Foundation Exceptional Student Fellowship

Target All-Around Scholarship

The Collegiate Inventors Competition

Tylenol Scholarship

GRADUATE STUDENTS

Even if you're a dissertation-writing, paper-correcting, coffee house–frequenting grad student, there still remain plenty of degree-enabling, debt-liberating, big money–accumulating scholarship opportunities—for just about everything except excessive hyphen-using. Graduate-level scholarships (often referred to as fellowships) are available for students enrolled in most master's degree programs, as well as for students pursuing advanced degrees in very specific academic fields or professional disciplines such as law, business, and medicine. Some prototypical graduate awards include

▌ The Hertz Foundation Fellowship, which awards a full tuition scholarship and $25,000 toward a graduate degree in the physical sciences;

▌ The Harry S. Truman Scholarship, which awards a $30,000 assistance package to students pursuing graduate degrees in government or public service;

▌ The Little Family Foundation MBA Fellowship Award, which provides $10,000 toward a graduate business degree at 19 top business schools;

- The Jacob Javits Fellowship, which awards four dozen scholarships worth $25,500 each to students pursuing master's degrees or Ph.D.s in fine arts, humanities, and social sciences;

- The National Defense Science and Engineering Graduate Fellowship, which doles out $18,500 to $20,000 to 100–150 science and engineering students.

The general rule is that the further you go along in your education (into the realm of doctorates and post-docs), the more specialized and field specific the awards tend to be. When scholarships and fellowships are less field specific, they often target particular categories of graduate studies, like the humanities, the sciences, or professional fields. Some graduate scholarships and fellowships require that applicants already be enrolled in graduate school; others specify that students apply before they begin their graduate studies or during the end of their undergraduate years.

ADULT/NONTRADITIONAL STUDENTS

Adult students who decide to return to school (typically defined as students age 25 or older) can generally apply for the same scholarships that younger college students apply for, because most scholarships for undergraduates don't have age requirements. Thus, adult learners on a nontraditional track will search for scholarships in much the same way as traditional-aged undergraduate students. Adult students also have particular scholarships earmarked especially for them—many sponsored by professional organizations, corporations, foundations, or continuing education schools—that take into account their broader life experiences. A few examples of such scholarship awards include:

- Orville Redenbacher's Second Start Scholarship, which awards 25 scholarships of $1,000 each to adult students over age 30;

- Barbara Thomas Enterprises Scholarship, which provides a $5,000 scholarship to a single parent enrolled in a health information management or technology program;

- Talbots Women's Scholarship Fund, which awards five $10,000 scholarships and fifty $1,000 scholarships to women returning to college later in life to finish their undergraduate degrees;

- Golden Key Adult Scholar Awards, which provides $1,000 awards to adult students over the age of 25 who are members of the Golden Key Honor Society.

AMAZING GRACE

 Grace MacDowell-Boyer of Cedar City, Utah, a 44-year-old mother of six, was awarded a $2,500 scholarship from the All-USA College Academic Team program, a prestigious national scholarship program for college undergraduates. After years of volunteering with children with learning disabilities, Grace, who has three autistic children, decided to get a degree in psychology—for which she researched the effectiveness of videotaped self-modeling in children with autism. Of the 20 winners of this national scholarship award, Grace was the only grandmother.

ASK THE COACH #7

Are there scholarships for distance learning?

Many scholarships that leave the choice of college up to you specify that the award money must be used at an accredited school and as part of a two- or four-year degree program. As long as your particular distance-learning or online institution meets these requirements, you should be able to use most scholarship awards. For distance-learning students in degree programs that take longer than four years, the usability of such scholarship funds may be more limited. As for scholarships earmarked especially for distance-learning students, a prevalent source of such funding, as well as information on outside funding sources, is the specific colleges and universities that offer substantial distance-learning degree opportunities. ■

▌ THE SCHOLARSHIP FUNDERS

We now know that students of all ages can play and win the scholarship game. But the question remains, where does all of this wonderful scholarship money come from? Does it fall from the sky? Is it found under the collective sofa cushions of dotcom billionaires? Actually, the primary sources of scholarship funds include the federal government, state governments, private sponsors, as well as individual colleges, universities, and technical/trade schools.

THE FEDERAL GOVERNMENT

The federal government is the largest single source of financial aid, but a large proportion of federal financial aid dollars takes the form of entitlements (such as Pell Grants) or subsidized loans (such as Direct Stafford Loans). Because of the enormous resources of the federal government, however, there are significant amounts of merit-based scholarships for the taking, if you know where to look. For the high school senior going on to college, for example, the Robert C. Byrd Honors Scholarship program can provide thousands of dollars in scholarship funds. For college undergraduates, there are programs funded by a variety of individual governmental departments and agencies, not just the U.S. Department of Education. For graduate studies, the government provides large awards to "underrepresented" students (typically women and minorities), to students in select academic fields, as well as to those pursuing grad studies or research in areas deemed critical to national interests. See Ask the Coach #8 for more on the range of scholarships awarded by specific government agencies.

ASK THE COACH #8

Do U.S. government agencies provide scholarship funds?

Because the various federal government departments and agencies have different agendas to promote, you can expect a variety of less visible scholarship awards with very specific eligibility requirements. For example, the National Security Agency and the Department of Agriculture offer full-ride scholarships to a limited number of qualified applicants, but  they require that recipients become employees after completing their education (sort of like the military ROTC programs). Other agencies, such as the U.S. Customs Service and the Bureau of Alcohol, Tobacco, and Firearms, provide some money to encourage select students to go on to careers in law enforcement. NASA funds Space Grant Consortium scholarships in various states to encourage undergraduate research related to science. And for the younger crowd, the Army, Navy, and Air Force fund scholarship awards for students in grades 9–12 who submit outstanding research papers and participate in the 48 Junior Science and Humanities Symposia. Other federal organizations that award merit scholarships include the National Space Foundation and the National Institutes of Health. For more information on scholarships affiliated with U.S. government agencies, see ScholarshipCoach.com (keyword: USGOVTAGE). ■

STATE GOVERNMENTS

Each state has one or more agencies that oversee the scholarships distributed by the state and administer any state financial aid programs. In the last several years, these agencies have had increasing dollars to spend on merit scholarships. According to recent data collected by the National Association of State Student Grant and Aid programs, state government spending on merit-based scholarships increased 457 percent from 1982 to 1997.

The kinds of merit scholarships available vary greatly from state to state. You will typically find academic scholarships—usually based on grades, test scores, and class rank—that are automatically awarded to *every* student who meets the specified criteria. Georgia's HOPE scholarship program (which is different from the federal HOPE Scholarship tax credit discussed in Chapter 1) has been the poster child in this regard. Since this program began in 1993, more than 500,000 Georgians with a GPA of 3.0 or higher have received more than $1 billion in merit scholarships. Not to be outdone, Alabama, Florida, Kentucky, Louisiana, Maryland, Michigan, New Mexico, Texas, and Washington have either recently enacted new merit-based programs or have dramatically expanded funding for existing programs.

In Appendix B, I provide a list of state agencies, along with their contact information. Check for updates at ScholarshipCoach.com (keyword: STATEGOV).

And just about every state targets different groups of students for awards that encourage study in needed

State agencies in Oregon and Vermont administer many private-sector scholarship programs, too. If you happen to reside in these states (or will be attending school there), these offices are good information resources.

professions (such as health care and teaching), give a financial boost to underrepresented minority groups, or honor and assist the families of public officers (usually police and firefighters) and military personnel killed in the line of duty. Some states require service to the state after graduation (in the profession for which you earned your degree) in exchange for certain scholarship awards. Some of these state-sponsored merit scholarships are usable only at public institutions, and most require that recipients attend an in-state school.

PRIVATE SPONSORS

Scholarships are funded by a variety of private sources and for a variety of ideological and public relations reasons. Fortune 500 corporations, as well as other sizable companies, are a major source of scholarship dollars. Some of the largest privately funded merit scholarship programs in the country are sponsored by such corporate icons as Coca-Cola, Discover Card, Intel, Siemens, Target, Toyota, and Wal-Mart. Companies sponsor these programs not only to help students (and thus contribute to the education of America's future workforce), but also because of the public relations and product promotion benefits that accrue. In addition, a lot of companies offer separate scholarship programs and tuition benefits to employees or their families. These employee scholarship and benefits programs affect a significant percentage of the workforce and are a major source of assistance for college.

Wealthy individuals and family foundations (for example, the William Randolph Hearst Foundation, sponsor of the U.S. Senate Youth Program) are another prime source of scholarship funding. They are generally concerned less with generating publicity than with advancing their particular goals for influencing society or perpetuating the memory of a loved one by funding the education of new generations of students with similar interests and ideals. Some large corporations also set up separate foundations to signify a separate focus on philanthropy. The Coca-Cola Scholars Foundation is a prime example of this practice.

Most fraternal lodges, service groups, veterans associations, and other patriotic and civic organizations—such as the American Legion, Elks Club, Jaycees, Optimist International, Rotary Club, and Veterans of Foreign Wars—sponsor some type of scholarship program. The same goes for fraternities and sororities. The national headquarters of these groups run nationwide programs, while local chapters frequently sponsor their own smaller initiatives. In addition, student activity organizations—such as Boy Scouts/Girl Scouts of America, Key Club, 4-H, and the National Honor Society (NHS)—either have their own scholarship programs or participate in the programs of other organizations that support their values. On the local level, prominent businesses, banks, credit unions, chambers of commerce, newspapers, television stations, and religious groups are frequent scholarship sponsors.

The Western Sunbathing Association, a regional chapter of the American Association for Nude Recreation, provides $1,000 scholarships to members' children who write an essay on "What Nudism Means to Me." I suspect the reward ceremony requires only "casual" attire.

Special-interest associations and foundations are another abundant (and often overlooked) source of privately funded scholarship dollars. These organizations include business, industry, and professional groups; ethnic, religious, and minority organizations; military, commemorative, and disability associations; sports and hobby alliances and leagues; labor unions; and so on. These diverse groups frequently have definite ideas about who they want to give their scholarship dollars to: An applicant's ultimate eligibility for any particular scholarship is often narrowly defined by the agenda of the scholarship providers, who typically seek to award scholarships to students whose past circumstances or future goals seem to mesh with this agenda.

COLLEGES, UNIVERSITIES, AND TECHNICAL/TRADE SCHOOLS

The vast majority of colleges, universities, and technical/trade schools offer some type of merit-based scholarship awards. The University of Texas at Austin, for instance, awards about 7,000 merit-based scholarships, totaling roughly $15.3 million each year. And because of the increasing competition for strong applicants, the trend is toward increased institutional funding for such merit award programs.

College-sponsored scholarships can be given out by the financial aid and admissions offices, as well as by individual departments. These scholarships range from a few hundred dollars to the entire cost of tuition, books, room, and board. Some merit scholarships may reward all-around achievement, whereas others may be for achievement in a specific field, such as the performing arts.

Schools such as Harvard do award cash prizes for select achievements (although not technically merit scholarships) to students who are already enrolled.

Presently, Ivy League institutions do not award merit-based scholarships. This doesn't mean that some of the most competitive schools don't offer merit-based scholarships. Top schools that do offer college-sponsored merit awards include Caltech, the University of Chicago, Duke University, Emory University, and Rice University (see Ask the Coach #19).

▋ THE SCHOLARSHIP ADMINISTRATORS

Guess what. . . . The people who fund the scholarships aren't always the same people who run the scholarship programs. When the source of scholarship funding is separate from the organization that oversees the application process, the latter group is referred to as the scholar-

For scholarship contests sponsored by service organizations, fraternal lodges, veterans' associations, or family foundations, the organization that puts up the money typically administers the contest as well.

The National Association of Secondary School Principals administers the Prudential Spirit of Community Awards, the National Honor Society Scholarship, and the Principal's Leadership Award.

ship administrators. These folks are the gatekeepers who guard the entrance to the scholarship Promised Land.

Who are these administrators? Well, that depends on the particular scholarship program. Many corporations, for instance, outsource the logistics of running a scholarship to a group that specializes in conducting such programs. Such groups include the Citizens' Scholarship Foundation of America (CSFA), the American Association of School Administrators (AASA), the National Association of Secondary School Principals (NASSP), and the National Science Teachers Association (NSTA).

In fact, some scholarship programs—such as the Intel Science Talent Search, administered by Science Service—are created entirely by these third-party organizations, who seek out corporate sponsors to fund their pet programs. So when you and/or your school receives a winner's check, it will likely be from one of these scholarship-creating organizations, rather than from the sponsoring company itself.

▌ APPLICATION JUDGES

Here's another heads up: The group that funds or administers the scholarship program does not always judge the merits of the scholarship applications. Anywhere from a single judge to hundreds of judges (if you figure in all the judges at the state levels of a big national program) may be responsible for evaluating entries. Furthermore, different scholarship programs employ different types of judges.

For scholarships administered by the third-party organizations I mentioned, judges are generally drawn from the ranks of current or former teachers, school administrators, and organization staff members. High-profile national scholarships administered by these types of organizations may also employ blue-ribbon panels for final judging; these panels generally include celebrities, government officials, and other notables.

On the local level, blue-ribbon panels typically include television and radio personalities, successful entrepreneurs, and professional athletes. In contests that use this method of judging, a limited number of finalists are usually preselected and then presented to the blue-ribbon panel for final evaluation.

For scholarship programs administered by corporations themselves, public relations personnel may select the winners. Programs conducted by service organizations, fraternal lodges, associations, and foundations are likely to be judged by members of the organizations.

Understanding who the judges are and what they expect can give you a strategic edge when you're preparing your entry. We'll explore this advantage later. For now, suffice it to say that although scholarship contests are mostly judged on the published judging criteria, certain "hidden" criteria often enter the mix. (See Chapter 6 for more on this topic.)

■ TARGETED SCHOLARSHIP AWARDS

Think of the narrowly targeted scholarships as icing on the cake. There's plenty of cake–that is, broader, wide-open scholarships–for all. But for those who track down these specialized awards, the results can be finger lickin' good.

Now that we've explored who can play the scholarship game and the key individuals and groups who influence its outcome, we can take a closer look at how certain scholarship programs target particular types of applicants—namely, those who have personal characteristics consistent with the agendas of the organizations that pay the bills. Keep in mind that there are plenty of general scholarship programs out there that *don't* have particularly narrow eligibility targets and are therefore open to a wide array of students. In this section, however, we explore the major categories of scholarship targeting, so that you'll be better able to find those targeted scholarships that are a bull's-eye for someone like you.

Geographic Region

Perhaps the most common type of applicant targeting is based on geographic region. On the local level, particular awards may be designated to students from specific districts or communities. This is especially true of scholarships sponsored by local businesses and organizations that hope to benefit from the publicity and community goodwill. Scholarships targeted at students from a particular state or several states are also common. The McDonald's restaurant owners of the New York tri-state area, for example, fund the McDonald's Golden Arches Scholarships. (Do you want fries with that scholarship?) These 100 awards of $1,000 each are open only to residents of New York, New Jersey, and Connecticut.

Organizational Membership

Some scholarship contests are open only to members of particular organizations. The National Honor Society scholarship program, for instance, offers hundreds of $1,000 scholarships for society members in grade 12. Other national youth-oriented organizations that provide or administer member-only scholarship awards include the Boy Scouts and Girl Scouts, Key Club, 4-H Club, Junior Achievement, National Council of Youth Leadership, Golden Key International Honor Society, and American Radio Relay League, as well as career exploration programs such as the Future Business Leaders of America (FBLA) and the

In Chapter 4, I discuss the virtues of expanding your scholarship eligibility by joining organizations in areas of interest that award member-only scholarships.

Future Farmers of America (FFA). Many of the special-interest associations discussed earlier in the chapter also require that scholarship recipients be members of the association.

Family Affiliation

Other scholarships are limited to students who are affiliated (through their parents or ancestors) with particular groups, as well as historical figures or events. For instance, the Descendants of the Signers of the Declaration of Independence Scholarship provides college cash to undergrad and grad students who can prove they are direct descendants of one of the Signers. (When someone tells you to "put your John Hancock right here," if that is actually your name, you might just qualify!)

Some corporations offer scholarships as an additional benefit to employees and their families. ABC/Capital Cities, for instance, conducts a scholarship program open only to dependent children of company staff. These employee-focused scholarship programs tend to be sponsored by companies with more than 500 employees and other large, well-established business entities.

A number of scholarships are aimed at students whose families have a military affiliation. Such programs may specify that the parents or ancestors of applicants be war veterans and may even specify further requirements (service in a particular war or service division, death or disability, etc.). The First Cavalry Division Association Scholarships are given to children of soldiers who died or were fully disabled from injuries while serving in the First Cavalry Division during and since the Vietnam War or during the Persian Gulf War.

College and Career Goals

Some scholarships, especially those sponsored by industry groups or professional associations, are designed for students with particular college plans or career and vocational interests. Foundations with specific societal goals in mind also frequently create these types of programs. The Washington Crossing Foundation, for instance, targets students with "an interest in government service." Like many scholarships, this government service specification is very broad: Past winners have included students interested in becoming public prosecutors, senators, National Park Service botanists, army doctors, high school teachers, and everything in between.

As a general rule for high school students and young undergraduates, even if you are only marginally interested in a particular field or career, you should not hesitate to apply for the scholarship. Although most scholarships of this type specify that applicants have a "genuine interest" in the given field, judges recognize that for applicants in their teens, or even early twenties, virtually nothing is etched in stone. Interests can, and often do, change. Although these scholarships may require that you take some courses or major in a related area of study, there's nothing preventing you from later pursuing a different track. Other scholarships may require merely that you demonstrate your interest through extracurricular activities or by joining your field's professional association (which can, in fact, open up additional scholarship opportunities to you).

Race, Ethnicity, and Denomination

Plenty of scholarship money is also available to students who are members of ethnic minority groups, such as African Americans, Asians, Hispanics, or Native Americans. Some scholarships are open to members of any ethnic minority, whereas others are targeted at a particular group. A term that is used in some of these scholarship competitions that can make things a bit more confusing is "traditionally underrepresented ethnic minority"—a specification that generally does not include Asians or Asian Americans. Other scholarship programs seek to "promote ethnic diversity and cultural awareness," but they *don't* actually require that all award recipients be part of an ethnic or minority group.

Unfortunately, many scholarship seekers believe that if they are not members of an underrepresented minority group, they are not eligible for scholarships targeted for students with a particular ethnicity. This is far from the truth: *A high proportion of fraternal organizations based on a particular ethnicity offer scholarships to students who fit their own ethnic profiles.* Whether your heritage is Chinese, Cuban, Danish, Japanese, Italian, Norwegian, Laotian, Polish, Swiss, Greek, Armenian, Cambodian, Filipino, Slovakian, Puerto Rican, French, Hawaiian, Portuguese, Vietnamese, Indian, or Korean, or is based in some other part of the world, you can frequently find ethnically targeted college scholarship programs.

There are, in fact, actual scholarships for students with each of these ethnic backgrounds.

Your religious denomination can yield surprising scholarship opportunities as well. Whether you are Baptist, Lutheran, Methodist, Presbyterian, Roman Catholic, Jewish, Bahai, Muslim, Eastern Orthodox, Sikh, a Christian Scientist, or even an atheist or agnostic, there may be money for college based on your religious beliefs or your membership in a church, synagogue, temple, or mosque.

Gender

Never assume from the name of a scholarship alone that the scholarship is open only to one gender. I won an award from the National Association of Press Women in a journalism contest that was open to both males and females.

Some scholarship contests, especially those sponsored by various women's groups, are open only to female applicants. The Business and Professional Women's Foundation Career Advancement Scholarship Program is targeted to female undergrads, age 25 or older, who are upgrading their skills, training for a new career, or planning to enter the job market. As you might expect, scholarships open only to male students are not as common. (My estimate is that there is an approximately a 4:1 ratio of women-only awards to men-only awards.) For some scholarship contests open to both sexes, however, the criteria may specify that one male national winner and one female national winner be selected in each category.

Disabilities

A variety of national advocacy groups for people with disabilities, several giant pharmaceutical companies, and particular foundations and associations provide scholarships specifically for students with disabilities. If you or a loved one has a hearing or speech impairment, a visual impairment, asthma, attention deficit disorder, dyslexia or other learning disability, epilepsy, diabetes, autism, sickle cell disease, or hemophilia, or if you are paraplegic or use a wheelchair, there may be additional college money to help level the playing field.

See Ask the Coach #17 for scholarship search techniques specifically for students with disabilities.

Employment, Activities, and Hobbies

Did you ever think that working part-time flipping burgers or carrying golf clubs could earn you a college scholarship? A variety of scholarship programs reward all sorts of student employment. The activities and hobbies you pursue in your spare time can also earn you big scholarship dollars. Such pursuits include bowling, amateur radio, aviation, dog shows, horseback riding, scuba diving, sewing, surfing, astronomy, music, artistic endeavors, sports, and foreign languages, to name a few. I've even seen scholarships for duck calling!

The Burger King/ McLamore North American Scholarship, for instance, requires part-time work as a high school senior while maintaining at least a B average.

■ SCHOLARSHIP APPLICATION COMPONENTS

The application process for merit scholarships tends to focus on either your **current performance** on specified tasks (such as writing, artwork, oratory, or web page design) or your **past achievement** in particular areas (such as extracurricular activities, academics, athletics, or community service). In both instances, there are a series of application components that are commonly used, each of which is discussed below.

Essays and Short Answer Questions

Most scholarship essays are required to be between 300 and 1,500 words long, with 500 words the average. Scholarship essays aren't usually required to be longer than this, because most organizations don't have the staff to devote to judging lengthy expositions. Some scholarship applications also include short answer questions that demand especially brief responses—usually 150 words or less. This is good news: Less work for you, and more scholarship bucks per word!

Sample Work and Project Submissions

Some scholarships, especially those for writing or the visual arts, require you to submit samples of your work, such as portfolios or clippings. The Scholastic Art and Writing Awards, for instance, have students submit sample work in each of 24 categories of competition. Science-oriented scholarship programs (other than those for graduate school) most frequently require the submission of a project. The Duracell/NSTA Invention Challenge requires you to submit an invention that runs on Duracell batteries; more elaborate programs, like the Intel Science Talent Search, want an in-depth scientific research report on a subject of your choosing.

Extracurricular Activity Lists

When scholarship programs ask for information about extracurricular activities, they basically expect a summary of everything you do outside of class time. This includes school clubs, sports, jobs, independent projects, volunteer activities, and everything in between (except trips to the mall). Some programs distinguish between different types of extracurricular activities, such as school-related activities and community activities.

Most applications request that you submit such activities in a list format. Some contests limit you to the space provided on the application; others let you attach additional sheets. In addition to a brief description of each activity, you may be asked to note how much time you devoted to the activity; what, if any, leadership positions or offices you held; and what awards or honors you received from the endeavor.

Because of the substantial overlap in application requirements, applying for multiple scholarships is a lot less work than you might expect.

Grade Transcripts

As I mentioned in Chapter 1, many scholarship programs don't even look at your grades. When they do request grade information, they often require the submission of a grade transcript. The transcript can be either official (signed, stamped, and sealed by the registrar) or unofficial (just a printout of your grades to date). It's always a good idea to have extra copies of your transcript on hand for last-minute scholarship submissions.

Letters of Recommendation

Some scholarship applications may request one letter from a teacher or professor at your school and another from someone who knows you in a different capacity (employer, coach, club adviser, etc.).

Just as they are in the college admissions process, letters of recommendation are an integral part of many scholarship applications. Some contests ask letter writers to answer specific questions or evaluate the applicant in terms of the judging criteria. Others give letter writers free rein. Most scholarship applications do not specify a word limit for recommendation letters.

Commonly, scholarship programs that request recommendation letters ask for one or two—three letters for one application is generally the most you'll be asked to provide. The vast majority of contests allow you to choose the people you want to write recommendations for you. If you can't off the top of your head think of someone who would write you a strong recommendation, don't worry. In Chapter 10, I'll show you how to sow the seeds for a bountiful harvest of great recommendation letters.

Interviews

Scholarship interviews can take place over the phone or in person. They can be conducted by an individual interviewer or by a panel of judges. For prominent national scholarship contests, such interviews generally occur only after a number of finalists have been selected from the pool of applicants. In contrast, local competitions may make interviews an integral part of the preliminary judging. Judges may also use interviews to group winners into different *levels* of awards, separating top scholarship winners from recipients of smaller prizes.

See Chapter 12 for the secrets of the scholarship interview.

Auditions

Auditions typically are held for scholarships related to the performing arts or oratorical scholarships. In the music portion of the Arts Recognition and Talent Search, for instance, finalists for five levels of awards are flown to Miami, Florida, for live auditions. For science-focused competitions, the "audition" may involve a formal presentation of scientific findings from research a student has conducted. The most strenuous audition-type event I've faced was in the Century III Leaders program, when I attended a three-day national meeting. While all of us nerve-wracked state winners debated and proposed solutions to societal issues, the judges sat coolly in the background, evaluating each of us. Auditions this elaborate, however, are the exception.

In the end, I took home the top prize— worth $11,000.

Awards and Honors

Although they are far less prevalent than essays, lists of extracurricular activities, or recommendation letters, summaries of any awards and honors a student has received may also be requested on the application form. The definition of what exactly constitutes an "award and honor" is typically vague. Generally, you want to include not only trophy-type awards, but also honors that are less tangible (such as when you represented your school at a conference on reducing youth violence).

In Chapter 11, I'll show you how to use awards and honors lists to further your strategic objectives.

Test Results

When students see the words "test results," they naturally think in terms of the PSAT, SAT, or ACT—those annoying standardized tests designed by some wicked exam writer in a diabolical plot to bring pain, suffering, and multiple-choice bubble-forms into the lives of otherwise happy high school juniors and seniors. When you are required to submit test scores—typically for hardcore academic scholarships—you will need to submit copies of official results from the test maker or will merely need to write your scores on the application form.

Sometimes, there are test scores relevant to scholarship applications that have nothing to do with those heinous tests you take to get into college. The Century III Leaders program, for instance, administered a 50-question exam on current events. Scholarship programs that involve foreign language achievement may administer written or spoken tests. (*¡Ay caramba!*) The inclusion of such specialized tests, however, is relatively unusual.

■ STEER CLEAR OF (MOST) ENTRY FEES

Unlike the hefty application fees that colleges typically charge, scholarship contests generally don't cost anything to enter. On occasion, you might be asked to pay a small processing fee (for example, the National Honor Society Scholarship charges $4), but this is unusual. In fact, the only scholarships I've seen that cost anything more than a couple bucks to apply for are performance-oriented competitions that involve live auditions. For such programs, entry fees may be in the $25 to $35 range.

In many instances, your school may be willing to pay such entry fees for you.

If you happen to find an unfamiliar scholarship contest that charges substantial entry fees, proceed with caution. Scholarship scams do exist. Signs that a contest could be a scam include guarantees that you will win, a sketchy application process, and numerous typos on official forms. Furthermore, just because a "foundation" or "association" with an official-sounding name sponsors a particular scholarship, don't assume it's legitimate. If you suspect that a scholarship could be a scam, contact the Better Business Bureau (www.bbb.org), the Federal Trade Commission (www.ftc.gov), or your state's Bureau of Consumer Protection, or else steer clear altogether.

SPENDING YOUR MERIT SCHOLARSHIPS

The moment you find out that you've won a scholarship is truly awesome. I highly recommend it. One time, when I was playing pool with friends at a local pool hall after school, I got a phone call from my parents. They told me I had just won a $10,000 award. How ecstatic was I? Ecstatic enough to run the table!

The $10,000 I had just won was a **portable merit scholarship**, meaning that it could be used at any accredited vocational school, two-year college, or four-year college in the U.S. I used the money at Harvard, but I could just as easily have claimed it at my hometown college, the University of Oregon, or anywhere else. Portable scholarships are the crown jewels of the financial aid system because you don't have to sacrifice college choice.

*The key word here is **accredited**. I could use the money at any legitimate institution of higher education, but not at the Ben Kaplan School of Buying a Brand New Car.*

Although many scholarships specify **full portability**, some local ones may be only **partially portable**. This means that you have to use the award at a school in your immediate area or home state. Partial portability is a common characteristic of scholarships and grants sponsored by state and local governments.

ASK THE COACH #10

Is scholarship money taxable?

The good news is that scholarship money spent on tuition, books, school fees, and other course-related expenses is usually not taxable. As long as you don't spend the money on such things as room and board, clothing, or transportation (expenses that generally cause scholarship money to become taxable), the government shouldn't take a bite out of  your winnings. This is another big benefit of winning scholarships: For you or your parents to contribute $1,000 to your education, your family would need to earn significantly more than $1,000—because of all the state and federal (and maybe even local) income taxes that must first be paid. To put it another way, each dollar derived from scholarship winnings is worth quite a bit more than a dollar earned from your after-school job or your parents' employment—specifically because Uncle Sam doesn't take a cut out of your winnings. ■

School-specific scholarships, on the other hand, can be used only at a particular institution of higher education. If you choose not to attend the earmarked school, you can't claim the award. School-specific scholarships are less desirable than portable ones, since you're limited in where you can use the money. If, however, you get a school-specific scholarship to the college you actually *want* to attend, the fact that the award isn't portable doesn't matter.

The techniques I outline throughout this book will help you find and win both portable and school-specific awards. But because I believe that financial considerations shouldn't dictate which school you choose, I've put special emphasis on portable merit scholarships that you can use at *any* institution—including the college of your dreams.

CHAPTER 2 SUMMARY AND KEYWORDS

Money Availability: There is scholarship money for high school students, their younger siblings, college undergrads, graduate students, and adult/nontraditional students—representing talents, activities, interests, accomplishments, and affiliations in many areas and fields. There are even scholarships available for distance-learning programs. The further along you go in your education, the more specialized and field-specific the awards tend to be. ■

Scholarship Providers: Federal and state governments, private sponsors, and colleges provide scholarship funds. Private sponsors include corporations, individuals and family foundations, fraternal and service groups, student activity organizations, and a wide variety of special-interest associations and foundations. Money from these funders is advanced for all kinds of ideological, altruistic, and public relations reasons. ■

Scholarship Administrators and Judges: Funders do not always run their own scholarship programs. They sometimes outsource the logistics of the program to third-party administrators. The application judges may be yet a different group. You need to understand who does what for each scholarship program when you are formulating your application strategy. ■

Targeted Awards: In addition to numerous general scholarships that vast numbers of students can apply for, more specific scholarships with a narrower target audience are also available. Organizations may target specific students according to such factors as geographic region; organiza-

tional membership; family affiliation; college and career goals; race, ethnicity, and denomination; gender; disabilities; and employment, activities, and hobbies. ■

Scholarship Application Components: Some scholarships focus on current performance; others emphasize past achievement. Scholarship applications may include essay and short answer questions, sample work and project submissions, lists of extracurricular activities, grade transcripts, letters of recommendation, interviews, auditions, summaries of awards and honors, and test results. ■

Entry Fees: Most scholarship applications don't require entry fees; the small number of bona fide scholarships that do generally charge only a few dollars. Some performance-oriented scholarship competitions may charge higher fees, but the student's school may pick up the fee. All other entry costs may be a scam, and suspect applications require due diligence before paying and applying. ■

Spending the Money: *Portable* scholarship money can be used at any accredited school. *Partially portable* awards are limited to use at schools in your home state or immediate geographic region. *School-specific* scholarship winnings can be claimed only if you enroll at a particular college. ■

Taxes: Scholarship money is usually not taxed if it is used for tuition, books, and fees. This makes $1,000 in scholarship winnings much more valuable than a $1,000 (before tax) paycheck. ■

SCHOLARSHIPCOACH.COM KEYWORDS

For more information on a scholarship or topic mentioned in this chapter, enter the associated keyword in the keyword link box located in the Coach's Locker Room section of ScholarshipCoach.com.

Scholarship/Topic	Keyword
All-USA College Academic Team	ALLUSACOL
American Legion Oratorical Contest	LEGIONORA
Barbara Thomas Enterprises Scholarship	BTHOMAS
Barry M. Goldwater Scholarship	BARGOLD

BMI Student Composer Awards	BMICOMP
Burger King/McLamore North American Scholarship	BURGER
Business and Professional Women's Foundation Career Advancement Scholarship	BIZWOMEN
Canon Envirothon	ENVIRO
Coca-Cola Scholars Program	COKE
Collegiate Inventors Competition	COLINVENT
Descendants of the Signers of the Declaration of Independence	SIGNERS
Discover Card Tribute Awards	DISCOVER
Dore Schary Awards	SCHARY
DuPont Challenge	DUPONT
Duracell/NSTA Invention Challenge	DURACELL
Elie Wiesel Prize in Ethics	WIESEL
ESPN SportsFigures Scholarship	ESPN
Executive Women International Scholarship Program	EXECWOMEN
First Cavalry Division Association Scholarships	FIRSTCAV
First Nationwide Network Scholarship Program	FIRSTNAT
FTE Undergraduate Fellows	FTE
Golden Key Adult Scholar Awards	GOLDKAD
Golden Key Art Competition	GOLDKART
Golden Key Literary Contest	GOLDKLIT
Golden Key Performing Arts Showcase	GOLDKPERF
Harry S Truman Scholarship Program	TRUMAN
Hearst Journalism Awards Program	HEARST
Hertz Foundation Fellowship	HERTZ
Imation Computer Arts Scholarship	IMATION
Jacob Javits Fellowship	JAVITS
Jazz Club of Sarasota Scholarship Program	JAZZSARA
John Lennon Scholarship	LENNON

Karla Scherer Foundation Scholarship	SCHERER
Kemper Scholars Grant Program	KEMPER
Kodak Scholarship Program	KODAK
Little Family Foundation MBA Fellowship Award	LITTLEFAM
McDonald's Golden Arches Scholarships	BIGMAC
Miss Active Teen Across America	ACTIVTEEN
Morris K. Udall Scholarship	UDALL
NACA Regional Council Student Leader Scholarships	NACA
National Alliance for Excellence Scholarships	EXCEL
National Defense Science and Engineering Graduate Fellowship	NATLDEF
National History Day Contest	HISTDAY
Optimist International Essay Contest	OPTESSAY
Optimist International Oratorical Contest	OPTORA
Orville Redenbacher's Second Start Scholarship	ORVILLE
President's Student Service Scholarships	PRESSERV
Prudential Spirit of Community Awards	PRUDENT
Scholastic Art and Writing Awards	SCHOLART
State Farm Exceptional Student Fellowship	STATEFARM
Talbots Women's Scholarship Fund	TALBOTS
Target All-Around Scholarship	TARGET
ThinkQuest Internet Challenge	TQUEST
Toshiba/NSTA ExploraVision Awards	EXPLORA
Tylenol Scholarship	TYLENOL
United States Senate Youth Program	SENATE
U.S. Government Agency Scholarships	USGOVTAGE
Voice of Democracy Program	VOICE
Washington Crossing Foundation Scholarship	WASHCROSS
Young American Creative Patriotic Art Awards	PATRIART
Young Naturalist Awards	YOUNGNAT

What Parents Can Do to Help

INSIDE THIS CHAPTER

▋ Parents as scholarship searchers and research assistants

▋ Helping with strategy and organization

▋ Proofing the applications

▋ Being a good supporter and sounding board

▋ A letter from my parents

❚ SEVEN WAYS PARENTS CAN HELP

This chapter is written specifically for all the parents out there. If you're a student, however, it's also good for you to read it so that you can brief your parents on the details. Or better yet, read this chapter first, let your parents read it, and then discuss how to work together.

Parents

Some of my fondest memories of my scholarship quest were the experiences I shared with my parents. I remember finding out about one particular scholarship the very day the application was due, forcing me to scribble down my application responses even as my mom warmed up the car for a last-minute deadline dash. We then raced across town to turn in the barely completed form—the two of us acting like recent graduates of the Mario Andretti School of Scholarship Deadline Driving.

As for my dad, I think back to all of those late nights he spent—thesaurus in hand—copyediting and proofreading my scholarship essays:

> *Dad:* Is there a better word for *excitement*?
>
> *Me:* *Anticipation? Enthusiasm? Thrill?*
>
> *Dad:* How about *exhilaration*?
>
> *Me:* Dad, you da man!
>
> *Much exhilaration ensues.*

And then there were those moments when we'd all pounce on a letter that had just arrived from a scholarship organization, ripping it open like a pack of wolves. More often than not, the letter would say "Congratulations," and my parents would start dancing around the house, performing 70s disco moves that should never be done in public anymore (at least not by them).

If there was one thing I did right, it was this: I did a wonderful job choosing my parents.

The important thing to realize about the experience I've just described—other than the fact that dancing the "funky chicken" is no longer cool—is that both of my parents were very much active participants in my scholarship quest. We worked together. We cheered together. We got speeding tickets together. We were a team. And in this chapter, for all the parents reading this book, I describe the substantial role that you can play in helping your children win college cash.

For personal perspectives from parents who have been through the college scholarships game, visit ScholarshipCoach.com (keyword: PARENTS).

To write this chapter, I drew on a lot of the questions and feedback I have received from parents who attend my scholarship workshops. I know firsthand that parents are sometimes the most eager participants in the scholarship game—after all, mom and dad are usually the ones footing the lion's share of the bills!

When reading this section, please keep in mind that all of the possible tasks that I suggest parents can do also can be done by students themselves. If, however, you're a mom or dad interested in taking an active role in your child's scholarship quest, then all the better. I'll illustrate how you can spend your time most productively, while keeping a respectful distance from the application work that your child should be doing on his or her own.

HELPING WITH SCHOLARSHIP SEARCHING

Helping in the process of *searching* for scholarships is one of the best ways you can make a significant contribution to your child's scholarship success. From assisting

For details on how to locate scholarships that are right for your child to apply for, check out Chapter 4.

in an Internet search to visiting other high schools or colleges in your area, you can really help leverage and multiply your child's time. Scholarship searching is an ongoing process, and when you are able to discover new scholarships for your children to apply for, you allow them to focus more of their time and attention on the critical job of strategically completing each scholarship application.

For parents of children in high school, some additional considerations may prove useful. Because many high schools (my former school was one) use parent volunteers to staff the school's college and career center, enterprising moms and dads can gain special access to the school's scholarship resources. If you frequently volunteer at the school, try to volunteer at this center, where you'll likely find a cache of scholarship files, applications, and search resources (such as CD-ROMs and specialized directories). You will quickly accumulate a wealth of expert knowledge about the key scholarship resources at your school and will be in a better position to uncover scholarship applications that may be buried beneath a pile of dense paperwork on some counselor's desk.

It's always a good idea for parents to schedule time with a school counselor to discuss the scholarship resources available at the school.

Even if you, as a working parent, don't have time to volunteer, you may still have better access to certain high school resources. For instance, at some schools, particular scholarship resources are accessible to students only through their counselors. The counselors, however, may be willing to give interested parents direct access to these scholarship files. Another good strategy is to keep open lines of communication with other parents you know from your child's school or nearby schools, especially parents who seem particularly active in the school. Ask them what scholarships and scholarship resources they are aware of. Ask parents of older students what scholarships their children have applied for. And don't forget to peruse old graduation programs or school newspapers for mention of scholarship awards won by recent graduates.

If you don't know other parents who are particularly knowledgeable about this, try attending a PTA meeting, and talk to the parents there.

If you're the parent of a college student, especially one attending college away from home, keep in mind that your child may be able to apply for scholarships in the area he or she is attending college as well as in your home area. A great thing to do is to divide up the scholarship search workload geographically. Have your child seek out resources at his or her college and in the community where the college is located, while you search for scholarship opportunities in your immediate area.

Discussing the scholarship application process with parents after one of my tour workshops.

STRATEGIZING WITH YOUR KIDS

An important point to emphasize to your children is that scholarship applications aren't thrown together haphazardly. The best ones are strategically crafted. Therefore, one of the most important roles you can play is to help your child work out a strategy for each scholarship application. Read Chapter 7 and discuss as a family what type of applicant portraits you are trying to paint in each case. Just as portraits of a person can look different depending on how he or she is dressed, posed, and lit, the "look and feel" of each of your applications may be perceived differently by the judges of separate awards.

Review Chapter 6 with your children to make sure they have taken into account the specific agenda and mission of each scholarship sponsor and considered the universal criteria that influence scholarship judging for each award.

Help your children brainstorm who would write the most suitable recommendation letters for each type of scholarship, and assist them in getting together strategic background materials for their recommendation writers, as I describe in more detail in Chapter 10.

PROVIDING RESEARCH ASSISTANCE

If you have younger children as well, get them involved in the process of helping their older siblings in the scholarship game. It's sort of like playing in the minors before being called up to the majors. They'll be that much further along when it's their turn to bat.

Writing a good scholarship essay sometimes involves compiling background information before a student starts writing. This is yet another way that parents can make a significant contribution. The Washington Crossing Foundation scholarship program, for instance, asked applicants to describe in an essay on government service any inspiration "derived from the leadership of George Washington in his famous crossing of the Delaware." Well, at the time, I knew very little about this historic event (except that apparently, as the famous painting shows, he crossed it standing up in a boat). So on the way back from running some errands, my parents stopped by the local public library to photocopy some encyclopedia articles and check out some books about this time period in American history.

In another scholarship application, which required a "what-would-you-do" type essay, I wrote a piece that suggested potential reforms to the American school system. Obviously, it was important that I be up-to-date on the latest developments in the educational reform movement, so my dad conducted a few electronic searches for the latest newspaper, magazine, and journal articles on the topic. My mom found the articles in a university library and made copies for me.

Of course, a lot of this background research I conducted on my own, too. But during very busy times, having this assistance from my parents was a lifesaver, because it let me focus my energy on developing application strategies and crafting the actual application and entry materials so as to have the best chance of winning awards.

Note to students: If your parents help you out in this way, be sure to say "thank you" often, and remember to take out the trash whenever possible!

KEEPING THINGS ORGANIZED

Because some scholarship organizations may be reachable only by phone during hours when your child is in class, it's especially helpful if you are able to make a few follow-up phone calls on his or her behalf.

Managing the stacks of paperwork and keeping track of the various deadlines can test a student's organizational skills (or lack thereof)—especially when he or she has to write two papers, study for three tests, and complete two scholarship applications all in the same week. During these busy times, my parents often helped me in my scholarship quest by sending out letters on my behalf or making phone calls to request scholarship application packages. If I was extremely busy when these applications arrived, they would even help by filing them away and marking the deadlines on a big scholarship calendar that we hung in my room.

BEING A GOOD SOUNDING BOARD

Sometimes, when filling out a scholarship application, I would get a nasty case of "activity amnesia": I couldn't think of a single appropriate activity or credential to describe. Here's another place where you, as a parent, can be helpful—serving as the extra "memory card" for your child. Since you've been there for many of your daughter's or son's projects, you may be able to recollect important experiences or details that he or she has forgotten. If your child has left out an important experience that would work great in a particular essay, chances are you can help jog his or her memory.

Being a sounding board also means helping your child prepare for any upcoming scholarship interviews. As I describe in Chapter 12, you can play the role of interviewer and pepper your child with practice questions, helping him or her think up persuasive on-the-spot answers.

If you use other skills as part of your job, contribute these strengths as well.

In addition to helping with all of the tasks I've mentioned, parents can be an important source of general feedback on an entire scholarship application. When serving in this capacity, try to offer suggestions, rather than criticism—highlight what you like about the application as much as what can be improved. (Tip: Avoid words like "sucks.")

REVIEWING THE APPLICATION

If you do a lot of writing as part of your job, you might make a great scholarship application copyeditor and proofreader. Aside from my own last-pass reading, my dad conducted the final copyediting and proofreading for most of my submissions. (In fact, he proofread this paragraph—so blamme himm if ya finda typpo.) You can identify grammatical and punctuation corrections, provide ideas for reorganization, and offer content suggestions, but don't make the mistake of inserting *your* voice in place of your child's—a big "no-no" that scholarship judges are adept at detecting.

Grandparents may also be good resources for help with scholarship searching or proofreading.

ASK THE COACH #11

How can I motivate my child to pursue scholarships?

I'm no expert on parenting, but let me relate to you some successful motivational techniques that other parents have used. First, many parents have suggested sitting down as a family and making sure that your kids understand the impact of college costs on the family's overall finan-

cial situation. Show them how playing the scholarship game—and playing to win—can make a big difference.

Second, emphasize the secondary benefits of winning college scholarships. Explain to your children that by *not* having a large debt burden to service, they will have more freedom during and after college— freedom to pursue the activities they feel passionate about, seek the jobs that are the most fulfilling (and fun), or even take some time off to travel and see the world.

Third, show them all the different types of scholarships out there and convey that you really think they can win scholarship money. Emphasize that you don't have to be a whiz kid to win these awards and that there's a strong learning curve—they don't have to be Mr. or Ms. Perfect to begin with and will improve over time. Relate to them my own scholarship success story to show how possible this all really is, and begin to go through this book with them. Finally, communicate to your children that you'll support them in their scholarship quest any way you can, especially by performing many of the tasks I've outlined in this chapter. ■

Talk about being good supporters!

GIVING SUPPORT AND ENCOURAGEMENT

One of the most important things parents can do is be supportive, regardless of the outcome of any particular scholarship application. A common trait among successful scholarship applicants is that they know they are not going to win all—or even most—of the scholarships they apply for. They take things in stride, and apply for as many as they can to put the odds in their favor. So help your child laugh off any scholarship rejection letters that come in the mail (we all get them) and not waste energy thinking about the ones that got away. Remind your child that the most powerful question in any scholarship seeker's vocabulary is "What's next?" My parents were great in sharing my success, but they were even stronger in vanquishing any sense of failure that I occasionally felt about entries that were not as successful. Applying for scholarships is a lot like weightlifting or aerobics: More important than how you do on any given day is the fact that you stick with it over the long haul.

Parents

A Letter From My Parents

Dear Parents of Future Scholarship Winners:

When our son applied for his first scholarship, we probably felt similar to the way you do right now: We encouraged our son to apply and did whatever we could to help, but we really didn't expect a whole lot to come from it. When the scholarship checks did start rolling in, it was a wonderful surprise. The biggest shock, however, had nothing to do with all the money. It was something more important: the dramatic, even life-changing transformation we witnessed in our son.

You see, because of the personal nature of scholarship applications, just filling out these forms forced him to think about his strengths, to confront his weaknesses, and, most importantly, to dream about his future. In short, entering scholarship contests forced him to discover who he really was, and to begin developing a plan to fully realize his talents and passions. Not that this plan can't or won't change. Indeed, as any grown-up knows, it will change many times during the course of a lifetime. But it was this underlying sense of purpose and progress that led to Ben's many other successes, and that, most importantly, led him to discover the things that would make him most happy. The result was a gradual transformation in our son, as he took increasing control over his own destiny. This has been very inspiring for us, and has even influenced our own life decisions.

There are, of course, many other benefits to applying for scholarships—such things as enhanced writing skills, heightened self-promotional abilities, and substantially improved college applications (which dramatically increases the likelihood that your son or daughter will be admitted to the college of his or her choice). But these things paled in comparison to our son's personal growth. We also grew as a family through the transformational process of working together toward a common goal. The camaraderie of the quest has resulted in the forging of close ties—bonds that, we believe, supercede the expected parent–child relationship. Even when the scholarship money is used up, and the memories of award ceremonies become cloudy, these bonds live on.

If we can offer any advice to other parents it would be to play a supporting role—instead of directing the action. This is frequently the hardest lesson for a parent. Nonetheless, it is sometimes the most valuable thing you can do.

Likewise, keep encouraging your child to apply for college scholarships even if the first few bids are unsuccessful. As a family, we've come to realize that learning how to *win* first means learning how to *lose;* and in learning how to lose, you actually learn how to win. Furthermore, scholarship contest results should *never* be treated as an assessment of how good or talented your child may be. These contests are highly subjective and often unpredictable, and results should never be taken personally, or as a measure of self-worth.

In a nutshell, your role as a parent of a scholarship game player is a multifaceted one. It includes encouraging your child to apply for numerous scholarships, helping him to use time efficiently and meet deadlines, and supporting her in the midst of temporary setbacks. It may also include helping him or her fine-tune applications, conduct research, or express future goals and dreams. Moreover, being a part of your child's scholarship team will help you, as it helped us, to become a better parent. So even though the immediate need for college financing may motivate your child's search for scholarships, remember that regardless of outcomes, the effort is most definitely time well spent.

Best wishes,

Gary & Patana Kaplan

CHAPTER 3 SUMMARY AND KEYWORDS

Scholarship Searchers: Assisting with the scholarship search process is one of the best ways parents can contribute. This allows your children to focus on the application itself. Volunteering at the college and career center at your child's school can also facilitate this search. ■

Strategy Consultants: Parents can help their children craft a strategy for each scholarship. This includes helping them paint an application portrait, consider the specific agenda of each scholarship sponsor, evaluate the universal judging criteria, and brainstorm for people who would write good letters of recommendation. ■

Research Assistants: Interested parents can help out during a time crunch by gathering research and background materials the student needs for specific scholarship essays and applications. ■

Organizers: Managing paperwork and keeping track of deadlines are important functions for parents. Sending out application request letters and making phone call requests can also prove useful. ■

Sounding Boards: Parents should help their children recollect important experiences to describe on scholarship applications. Assisting with interview preparation and providing general feedback are also key ways parents can help. ■

Copyeditors: If you're comfortable with the written word, copyediting and proofreading your child's applications can be quite beneficial, but steer clear of inserting your own voice in place of your child's. ■

Motivators: You can motivate your children to play the scholarship game by discussing family finances, emphasizing lifestyle freedoms, conveying your belief in their abilities, and offering to help in any way you can. ■

Supporters: Being supportive—regardless of results—is critical. The process rewards those who stick with it. Teach your children to avoid dwelling on scholarships that don't pan out and to focus on the applications coming up in the near future. ■

SCHOLARSHIPCOACH.COM KEYWORDS

For more information on a scholarship or topic mentioned in this chapter, enter the associated keyword in the keyword link box located in the Coach's Locker Room section of ScholarshipCoach.com.

Scholarship/Topic	Keyword
Perspectives from Parents	PARENTS

PART II

Getting
Ready
to Play

Finding Your Own Pot of Gold

INSIDE THIS CHAPTER

▊ Principles of scholarship
  searching

▊ Using your school and beyond

▊ Secrets of Internet scholarship
  databases

▊ Canvasing your community

▊ Locating school-specific awards

▊ Search techniques for specific
  types of students

▋ THE SCHOLARSHIP RAINBOW

Legend has it that at the end of every rainbow is a pot of gold. So, college-cash seekers, you could lace up your shoes, get in your car, and whip out your best rainbow-tracking radar system . . . or you can use the powerful techniques outlined in this chapter to locate your very own pot of scholarship gold. (I'm sure you're seriously pondering which option I will suggest.)

In this comprehensive chapter, I describe some basic—and some not so basic—techniques for finding and researching scholarship programs. If you dutifully apply these strategies and tactics, you will undoubtedly find a treasure trove of scholarships that are just right for someone like you.

▋ FIVE PRINCIPLES OF SCHOLARSHIP SEARCHING

Before we delve into the specific search techniques, let's take a moment to reflect on the principles governing our search. Most people just jump into the search process, look into a couple of resources that are especially convenient, and then get overwhelmed—missing out on thousands of dollars in the process. But if you take the time to learn the proper search principles, you will be far more effective with your time and far less prone to frustration. Is it worth it to do this right? You bet it is!

PRINCIPLE 1

DIG DEEP TO FIND HIDDEN TREASURE

The principle of digging deep is derived from a simple fact: The harder *you* have to dig to find a scholarship (or to find out additional information about it), the greater the odds that someone else won't. Does the digging pay off? Most definitely. This extra bit of work can translate into significantly more scholarship winnings for you.

Consider two examples: First, say you spend extra hours tracking down a scholarship that is very hard to find. You could expect that if it took you that long to find it, chances are that it would take others just as long. But many scholarship seekers aren't as diligent as you, and would give up before striking pay dirt. So you could expect this scholarship to have fewer entries than a comparable one with better publicity. Fewer entries translate into better odds of winning. So putting the added investment into research, by digging extra deep, really does tilt the odds in your favor.

Now let's examine a second example: You're applying for a well-known national scholarship, and you take the time to research more information about it than what's contained on the entry form and brochure. It takes some doing, but you locate some sample essays written by past winners. What is the result? This added information gives you a better understanding of what the scholarship judges are looking for, and as a result, your odds of winning become much better than those of other less-prepared applicants. Once again, the extra investment in research can pay big dividends.

Because the deep digger finds the hidden treasure, it is always a good strategy to invest your time into fully exploiting the search techniques and action steps covered in this chapter.

KNOW THYSELF

Is the "know thyself" principle a warm and fuzzy New Age concept about getting in touch with your inner child or discovering your masculine or feminine side? Uh, no. Actually, it's a way of assessing yourself that is directly applicable to your scholarship search efforts.

There are aspects of your activities, personal information, credentials, affiliations, and background (and of your family, too) that you aren't aware of, don't know fully about, or didn't realize could make you eligible for additional scholarship awards. You might not know off the top of your head, for instance, which Army division your father served in during the Vietnam War. You might not know the names of all of the business or professional associations and organizations your mom is a member of. Maybe you just had no idea that the church you attend is part of a larger religious association. Knowing such things could help you discover that you are eligible for many additional scholarship awards.

It is important, therefore, to ask questions and interview family members, and analyze your own involvements and tangential affiliations. This knowledge can lead you to lucrative scholarship opportunities that you might not have even thought of seeking.

Later in the chapter, I'll give you some tools for doing this.

CAST WIDE, YET FOCUS NARROW

Some students seek out only scholarship opportunities that have very broad eligibility criteria—in other words, scholarships that a wide range of people can apply for. Conversely, other students look for nothing but scholarships that are open only to students with a unique personal characteristic, such as a particular disability, hobby, or ethnic background. Which approach should you follow? Well, my scholarship-seeking friend, you should do *both*.

Those who search only for broad, generic scholarship programs miss out on awards that may be designed specifically for someone with their unique characteristics—programs that are often less competitive because very few people can apply for them. On the other hand, those who focus solely on scholarships for students with a notable personal characteristic—such as scholarships for undergraduates with asthma—lose perspective on the vast forest of scholarship money that is accessible to all. To avoid leaving any potential scholarship money untapped, cast a wide net, yet focus narrow, too.

This principle also can be applied to scholarships with a particular geographic focus. Don't look only for nationwide scholarship programs, and don't search solely for community- or district-specific scholarships, either. Savvy scholarship searchers seek both national and local awards.

SEARCH TOMORROW, TODAY

When you go to the grocery store, you can buy food for just your next meal—or you can plan ahead and get ingredients for meals later in the week, too. The same is true for scholarship searching. When you are already putting in the effort to mount a scholarship search, you might as well leverage your time by searching for scholarships for future years (for example, a high school junior might search for scholarships that both high school seniors and college freshmen can apply for). Keep in mind that just because a scholarship is well publicized this year doesn't mean that it will be easy to find in future years (perhaps the program's promotional budget will be slashed). Planning ahead in your scholarship searching thus helps you locate and keep track of funding sources that may fall off the screen of your scholarship search radar in future years.

Finding out about scholarships for future years serves another important purpose. When you can locate such scholarships now—and examine the judging criteria right away—you have time to enhance your record in key ways to better position yourself to win the award in the future (perhaps by joining an appropriate club, getting a relevant internship or job, or volunteering for a related community service program).

This is especially important for middle school students, as well as high school freshmen, sophomores, and juniors.

I also recommend procuring applications right away for scholarships that you may consider applying for in future years. Although you will eventually need to get an updated application, seeing the form in advance helps you better prepare.

Searching for tomorrow also means seeking out scholarships for students affiliated with particular clubs, organizations, associations, or leagues that you aren't yet a member of, but that you *could* join in the near future, to learn new things and make new friends (while reaping the additional scholarship benefits).

As a high school student, for instance, you could join Junior Achievement, 4-H, Beta Club, Future Farmers of America, Future Business Leaders of America, the Key Club, or the National Honor Society and thereby make yourself eligible in the future for a wide range of scholarship awards.

As a college student, you could join Golden Key or the National Association for Campus Activities (NACA), or seek out student membership in professional organizations and societies related to your future career (that just so happen to offer scholarships to their members). Looking to the future in your scholarship search enables you to take steps to expand your future scholarship eligibility.

THE FLOOR IS NOT YOUR FRIEND

How many of you are guilty of the following organizational system? You need to find that absolutely critical sheet of paper, that utterly important binder, or that badly needed notebook containing the handwritten phone number of that hottie in your English class, so you start tearing through the piles of clothing and other items that litter your floor. (Yeah, I've been guilty of this, too.)

When it comes to embarking on a major scholarship campaign, however, this organizational approach will create a lot of extra work for you in the long run. Instead, try to get organized from the beginning. As you come across contact information for various scholarships, take steps to acquire the application materials *immediately*. (This is

If you're mailing an application request letter, it's generally a good idea to include a self-addressed stamped envelope.

When you are sending out a considerable number of letters all at once, it's easy to place a letter in a wrong envelope. Always double-check that the envelope and letter match.

also added insurance in case deadlines have been moved up unexpectedly.) If you've located a website affiliated with a particular scholarship, check the site for application forms and materials to download (an easy process). If you have a phone number for an organization, use it to request an application. If these first two methods are not possible, you will need to request an application via e-mail, fax, or good ol' "snail mail" (a.k.a. the U.S. postal service).

To economize your letter-writing time, develop a form letter for requesting applications. This letter doesn't need to be too fancy, although it should probably be computer printed or typed and in a standard business format. If you are provided with the specific information, address the letter directly to the contact person in charge of the scholarship (including his or her title, in case a new person has assumed the job). If no specific contact is named, write "Attention: Scholarship Coordinator" on the top line. Also make sure you clearly state the name of the scholarship application you are requesting, since some organizations administer many scholarships. In addition to your mailing address, be sure to include your phone number, fax number (if you have one), and e-mail address. In general, make it as easy as possible for the scholarship administrator to reach you.

When you request a scholarship application, keep notes on what you did (such as who you talked to during a phone call) or print out an extra copy of your request letter, and file such items (along with any information you've already accumulated about the scholarship) in a three-ring binder labeled "Application Requests." Be sure to jot down the date you made the request. This way you'll be able to keep track of any applications you don't receive. If you haven't received a response from the scholarship sponsor within three weeks, place a follow-up call or send another letter.

I found it helpful to mark the deadline of each scholarship on the folder in big, bold letters so I could see these key dates at a glance.

When scholarship applications arrive in the mail, remove the corresponding scholarship information you filed in your Application Requests binder and start a separate file folder for each scholarship. If you have access to a filing cabinet, it's perfect for organizing these folders; otherwise a cardboard box will work just fine. Divide your filing space into two sections: one for scholarships with deadlines that are in the current school year and another for scholarships that you may apply for at a later date.

Before filing away materials, read over all of the guidelines, rules, and judging criteria for each scholarship. This way, you won't be surprised by anything later.

Staying organized and on top of things may sound like a good bit of work, but it will save you hours and hours down the road—and may mean thousands of extra dollars for your education. How's that for motivation?

■ TEN "SHOW ME THE MONEY" ACTION STEPS

In the blockbuster movie *Jerry Maguire,* a wide receiver played by Cuba Gooding Jr. demands that his sports agent, played by Tom Cruise, repeatedly shout four now famous words: "Show me the money!" And it's about time we did the same. So on the count of three, say it with me. One . . . Two . . . Three: *"SHOW ME THE MONEY!"*

Are you psyched up? Adrenaline pumping? Feel a little ridiculous for shouting at a book? Good. You're ready to discover the ten "Show Me the Money" Action Steps— a powerful sequence of search techniques and tactics that will help you locate a cornucopia of scholarships right for you.

ASSEMBLE YOUR SCHOLARSHIP SEARCH TOOLS

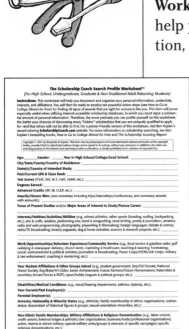

One of my roommates from college loved his tools, plain and simple. He had a special toolbox that he kept in our dorm room that contained mechanical and power devices of all shapes and sizes. The guy could entertain himself for hours in a Home Depot.

What he taught me (besides the virtues of "more power") was this: Before you start a project, you've got to have the right equipment. This is true whether the project is fixing a leaky sink or embarking on an exhaustive scholarship search.

The first tool that you, a college-cash seeker, will want to use is the **Scholarship Coach Search Profile Worksheet**, presented in Appendix A. The worksheet will help you document and organize your personal information, credentials, characteristics, interests, goals, and affiliations (including your family affiliations). It will prompt you to track down a lot of personal information, some of which you won't know off the top of your head, that can prove useful in locating scholarships. This detailed information will be especially useful when you search for scholarships with specific eligibility requirements that fit your unique profile, since the more precisely you describe yourself, the better your chances of discovering "hidden" scholarships that few of your peers will be able to find. So take a few moments right away to fill out the worksheet as best you can. Later, you will think of new things to include. Keep the completed worksheet handy; you'll draw on it in many of the other action steps.

A second tool to become familiar with is the one found at my ScholarshipCoach.com. website. Among the resources you'll find on the site are daily alerts for new scholarships and upcoming deadlines, opportunities

The keywords associated with the awards mentioned in this book are good places for many searches to start.

The Scholarship Scouting Report provides essential information about a broad range of scholarships that you can begin to apply for right away.

to ask me questions and chat online, useful interactive forms, as well as the Web Surfing Coach (an interface that features the most up-to-date scholarship search links and offers you guidance as you navigate the Web for scholarships). As I mentioned in the introduction, readers of this book have access to the Coach's Locker Room at the site, which features updates of the material in this book, keyword links to award contact information and other goodies, as well as additional special resources when they become available.

Another important tool that can help you jump-start the searching process is *The Scholarship Scouting Report*, written by yours truly. This innovative guidebook focuses on America's top scholarship opportunities—the programs important to any scholarship search. In this behind-the-scenes guide, I provide detailed descriptions of application requirements, judging criteria and eligibility rules, sample winning entries, as well as insider tips and interviews with judges, winners, and administrators associated with featured scholarships. Use the book not only to learn about specific scholarship programs, but to further familiarize yourself with the types of scholarships available and the various formats, components, and requirements of prototypical scholarship applications.

TAP INTO YOUR SCHOOL'S RESOURCES

Once you've got your major search tools, it is time to tap into local resources at your high school, college, or university. The reason schools are a bountiful source of scholarship information is that many scholarship sponsors send applications, brochures, and other materials directly to schools to get the word out about their programs. Your school is an especially good starting point for searches specific to your community or state, since search resources outside your region are unlikely to have as much specific information as your local high school or college. Application materials may be sent to principals, counselors, teachers, administrators, financial aid officers, professors, or department heads at your school.

High schools often have resources like a filing cabinet devoted to scholarship applications, a bulletin board that lists forthcoming deadlines, or a database of scholarship programs specific to your home state. At a high school, scholarship information is often centralized—typically at a college and career center, guidance office, or school library. Find out how your school works, and become an expert on the resources available.

Colleges sometimes publish their own manuals to scholarship and fellowship programs, or make such publications available over the Web.

Colleges and universities may have a centralized scholarship information source, but they also have additional information disbursed throughout the campus. The place to start, of course, is the financial aid office. But scholarship resources and information may also be located at various libraries on campus or at offices that help students pursue careers. At Harvard, for instance, the Office of Career Services had on hand a great deal of resources devoted to scholarships and fellowships. You also want to check with specific offices on campus related to your personal characteristics (such as offices for students with disabilities or international students).

You're likely to find a lot of course-specific scholarship information at individual departments associated with your major or area of study. For scholarships oriented toward specific academic fields, individual departments may have more substantial information than the financial aid office at your college. Academic department offices usually have information on scholarships controlled and awarded by the department itself (for students attending your specific college), as well as scholarships funded by private sources open to students from a variety of institutions. Several scholarship winners I've interviewed have mentioned that by asking specifically for scholarship and fellowship information at department

In addition to scholarships, graduate departments provide teaching assistantships or research assistantships to graduate students, which involve a tuition award and/or salary.

offices, they unearthed scholarship opportunities specific to their major that others in the department weren't even aware of!

Regardless of whether you attend high school or college, I suggest setting up a meeting with a general counselor or financial aid officer at your school for the express purpose of discussing scholarship opportunities. Tell your counselor or officer that you are serious about winning scholarships, and that you would be very grateful for any help, direction, and information that he or she can provide. It is always a good strategy to cultivate relationships with such individuals at your school. Because I did, I was informed of many programs and scholarship opportunities that I would have otherwise missed.

For those of you looking for a campus job, you may want to consider taking a paying job or volunteering in your school's guidance or financial aid office. One scholarship winner I interviewed said that by doing this, he dramatically increased his access to scholarship opportunities—*he* was the one who sorted and filed away scholarship applications received by the school! One financial

Ask your teachers or professors about any scholarships they have heard about. Instructors may know of scholarship programs and contests in their areas of expertise (especially fields like creative writing, journalism, science, or the arts).

Working in close cooperation with school counselors also helped him acquire excellent letters of recommendation for both scholarship and college applications.

GUERRILLA TACTIC

Work Your School's Scholarship Center

■ Take a job or volunteer in your school's guidance or financial aid office to increase your access to scholarship opportunities and resources.

aid officer I spoke with from Southern Oregon University said that she kept an eye out for (and passed along scholarship opportunities to) students who worked in the financial aid office.

Keep an eye out in the school newspaper for articles about students who have won particular scholarships. This is another good source for scholarship leads.

High schools and colleges also sometimes keep lists of past students at the school who have won particular scholarship awards. Seeing the awards that former students have won can yield a valuable list of potential scholarship programs—especially local ones. In addition, scholarship information letters and applications from past school years are often filed in binders for student perusal. If your school doesn't already keep a file of students who have won particular scholarship awards as well as old scholarship applications and letters, don't be shy about offering constructive input: Suggest that they start doing so immediately.

Many high schools and colleges also purchase scholarship search databases on CD-ROMs that are updated periodically or subscribe to database services available over the Internet. Keep an eye out and ask around for such resources. I discuss more about the specific databases available (at your school and elsewhere), and how to maximize your results, in the next action step.

SEARCH SCHOLARSHIP DATABASES

A database is really nothing more than a collection of information organized in such a way that makes it easy to search and find things. Scholarship databases, therefore, can streamline your search process by centralizing information about thousands of scholarships and putting this information at your fingertips.

It's even possible to search three seemingly different databases but actually be repeatedly searching the same scholarship data set. If you did this, you would uncover only a tiny portion of what's out there, while doing three times the necessary work.

More often than not, however, scholarship databases are misused. This misuse occurs because most people don't understand how these databases work and aren't aware of the strengths and weaknesses of each database they are using. Complicating the issue is the fact that more and more of these databases have sprung up, with practically every one claiming to have "the most scholarships" or the "highest dollar value of awards." As a result, it's harder than ever to figure out which databases you should spend your limited time on. It's no wonder that on my Scholarship Coach National Tour many scholarship seekers I met voiced their frustration with using many of these databases.

So my friends, you now have two choices: You can waste a lot of time with a trial-and-error approach—and make plenty of mistakes along the way—or you can read the rest of this section and let me do a lot of the introductory work for you! I have spent hundreds of hours examining these databases (I'm a regular party animal), and have interviewed dozens of scholarship database administrators, researchers, and programmers to uncover additional secrets.

In the sections that follow, I describe the fundamentals of how scholarship databases work, discuss some of the key features and limitations of these databases, show you how to access each database, rate each one on several key criteria, and then offer some tips and strategies for maximizing your results.

A Scholarship Database Primer

We can divide scholarship databases into two basic components. The first component is the information itself. The best scholarship databases contain not only the name and amount of each scholarship award, but also

a general description of the scholarship; information about the scholarship provider; a list of relevant contact names, numbers, addresses, and websites; and data on eligibility requirements, application materials, entry deadlines, and the number of scholarships awarded.

The second component of a scholarship database is the search mechanism— the system that helps you find scholarship information pertinent to you and filters out irrelevant listings. No matter how wonderful the overall scholarship information contained in a database may be, it's of no use to you if you can't find the scholarships that match your interests, talents, skills, background, and future plans. To help you find what you're looking for, information specialists who compile databases try to divide scholarships into certain categories and then make it easier for you to weed through these categories.

Scholarship databases come in a variety of formats, with different bells and whistles. Most scholarship databases are accessible on the Internet, on CD-ROM, or in print directories.

INTERNET DATABASES

The most widely used scholarship databases are accessible over the Internet and tend to have one of two search mechanisms for finding relevant information: a **matching system** or a **browsing system**. A matching system asks you to fill out a questionnaire and supply personal information (such as age, gender, GPA, organizational affiliations, and career information) relevant to scholarship eligibility. A browsing system allows you to sift through *categories* of scholarships that might interest you (such as browsing through all scholarships for adult returning students or scholarships for those interested in the visual arts). Browsing systems, however, give you more capabilities than you have when just reading a printed list of available scholarships; you can sort or filter the listings into broad and finer categories, allowing you to focus in on scholarships designed to recognize someone with your personal characteristics. In this system, however, you still do the matching yourself, one match at a time.

Each search mechanism has its advantages and disadvantages. The matching system saves you time by examining together, in a batch, all the information you have supplied—and then creating a list of scholarship

Filling out this questionnaire can take from less than a minute to 30 minutes (or longer if Internet traffic is heavy and you have a slow connection).

Most Internet scholarship databases are free of charge to users, although there are some notable exceptions that we'll discuss a little later.

prospects that seems to fit your profile. The main drawback of a matching system is that you are relying on three basic assumptions:

■ that the information in the database is uniformly accurate and timely for matching purposes (it generally isn't);

■ that the scholarship researchers have figured out the best way to categorize the information (they usually have not);

■ that the programmers who created the matching system thoroughly understood, designed, and tested a complicated set of filters and algorithms for including and excluding the right and wrong scholarship listings (wishful thinking at best).

In essence, because you see only the scholarship listings that the matching system *says* fit your profile, you do not know what scholarships you could be missing.

The strength of a browsing system is that it makes searching the database more *transparent*. Because you are visually sorting through all the listings yourself (with the aid of a computer to help you categorize the listings in useful ways), you can get a better feel for the types of scholarships contained in the database and better ensure that appropriate scholarships don't fall through the cracks. On the flip side, all of this takes substantial time, energy, and concentration; it's easy to get confused about what categories of scholarships you've already sifted through and lose track of awards that may be suitable for you.

Some Internet databases have both a matching system and browsing system. However, one typically functions much better than the other.

CD-ROM DATABASES

Additional scholarship databases are available on CD-ROMs, which can include both the matching and browsing systems. Many of these CD-ROMs are designed to be sold (or leased) to high schools, colleges, libraries, and state career information service offices, and generally cost anywhere from a few hundred dollars to a few thousand dollars on an annual basis. (Although the institution purchases the use of the CD-ROM, students don't have to pay to access it.) In fact, some Internet databases are scaled-down versions of these CD-ROM products. For the individual scholarship seeker, the best way to tap into CD-ROM databases is to inquire about their availability at schools, libraries, and career-related state agencies in your area.

PRINT DIRECTORIES

Later in this chapter, I'll clue you in to the relationship between certain Internet databases and particular printed directories.

Scholarship databases may also masquerade as big, thick printed directories that have all the excitement of worn-out, big-city phonebooks. Many of these printed directories are actually derived from the databases available online. A major drawback of printed directories, of course, is that they can become out of date almost as soon as they are published. Furthermore, using printed indexes typically found at the back of these thick volumes isn't as convenient or fast as electronic search tools. In general, if you are thinking about purchasing a particular print directory, try to determine the source of the data (often found on the copyright page). This way, you will know if a print directory is, for the most part, a less up-to-date version of an Internet database you've already searched.

Not All Databases Are Created Equal

When a mechanic checks out your car, he doesn't just glance at the paint job or kick your tires. He gets under the hood to check out what's going on in the guts of the machine—the parts that are hidden from view. Likewise, to truly understand how scholarship databases work, we have to examine some aspects of these databases that are unseen by the vast majority of database users.

The first thing to recognize is the distinction between a source database and a licensed database. A **source database** offers scholarship information that was researched and gathered on a firsthand basis by the company or organization that also provides students with access to the database. The scholarship information contained in a source database was not extracted from another database.

A **licensed database**, on the other hand, has been derived from someone else's database entries. The scholarship information in a licensed database was *not* researched or gathered by the company or organization that offers access to the database. Instead, a license fee was paid to use the listings (and sometimes even the search mechanism) from someone else's source database. It's kind of like copying someone else's homework, although it's totally legit.

This doesn't mean that licensed databases contain all the awards of the source databases from which they are derived. Because license fees typically depend on the amount of information being licensed—the more information, the greater the cost—licensed versions may not, in fact, include all of the scholarship listings contained in the original source database. Furthermore, a licensed database may not be updated as frequently as the original source database. While some source databases are updated daily, licensed versions of those databases may be updated only semi-annually or annually.

Why should you care about all of this? You should care because many databases—all of which go by different dotcom brand names—don't tell you up front whether their scholarship listings are source material or licensed. And if you aren't able to distinguish source databases from their licensed versions, you may think that you are casting a wide net by searching many different databases when in fact you are repeatedly searching

The source database may not be readily available to the general public. In such cases, you must access it via a licensed version.

the same limited set of scholarships. (That's when the frustration sets in.)

Once you can distinguish between source and licensed databases (I'll show you which are which in the next section) you can approach scholarship database searching in a smart, strategic way. In general, I recommend *first searching source databases,* because this ensures that you have access to the most comprehensive and up-to-date scholarship listings. As time permits, follow up your search of a particular source database by searching one or more licensed versions of that database.

GUERRILLA TACTIC

Search Source Databases First

■ When searching scholarship databases, first search source databases to make sure you have the most complete information. Then extend your search to licensed versions.

A licensed database may have a search mechanism that is superior to the source database from which it was derived, and may even contain a few additional listings.

Why search licensed databases as well? They can help make your search more complete and comprehensive. Because licensed databases may have different matching and browsing systems than the original source databases, this allows you to search essentially the same set of scholarship information in different ways, making sure that potential scholarship leads don't fall through the cracks. Furthermore, certain databases that are generally classified as licensed databases (and contain mostly licensed scholarship information) may actually have a small source component—with some new and original scholarship research added to the licensed scholarship listings.

Database Reviews and Profiles

Now that you understand the types of databases, it's time to get specific. In this section, I present, in alphabetical order, some of the most accessible and useful scholarship databases. I've placed special emphasis here on source databases that are available over the Internet, as well as additional databases that offer enough unique scholarship listings to make a search worthwhile. If there are notable licensed databases that add some important search features to a particular source database (a keyword search or unique filtering system, for example), I mention them as well. Most of the databases I describe are free—they don't charge you anything to search them (although you may get inundated with ads). If there happens to be a search fee, I've noted it in the text.

Keep in mind that each source database uses different methods for gathering scholarships and tends to be better at listing certain types of scholarships than others. Some databases employ students and stay-at-home moms to search the Internet and printed publications for scholarship leads. Others hire professional clipping services and librarians to perform the research and distill the information. Certain databases gather information from a survey or questionnaire mailed to a list of known scholarship providers. Others research new scholarships primarily by visiting scholarship-provider websites.

Some databases sell the personal information you supply to companies (particularly loan-related companies) that target students and their parents. Those concerned about privacy issues should check each site carefully to see if it's possible to "opt out" of such uses of your personal profile.

GUERRILLA TACTIC

Explore a Variety of Scholarship Databases

■ Because each scholarship database has access to different scholarships, search a wide variety of databases for the maximum number of quality scholarship leads.

There are just too many scholarships out there (especially on the local and institutional levels) for any one database to be considered comprehensive.

	Below Average	Average	Above Average
Content			
Detail			
Ease of Use			
Fit			
Flexibility			

As a result, each database has access to different segments of the scholarship landscape—with no one database listing any more than a small percentage of the scholarships actually available. Because of this, the savvy scholarship seeker knows to search more than just a couple of these databases. Just as you would sample many different foods in a buffet line, you want to search a wide variety of databases to better satisfy your appetite for college cash.

To give you an idea of what to expect from each database, I've rated them on several criteria I think are important. I rate the usefulness of the information contained in each database according to two different metrics: content and detail. **Content** encompasses the range of scholarships represented in the database, the overall size of the database, and the general applicability of the award listings to the typical scholarship seeker. **Detail** refers to how much specific information is contained in the listing for each scholarship (such as eligibility requirements, application guidelines, and entry deadlines) and the overall accuracy of that information.

I evaluate the mechanism for searching the database listings on three criteria: ease of use, fit, and flexibility. **Ease of Use** is based on an assessment of whether database searching is straightforward, streamlined, and generally user-friendly. **Fit** refers to a database's matching system. For a database to have good fit, you want it to exclude junk listings that clearly are not appropriate for you. At the same time, you don't want the matching system to be too narrow, causing you to miss out on potential scholarship prospects (especially when scholarships are commonly misclassified). Finally, **Flexibility** is a measurement of how easy it is to modify your search criteria (the personal information you have supplied) to widen and narrow your net while conducting multiple searches to query for different types of scholarships. I've also factored into this metric any special ways that the database provides to get at the information— such as the availability of a keyword search.

In cases where the database does not use a matching system, the fit criterion is not rated.

On each of these five criteria, I rate a database as

■ ABOVE AVERAGE, if it is generally better than other profiled databases;

■ AVERAGE, if it is roughly equivalent to most of the other databases; or

■ BELOW AVERAGE, if it is of lower quality in this category than its peers.

To rate a database, I conducted a series of prototypical searches in it. For databases available in multiple formats, the ratings are based on the online version.

Keep in mind that all these ratings and descriptions are based on a snapshot in time. Databases are continually refined, enhanced, improved, and revamped. (Indeed, I hope some of these databases may be improved in response to my ratings.) In addition, new databases do spring up from time to time, while old ones disappear, get absorbed into others, or change their Web addresses. To stay in touch with the latest information and updates, visit ScholarshipCoach.com (keyword: DATABASE).

So are you ready for the database profiles and reviews already? Well, make sure that your seat back is in its full upright position, your tray table is locked and stowed, and your seat belt is securely fastened. Let's go!

ScholarshipCoach.com not only links you to all these databases via the Web Surfing Coach, but also provides updates to these ratings, new database developments, and other features of interest to online searchers.

SCHOLARSHIP COACH.com
Your personal adviser for winning college cash

CASHE / Wiredscholar Scholarship Database
Available online at: www.cashe.com or www.wiredscholar.com/paying/content/pay_scholarship _search.html

The CASHE/Wiredscholar database is one of the elder statesmen of the scholarship database world. In fact, several individuals who worked on the development of what even-

	Below Average	Average	Above Average
Content			✔
Detail		✔	
Ease of Use	✔		
Fit			✔
Flexibility	✔		

Users of the Illinois Student Assistance Commission's "HigherEd Net" are actually plugged right into the CASHE database.

tually became the CASHE (College Aid Sources for Higher Education) database were later involved with some of the other databases listed in this section. This particular database uses a matching system to help you locate appropriate scholarships. Filling out the required questionnaire takes about 20–25 minutes and involves quite a few pull-down menus and browser reloads to get at the exact numerical codes used for matching.

There are currently two separate interfaces for using the same source database: one at cashe.com and another at the wiredscholar.com site. According to database managers, however, the older interface at cashe.com will eventually be phased out. Over time, I expect the newer database interface to become more straightforward and faster, especially since the database and website are now funded by Sallie Mae, a Fortune 500 company.

Unlike with most other databases, the results from searching this one do not appear right away. Instead, scholarship search results are e-mailed to you; it can take anywhere from 30 minutes to 2 hours for this to occur. Consequently, it is not particularly convenient to change search parameters and conduct multiple searches.

College Board / ExPAN Scholarship Database
Available online at:
www.collegeboard.org/fundfinder/html/fundfind01.html

Created by the College Board (the same lovable folks who administer all those standardized tests), the scholarship listings in this source database are based on the College Board's *Annual Survey of Financial Aid Programs*. The online version of this database is drawn from a portion of ExPAN,

You should investigate whether your school provides use of ExPAN. If it does, you will want to try the Fund Finder scholarship search feature.

	Below Average	Average	Above Average
Content	✔		
Detail		✔	
Ease of Use			✔
Fit		✔	
Flexibility		✔	

a guidance and college admission software product sold directly to schools. The free online database includes fewer scholarship listings than many of the other scholarship databases profiled here, and the search mechanism is fairly simple and straightforward, making it a quick and easy database to use. The database is updated only annually, with the information contained in the online version presently lagging one year behind the printed scholarship directory released each year by the College Board.

ASK THE COACH #12

Should I pay others to help me find scholarships?

There are two types of fee-based scholarship search companies: ones that provide you with a list of scholarships that "match" your profile and others that grant you access to members-only scholarship databases. The first type performs the scholarship searching for you. The second type lets you leverage off their research, but *you* still do the actual searching yourself.

There is nothing inherently wrong with paying a small fee for help with a scholarship search, but the fact remains that many of these services (with a few notable exceptions) don't usually have a high enough incentive to do the necessary research, legwork, and quality control to provide you with truly useful results.

In regard to services that provide you with ready-to-go scholarship lists, many such services don't have particularly good matching systems. Many students have discovered that the lists they get back include a lot of scholarships that don't seem to match them at all. In general, no one else can replace your own personal scholarship search, because no one else cares about your search results as much as you do.

The second type of service—one that simply provides access to a proprietary scholarship database—may or may not be worth the money. It all depends on the uniqueness of the scholarship listings in the database, the way the search engine functions, and the type of personal profile you are trying to match. The key thing to realize about such fee-based database access is that these databases themselves don't necessarily have any better information than what is available for free. Even if you pay to use them, you should still search the other free databases.

In general, before you plunk down any money, talk to others you trust who have used the search service you are considering. (You can check out reviews of such services at ScholarshipCoach.com.) Unless the service offers something you can't find elsewhere, you will be better off saving your money, checking out my recommended free search sites, and applying all the search techniques outlined in this chapter. ■

CollegeQuest Scholarship Database
Available online at: www.collegequest.com

This source database is used to generate a number of Peterson's printed scholarship directories. The online version of the database is relatively small, and the matching questionnaire takes a modest 5–7 minutes to complete, depending on how many categories of personal information you choose to include in the questionnaire (the database permits you to include

	Below Average	Average	Above Average
Content	✔		
Detail	✔		
Ease of Use		✔	
Fit	✔		
Flexibility		✔	

Be careful about initially eliminating any categories of personal information since it can seriously affect your search results.

or exclude such categories). Only very brief information for each scholarship match is presented, and one persistent problem I had with the database was that a number of scholarships appeared to be misclassified. As a result, users of this database should expect to weed through a lot of "matches" that do not really fit them at all. Access to this database is also presently available through America Online (AOL).

FastAid / National Scholarship Research Service Database
Available online at: www.fastaid.com

Created by Dan Cassidy and the National Scholarship Research Service, FastAid is a source database that surfaced in the 1980s. In addition to all the standard listings that many other database sites have, FastAid is known for listing some of the more quirky or esoteric scholarship awards. A few annual print directories under the authorship of Dan Cassidy are generated from this database.

	Below Average	Average	Above Average
Content		✔	
Detail		✔	
Ease of Use	✔		
Fit			✔
Flexibility		✔	

The online questionnaire requires about 10 to 15 minutes to complete—a process that I found unnecessarily complicated by category selection boxes that function differently than those of other databases. My test student profiles, however, were matched fairly well: There weren't too many mismatches and the broader awards that my profiles were eligible for filtered through to my search results. The amount of information listed for each scholarship is adequate, but I encountered a few problems with the accuracy of information contained in some of the listings.

Fastweb Scholarship Database
Available online at: www.fastweb.com

Fastweb is easily the most "commercial" of the scholarship database websites, with consumer product offers interwoven into its scholarship results lists. The database features an easy-to-use interface, a personal user mailbox, and a regular stream of e-mail that advises the user of new awards that might match his or her profile. Because Fastweb is one of the better known scholarship websites, the database benefits from the fact that certain scholarship administrators and sponsors take the initiative to send the latest information on their scholarships directly to Fastweb. As a result, Fastweb's strong suit is that it is continually updated with newly created scholarships, although many of these are simply writing contests or sweepstakes.

	Below Average	Average	Above Average
Content			✔
Detail		✔	
Ease of Use		✔	
Fit		✔	
Flexibility			✔

The Fastweb database also flags scholarship listings with available online applications and provides entry deadline warnings in a user's mailbox.

The questionnaire used for scholarship matching is one of the lengthier ones—on the order of 20 minutes or more to fill out. Changing a profile to run multiple searches is straightforward. After running my test searches, however, I had the feeling that I wasn't provided with *all* the scholarship matches contained in the database; this feeling was further intensified by the stream of e-mail alerts in the form of "new scholarship" teasers (which weren't so new). To find out about these additional scholarship matches, I had to repeatedly log in to my Fastweb mailbox for details.

Grad
PhD
MA
Students

ASK THE COACH #13

Can graduate students find scholarships and fellowships in online databases?

Most of the databases profiled in this section have substantial scholarship listings for graduate students. In addition, two universities and one private organization have online databases of interest to graduate students in the U.S. and from around the world who seek scholarship funding. **The Cornell University Graduate Fellowship Notebook** (www.cornell.edu/Student/GRFN) features about 700 scholarship listings, with the majority of awards from non-Cornell sources. **New York University's Grants in Graduate Studies** (GIGS) database (www.nyu.edu/gsas/fininfo/gigs.html) focuses on grants provided by public and private groups for graduate and postgraduate students. You will also want to check out the scholarship, fellowship, and grant listings at the **Academic Research Information System** website (www.arisnet.com/newstu.html), which includes funding opportunities divided into six basic categories: creative arts, humanities, social sciences, natural sciences, biomedical sciences, and general. All three of these websites have only simplistic category-based browsing systems, so be prepared to read through a lot of very specific award listings. ■

FreSch Scholarship Database
Available online at: www.freschinfo.com

When using this small source database, you can employ the "Power Search" to match scholarships to your personal profile, or you can browse about 30 categories (with selected keyword searches). The latter is my preferred way. I found the Power Search feature to be problematic because of the extremely long time needed for results to be processed and web pages loaded, and the present lack of flexibility in

	Below Average	Average	Above Average
Content	✔		
Detail		✔	
Ease of Use	✔		
Fit		✔	
Flexibility	✔		

modifying or editing my search criteria. Although the user interface and entire website have a home-made feel to it, the database nevertheless includes some unusual scholarship awards that I could not find in other databases.

Reference Service Press (RSP) Database
Available online at licensee website (see box) and via CD-ROM subscription

I have not rated the ease of use, fit, or flexibility of this database, since it is most readily available through licensee websites that have their own interface and search mechanism.

The RSP database is one of the largest scholarship information treasure troves available. Because former professional librarians oversee this database, it tends to be accurate, uniform, and detail oriented. Unfortunately, it is no longer freely available online at AOL. To use all three

	Below Average	Average	Above Average
Content			✔
Detail			✔
Ease of Use	N/A		
Fit	N/A		
Flexibility	N/A		

of its funding subdatabases (for undergraduate study, graduate study, and professional/postdoctoral work), you have to access them (on CD-ROM or on the Web) at a school or other institution that subscribes.

Schools and institutions subscribe to the database through SilverPlatter Information, a database reseller.

A small subset of the RSP database is presently available directly to students (for a fee) through a new licensee (see box). Scholarship directories released by Kaplan Educational Centers (no relation to me) also use licensed scholarship listings from RSP, although such directories include only a relatively small portion of what's contained in the full database.

ADDITIONAL ACCESS TO RSP DATABASE

A newer website, **CollegeBroadband.com**, has licensed a small subset of the RSP listings for fee-based access. When I tested it, the cost for one month of access to the database was less than $10. School-specific awards are not contained in this licensed version. The search mechanism is a matching system, but certain locked fields somewhat limited my ability to modify search criteria. I found the user interface straightforward and attractive, but the matching system could benefit from an expanded questionnaire and a much tighter fit.

ScholarAid / Student Advantage Database

Available online at: www.scholaraid.com or www.scholaraid.studentadvantage.com

Listings from the Scholaraid / Student Advantage database are used to create a print directory released by The Princeton Review.

The ScholarAid / Student Advantage database has a large number of scholarship listings and features both matching and browsing search mechanisms. The matching system involves filling out an extensive questionnaire with a large number of eclectic personal information choices. (Are you parents incarcerated? Have you participated in soil judging?) The questionnaire is lengthy, taking about 25 minutes to complete; it is complicated by a user interface that is awkward at times. Editing your personal profile is easy, however, with convenient side tabs to get you to the appropriate section of the questionnaire.

	Below Average	Average	Above Average
Content			✔
Detail	✔		
Ease of Use	✔		
Fit		✔	
Flexibility			✔

The website's browsing system enables you to perform a series of keyword searches based on certain eligibility criteria. You can, for example, use keywords to find scholarships for a particular college (e.g., *Duke University*), academic discipline (*biology*), year in school (*graduate*), or geographic region (*San Francisco*). You can also combine keywords (*graduate biology*) for fewer, more specific listings. The amount of information contained in each award listing, however, is rather sparse.

Scholarship Experts Database
Available online at: www.scholarshipexperts.com

The Scholarship Experts database is the newest of the source databases I've tested. The database requires a fee (below $30) to search its basic listings (national and state scholarships) for one year. Its creators have attempted to take the best from the free search websites, while supposedly eliminating the worst. The scholarship listings in this database seem to be balanced between fairly well known scholarships and more eclectic listings, although I didn't come across lots of scholarships that I hadn't found in the other databases.

	Below Average	Average	Above Average
Content		✔	
Detail			✔
Ease of Use			✔
Fit		✔	
Flexibility			✔

The well-designed user interface for this database is what sets it apart; it includes such features as help screens, an option that allows you to choose how many years' worth of results (1–4 years in the future) you want to search for, and the ability to pick up where you stopped, if you suddenly have to log off. Updating your profile for another search is fast and easy.

The database uses a matching questionnaire that takes about 20 minutes to fill out, but the fit from the matching process was only fair, as some clearly mismatched scholarship listings surfaced. My sample results suggested that the additional fee charged for "premium" access to local and institutional awards would not benefit very many searchers at present.

Scholarship Resource Network (SRN) Database

Available online at:
www.srnexpress.com/scholarships/index.cfm

The full commercial product is sold directly to high schools and colleges and is more robust and highly regarded than the free online version. If you have a chance to use it at a subscribing school, I recommend that you do so.

There are two versions of the Scholarship Resource Network (SRN) database: the full database that is part of the SRN/PC software sold to schools and an abbreviated subset of this searchable database (called SRN Express) that is available online for free at the Web address shown above. Additional online versions of SRN Express have been licensed to other websites (including FinancialAid.com and AbsolutelyScholarships.com).

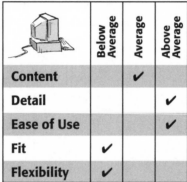

	Below Average	Average	Above Average
Content		✔	
Detail			✔
Ease of Use			✔
Fit	✔		
Flexibility	✔		

The strong point of this database is its detailed and complete listings on each scholarship match. The online version features two "quick search" options— by course of study and state of residency—that can come in handy. Although the Web version is fairly easy to use, the questionnaire for the online matching system does not have enough specificity for a tight fit and is difficult to save or modify.

ASK THE COACH #14

Are there any special scholarship databases for minority students?

All of the databases described in this section include scholarships for minority students. Two additional database websites also might be worth a visit. **The Minority On-Line Information Service** (www.sciencewise. com/molis), has a scholarship database specifically for minorities; it uses a subset of SRN Express. The **ScholarSite** website (www.scholarsite.com) features a small, bilingual search database (English and Spanish) that has a high concentration of scholarships for minorities (as well as some scholarships for those of every ethnicity). ■

Scholarships 101 Database

Available online at: www.scholarships101.com

As one of the Web's largest scholarship databases, the Scholarships 101 database has been licensed by dozens of websites, including such frequently visited terrain as USNews.com (see box) and Monster.com, as well as many financial aid and college-focused sites, such as Scholarships.com, Scholarships-USA.com, and GoCollege. com. (The database is also available on CD-ROM.) The strength of the Scholarships 101 database is the sheer number of its listings. The detail of each award listing, however, is only mediocre.

	Below Average	Average	Above Average
Content			✔
Detail		✔	
Ease of Use		✔	
Fit	✔		
Flexibility	✔		

A little known piece of scholarship trivia: Many of the listings in the Scholarships 101 database have been compiled by a crew of stay-at-home moms hired to track down scholarship leads.

Be aware that one of the key drivers of search results in this database is the inclusion of a particular academic major. In the first sample search I conducted (which took about 15 minutes) I followed the site's recommendation and didn't list a potential academic major. This returned a lot of mismatched scholarship hits. When I did declare a sample major—after experiencing some difficulty logging back in to modify my profile—a smaller number of more closely matched awards turned up. This result was much better except that many of the scholarship listings open to the greatest number of students were suddenly missing.

ADDITIONAL ACCESS TO SCHOLARSHIPS 101

The online version of **U.S. News & World Report** features a scholarship search (www.usnews.com/usnews/edu/dollars/scholar/search.htm) that makes use of listings licensed from the Scholarships 101 database. The *U.S. News* search uses its own search engine that, in my opinion, does not perform particularly well. The part of the search that is useful, however, is the "Quick Search" feature, which is really a browsing system. This feature provides you with visibility into the database by categorizing the scholarship awards into a half dozen scrollable menus (Ethnic, Athletic, Art, Corporate, Organizational, and Military). The site offers additional flexibility in searching for awards, without requiring the time to register any personal information.

Wintergreen/Orchard House Scholarship Database
Available online at licensee websites (see box)

The ubiquitous Wintergreen/Orchard House (WOH) database is available through licensees who use this content for their websites or print directories. In this database, a high proportion of the scholarship listings are awards with very specific and limited eligibility criteria. Most licensees update their listings only on an annual or semi-annual basis. Some use the data as is; others add some additional scholarships of their own to the database, while removing any listings that they learn (direct from scholarship providers) have been discontinued. Because a search mechanism does not accompany the WOH database license, the Ease of Use, Fit, and Flexibility ratings depend solely on the individual licensee.

	Below Average	Average	Above Average
Content		✔	
Detail		✔	
Ease of Use	N/A		
Fit	N/A		
Flexibility	N/A		

ACCESS TO WINTERGREEN/ORCHARD HOUSE

Licensed versions of the Wintergreen/Orchard House database are available for use at two college application–related Internet portals: **CollegeNet** (www.collegenet.com/mach25) and **CollegeLink** (www.collegelink.com/clnk/scholarship).

CollegeNet provides a "Mach25" browsing system in which you set a series of filters (based on age, gender, year in school, and whether to include or exclude school-specific listings), and then browse through different categories and subcategories of awards while the filters do their job. There is also a keyword search that can help you home in on the exact type of awards you are looking for. According to site administrators, the site is developing an advanced logic-based matching system.

CollegeLink also uses a browsing system for its scholarship search. You can use "Quick Search" to find scholarships based on award name, school, and organization, or you can perform a category search within a dozen categories. Selecting the "other" category allows you to view roughly 60 percent of the database content. Additional search features are also being planned.

CollegeNet and CollegeLink do not conduct proactive scholarship research of their own, but will add and delete scholarships or update existing detail information in response to input from scholarship providers and users of the sites.

Essential Database Search Techniques

If you don't know what you're doing when using these databases, the likely result is that you will allow bunches of suitable scholarships to fall through the cracks. To prevent this, there are a few things you should and should not do.

First, when these search databases ask you to define your personal characteristics, recognize that matching systems in databases take your choices *very literally*. For instance, suppose that you are skilled at playing the saxophone and indicated this on a database questionnaire. In your search results you would find scholarships directly related to the saxophone, but you might not find scholarships related to participation in band class or general musical ability. In many cases the database matching system isn't smart enough to realize that saxophone playing is a subcategory of band and music. How do you combat this? You make sure that in addition to checking the *saxophone* box, you also check the *band* and *music* boxes.

In many databases, holding down the CTRL key allows you to select multiple items from the same category field. But be careful: Forgetting to keep holding it down on subsequent clicks will erase your prior selections.

Even if you are only marginally interested in a particular career, undergraduate major, extracurricular activity, or type of college, include these parameters as part of your search.

Complicating the issue is the fact that you can't always select as many items on the questionnaire as you would like. (Some databases allow you to select only two or three options in a given category.) In such instances, conduct several searches in the database and vary the information contained in your questionnaire each time around. If the design of the questionnaire doesn't allow you to easily vary your personal information, reregister for the database under a different name (and e-mail address if need be) and complete a fresh questionnaire with new information.

Some databases ask you if you want to exclude scholarships whose deadlines have already passed. It is generally not a good idea to exclude these scholarships. Application deadlines often change, listings can be a couple years old, and there's no guarantee that the deadlines stated in the database are correct. You also want to know what awards will be coming up again in future years that you might still be eligible to apply for.

Make sure you don't lose any information while completing online forms. Be aware that many database questionnaires need to be completed in one sitting. If you allow too much time to elapse between entries (such as leaving your computer to grab a snack) you may have to reenter all your choices all over again.

One last bit of advice: Conduct searches very specific to your characteristics, but perform fairly generic database searches as well (in which you specify minimal information about yourself). Specifying a lot of very specific information can cause some databases to omit widely accessible scholarship programs—the ones that most high school seniors and many undergraduates are eligible to apply for. (In an ideal world this wouldn't happen, but the matching "logic" behind some databases is not always the most logical.)

ASK THE COACH #15

What Internet resources are available for Canadian students?

You're in luck! There are a variety of helpful Web resources for Canadian students looking for scholarships (or "bursaries" as they are sometimes called in Canada). Here are some sites that you will find especially useful. For the latest updates on these sites and others, visit ScholarshipCoach.com (keyword: CANADA).

Association of Universities and Colleges of Canada Online
www.aucc.ca/en/programbody.html

This website allows you to view scholarship programs administered by the Association of Universities and Colleges of Canada (AUCC) both alphabetically and by category. At last count, the AUCC administered more than 150 scholarship programs for Canadian students—for both undergraduate and graduate study—with most programs awarding multiple scholarships.

GraduateAid.com
www.graduateaid.com

This scholarship search site features a simple browsing system in which users categorize scholarships by college name or study program. Brief descriptions are included for each scholarship listing, with a limited amount of e-mail and Web addresses also included in the contact information.

ScholarshipsCanada.com
www.scholarshipscanada.com

To use the matching system on this site, you fill out a quick questionnaire that takes about 7–8 minutes to complete. The information on your questionnaire can be saved, and awards can be sorted by entry deadline or scholarship value. Test searches I conducted on this site yielded a substantial number of scholarship leads.

Simon Fraser University Graduate Awards Database
http://fas.sfu.ca/projects/GradAwards

This database is designed for students pursuing graduate school and post-doctoral studies. The site isn't going to win any Web design awards, but the scholarship information is efficiently presented. You can browse the database by academic department and deadline date, and you can perform keyword searches.

Student Awards Scholarship Search
www.studentawards.com

This site features a fairly large scholarship database and is designed for Canadian students studying in Canada, the U.S., or internationally. To perform a search for matching scholarships, you fill out a 20-minute questionnaire. Once you have input your information, it takes about 3 minutes to receive a matching list of scholarships.

University of Waterloo Scholarship Information File
www.adm.uwaterloo.ca/infograd/Scholarships/scholarship.html

Maintained by the University of Waterloo's Graduate Studies Office, this scholarship database contains award information for undergraduate, graduate, and postdoctoral studies. The scholarship listings include information on eligibility requirements, the value of awards, and any applicable deadlines.

Strengths and Weaknesses of Scholarship Databases

Although scholarship databases are great places to begin your search, they are just that—*starting points*. Some students assume that after performing a few database searches, they've found all the scholarships they are going to find. Wrong! Wrong! Wrong! Taking this approach is like hearing a few tunes on the radio and concluding that you've discovered everything there is to know about music. Fact: *Programs listed in Internet databases make up only the very tip of the scholarship iceberg.*

Some scholarship databases, for instance, have an unusual number of listings for local scholarships in Maine because they have input all the scholarships from the Financial Authority of Maine (FAME) website.

Actually, it's not even the tip of the iceberg; it's only one drop of water off that tip.

Although database searches are a quick way to accumulate a list of scholarships, they do have substantial limitations. First, these types of databases are way behind the curve when it comes to local and state scholarships. Many of these databases have uneven coverage of local areas, since it is difficult and costly to accumulate local information. What local information they do have is often there because a researcher has found a particular local database or directory of awards and has input those listings (after independently verifying them, we hope).

Second, don't expect timeliness with newly created scholarships. If these databases do include new scholarships, it's usually because scholarship providers took the initiative to submit information directly to them. Even really large scholarship programs can take quite a while to make their way through the grapevine before they are found in most databases.

Third, these databases are much better at helping you find scholarships that are easy to pigeonhole in particular categories. It's much simpler to match students with scholarships that have quantifiable judging criteria, such as GPA, than ones with more amorphous requirements, such as "strong character." Some of these harder-to-define scholarships, however, may be some of the best scholarship opportunities available for someone with your personal profile.

Finally, be aware that these database companies typically don't have big research departments (it's usually just a few people). Although they are skilled at locating scholarships, there's only so much that can be done with a limited number of personnel.

The bottom line is this: *Scholarship databases are powerful search tools to use, but don't use them to the exclusion of other search methods.* The best way to conduct a truly comprehensive search is to use all ten of the action steps described in this chapter.

Study
Abroad

ASK THE COACH #16

How do I find scholarships for study abroad?

The following resources will be useful both for American students enrolled at U.S. schools who wish to study abroad for a limited amount of time and for American students who wish to enroll directly in a foreign institution.

International Study and Travel Center Study Abroad Scholarships
www.istc.umn.edu/study/scholarships.html

Run by the Office of International Programs at the University of Minnesota, but useful to all students, the online International Study and Travel Center features a straightforward study-abroad scholarship search. To use the search, you simply specify the region of the world you'd like to study in, the type of program you're looking for (classroom, research, or internship), any special subject interests (language, business, arts, etc.), and any applicable eligibility categories.

International Institute of Education
www.iie.org/help/search.htm

This free search enables a student to browse sections of a scholarships, fellowships, and grants database for studying abroad. To search, remove the "X" on "IIE Resources" and place an "X" on "Financial Resources for International Study." Searches are possible using a variety of criteria, but for this particular search mechanism, it's better to keep your criteria extremely broad.

Foundations and organizations related to your particular country of interest are also a good bet. To find these organizations, consult your foreign language teacher, professor, or your school's study-abroad office, or use the techniques described in Action Step #10 to locate such groups.

The institutions themselves that run various study-abroad programs are also a good source for scholarships. You can find a directory of study-abroad programs at www.studyabroad.com or www.goabroad.com/studyabroad/search.cfm.

The determined seeker of study-abroad funding will also explore programs run by foreign embassies in the U.S. Many countries do provide cultural and educational exchange programs, and often ones funded by their home governments or some other sponsor. Visit www.embassy.org/embassies/index.html for a list of home pages of all U.S.-based embassies.

Foreign universities you are considering attending may also have some scholarship and grant programs for students from other countries. For links to university and international office websites, organized country by country, visit www.usc.edu/globaled/eecu.

In addition, I should mention that some of the largest sources of funding for study abroad include the Rotary Foundation Ambassadorial Scholarships (for students with at least two years of college-level coursework) and the U.S. Student Fulbright Grants (for graduate students). Both of these award programs are highly competitive. ■

POLITELY RAID OTHER SCHOOLS' RESOURCES

What if your school doesn't have particularly good scholarship resources? Not to worry! The enterprising scholarship seeker—that's you—doesn't let a few little inconveniences stand in his or her way. Instead, simply do what you would do if the corner grocery was sold out of your favorite junk food: GO TO ANOTHER STORE! This means visiting other high schools, colleges, and universities in your district (or beyond) to tap their scholarship resources, too.

In fact, I highly recommend taking these field trips even if your school has *all* of the aforementioned scholarship resources. As we've seen, when it comes to scholarships, information distribution is far from uniform: The school across town may have a list of scholarship programs that just never made it to your neck of the woods.

During my own scholarship search, I made sure to visit other schools in my area on a regular basis. (If you have friends at other schools, they can fill you in on the resources that are available.) Of course, I didn't exactly get all decked out in my school colors and insignia when visiting rival high schools. However, even if I had mentioned that I was from a different school, I think most counselors and parent volunteers would have still been willing to help me.

And guess what—you can "electronically visit" other schools without actually going there in person. Increasing numbers of high schools and college guidance and financial aid offices are putting scholarship information on their websites for their students to access. So locate the appropriate Web addresses for other schools in your area, and check out the scholarship information posted there (most don't require passwords to access the information). In addition, you should seek out the websites of schools in your state or beyond that are especially known for strong counseling or financial aid departments, large budgetary allocations, or extraordinary college planning programs. In the Internet age, you don't have to actually attend a school to benefit from its scholarship resources.

GUERRILLA TACTIC

Travel the Internet to Scout Other Schools

■ Seek out websites for schools with strong guidance offices and scholarship resources, and tap into the information they provide for their students.

ACTION STEP 5

CANVAS YOUR COMMUNITY

Now that we've tackled school and Internet resources, let's extend our scholarship search techniques to your community. Our goal is to locate those hard-to-find *local* scholarship programs—the programs that often have the fewest entries and thus give you the best odds of winning.

Community Groups

Some church-affiliated colleges will offer additional matching scholarships to enrolling students who have received scholarship funds from local congregations.

A good place to start locally is with a variety of community groups. Service organizations, veterans associations, religious groups, and fraternal lodges are frequent sponsors of scholarship programs on the local level. Here are some noteworthy organizations that you should query:

American Legion
Boy Scouts/Girl Scouts of America
Chamber of Commerce
Daughters of the American Revolution
Daughters of the Confederacy
Elks Club
4-H Club
Key Club
Kiwanis International
Knights of Columbus
Lions Club
National Honor Society
Odd Fellows and Rebekah Lodges
Optimist International
Rotary Club
Sons of the American Revolution
Soroptimist International
Unions (local chapters)
Veterans of Foreign Wars
YMCA/YWCA

For each of these groups, approach the local chapter in your city, state, or region. If you can't locate a local chapter, try contacting the national headquarters. If you do so, be aware that each local chapter is its own entity: The national headquarters may not be aware of all the programs that local chapters sponsor. So perhaps the best strategy is to ask the national headquarters about any national programs they may sponsor, and then to request contact information for the local chapter nearest to you.

Local Businesses

The Seattle, Washington, Chamber of Commerce is one group that administers an impressive scholarship program.

Businesses in your area with the highest profile or strongest community presence (especially with young people) are another good place to look for local community scholarship programs. Pay a visit to your local Chamber of Commerce; it may be aware of businesses in your area that sponsor (or might be interested in sponsoring) scholarships.

Have your family keep an eye out for scholarship programs advertised on television, in magazines, and in your local supermarket. Producers of consumer goods often promote their scholarships in such locations.

Radio and television stations, newspapers, and department stores are scholarship sources that often come up on the local level. Banks, credit unions, and other financial institutions in your community are also frequent scholarship providers. Ask to speak to the manager, and inquire whether the institution is sponsoring any scholarship contests.

Banks present another opportunity for scholarship seekers. Because they often hold the scholarship funds for other community groups and businesses, they may know of various scholarship programs that are available in your community. Speak to the manager of the bank, and inquire who at the bank might be aware of funds and trust accounts set up for particular community scholarships.

Local Chapters of Dollars for Scholars

About 140 colleges around the country have agreed to provide matching or additional funds for Dollars for Scholars award recipients.

An additional potential source of local scholarship funds and information that has sprung up in recent years is Dollars for Scholars, a national network of community-based, volunteer-operated scholarship foundations. Dollars for Scholars is managed in association with the Citizens' Scholarship Foundation of America. A primary goal of the program is to raise scholarship money for local

GUERRILLA TACTIC

Interview Local Bank Managers

■ Because local banks often hold fund accounts for community scholarship programs, ask bank personnel about any scholarship funds they help manage or are aware of.

For an updated list of all Dollars for Scholars chapters and their contact information, visit ScholarshipCoach.com (keyword: DOLSCHOL).

students and coordinate the application for and distribution of local scholarships through a central source. For this reason, a Dollars for Scholars chapter in your community could be a good source of information about local scholarship programs. Currently, nearly 900 chapters are located throughout the nation, and about 120 new chapters open each year.

SEEK OUT GOVERNMENT SOURCES

To take this action step, start out by contacting the government agencies in your state responsible for administering scholarship and financial aid programs. Such functions may be centralized in one agency or in two or more agencies. A complete state-by-state listing of such agencies is given in Appendix B. I recommend starting with the website address, since a good deal of information can now be found online. Follow up with phone calls, e-mails, or letters as needed.

Contacting these agencies is especially useful if you are considering an in-state college (because state-funded scholarships usually require that funds be used at an in-state school). But when you contact the various administrators, bureaucrats, and program managers, don't just ask them about the scholarship programs their agencies administer. Because these individuals often know a great deal about other scholarship opportunities in your state, tap their brains for additional college cash possibilities.

If you know the field you plan to study, you can extend your government-focused scholarship search to the specific federal agencies that have jurisdiction over or are directly involved in this field.

Special Government Programs for High School Students

For a list of the Byrd scholarship coordinators in all 50 states, visit ScholarshipCoach.com (keyword: BYRD).

If you are a high school senior who has strong grades, test scores, and extracurricular involvement, you should be aware of the Robert C. Byrd Honors Scholarship. Each state establishes its own application process and academic requirements, but typically applicants for this scholarship must have GPAs that rank in the upper 25 percent of their class and SAT scores above 1150 or an ACT score above 27. Each state is allotted a number of Byrd scholarships proportional to its population, with a substantial number of awards handed out in each U.S. congressional district. The dollar value of the scholarship depends on annual appropriations by Congress, but the typical award has been between $1,000 and $1,500 annually. Awards are renewable for four years (contingent on congressional appropriations), bringing the monetary value of the award to between $4,000 and $6,000. The Byrd scholarship is a federal program, but it is administered by state government agencies in each state.

If you haven't started a record for documenting your community service hours, here's a good reason to do so.

For high school students who have participated in community service or would like to in the future, an additional government-affiliated scholarship program to be aware of is the President's Student Service Scholarships. Each high school in the country may select two juniors or seniors who have contributed at least 100 hours of community service within one year. Student selected by their school receive a $1,000 college scholarship. (Once your school has selected you, there is no competitive application process.) The Corporation for National Service provides $500 per scholarship, matched with $500 from the local community. The surprising thing about this program is that *many schools fail to select any students for the award!* If you take it upon yourself to simply notify your school about the program, it just might get you an extra $1,000 for college.

Select finalists in the Coca-Cola Scholars Program may also be nominated separately for this scholarship award.

PURSUE ALL PERSONAL AND FAMILY AFFILIATIONS

Investigate whether each of the companies and organizations you listed on your Scholarship Coach Search Profile Worksheet, offers some type of scholarship program. For many of these groups, you will need to call the group itself to ascertain this information.

Pay special attention to your employer and your parents' employers. A lot of companies sponsor scholarship programs for their employees or children of employees. This is especially true of large companies that employ more than 500 people, or subsidiaries of these companies in both the U.S. and Canada.

Also, such companies often offer tuition benefits that have the same effect as a scholarship. For instance, some companies reimburse employees for educational costs after the successful completion of a course. To circumvent this potential cash flow dilemma, investigate whether the college billing office will allow you take an interest-free deferral if you provide evidence of your employer's tuition repayment policy (by submitting photocopies of the guidelines, along with contacts in your company's human resources department).

Furthermore, if your parents are members of any job-related organizations, such as unions, credit unions, or associations, investigate possible scholarships from those organizations as well. Locating programs with specific, limited applicant pools is as good as money in the bank. In fact, when it comes to such scholarship programs you could be the only applicant. (This *really* increases your odds of winning!)

Enlist your parents' help in looking for affiliation-based scholarships. Have them check with all of the organizations they belong to about the existence of scholarship programs.

ASK THE COACH #17

Are there any special ways to find scholarships for students with disabilities?

All ten action steps outlined in this chapter will help students with disabilities and medical conditions find scholarships, but certain sources of funding should be sought out with special attention.

A college's office for students with disabilities is a prime location for finding scholarships. At Penn State University, for example, the Office for

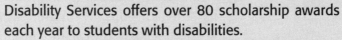
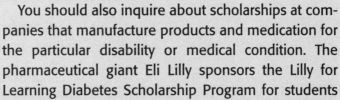

Disability Services offers over 80 scholarship awards each year to students with disabilities.

You should also inquire about scholarships at companies that manufacture products and medication for the particular disability or medical condition. The pharmaceutical giant Eli Lilly sponsors the Lilly for Learning Diabetes Scholarship Program for students with Type I diabetes. Parke-Davis, another pharmaceutical giant, sponsors the Parke-Davis Epilepsy Scholarship Award for high school seniors and college students. Schering/ Key Pharmaceutical, makers of asthma medication, sponsors the "Will to Win" Asthma Athlete Scholarship, and awards scholarships to student-athletes ranging from $1,000 to $10,000 in value. A variety of such companies offer these types of scholarship awards.

Furthermore, you should target associations and organizations related to your particular medical condition, since many of these groups have some type of scholarship awards program. Students with visual impairment, for example, will want to contact such organizations as the Association for Education of Blind and Visually Impaired, which sponsors an annual scholarship program. When you contact these organizations, target both the national headquarters and any state and local chapters located in your home area or the area in which you plan to attend college. Many individual chapters—such as those of the National Federation of the Blind—have their own scholarship programs that the national headquarters might not have information on. To find out what particular organizations are related to your disability or medical condition, use the techniques outlined in Action Step #10. ■

APPLY EFFECTIVE INTERNET SEARCH TECHNIQUES

In Action Step #3, we discussed how to harness the power of free Internet search databases, but this is only one aspect of what the Web has to offer. Now it's time for us to expand our Web-based search techniques by using well-known Internet search engines such as the following:

Google
www.google.com

AltaVista
www.altavista.com

Lycos
www.lycos.com

Excite
www.excite.com

As you know, finding websites is virtually impossible without engines that provide you with tools to quickly and easily search for information. They help you navigate your way through the Internet's information jungle. To use these engines effectively, however, you need to know a few key tricks. In this section, I will teach you these techniques by focusing on the most efficient ways for using these engines to expand your scholarship search.

Let's start by learning a little about how these search engines work. Although search engines don't store data from the websites themselves (except if certain pages are cached), they do create indexed references to website pages. Often this includes the page title, the Web address, as well as a summary description and list of keywords. Some Web search engines gather the summary description from the first few hundred characters of the page, whereas others look for common words or phrases on the entire page.

Using these search engines is fairly straightforward: Simply type words in the "Search For" box and hit the "Enter" key. I've found, however, that knowing how to properly use the syntax in a particular search engine—including quote marks, plus and minus signs, and capital letters—can make your scholarship searches considerably more effective. Check out the "Help" section of your favorite search engine for more specific tips on optimizing your technique.

Primary and Secondary Websites

As you search the Web for suitable scholarships, look for two types of sites: primary and secondary websites. **Primary websites** are the official sites put up by the organizations sponsoring or administering scholarship programs. In the past couple of years, increasing numbers of these programs have been making scholarship information (and even applications) available on the Internet.

If you happen to know the official name of a scholarship program, you have enough information to search for the primary website using the search engine techniques just discussed. If you don't know the official name of the scholarship, first try to search for it by including the word "scholarship" with whatever information you do know. If that doesn't work, try searching for the organization that sponsors or administers the scholarship. Once you get to the organization's website, you can search within the site for the scholarship program.

Of course, what you're really seeking are scholarships that you've never heard of before. You can find them by searching for generic categories of scholarships (such as ones aimed at particular career interests, fields of study, or hobbies), but the effectiveness of such an approach is limited.

Because many high school and college guidance offices create such sites for students at their schools (most without any password or school verification required), the result is a dramatic expansion in the school resources at your disposal.

This is where **secondary websites** come into play. Secondary sites are not official sites put up by scholarship sponsors or administrators, but rather sites that post lists of available scholarship opportunities. Scholarship listings are usually not the main focus of these sites, but instead are offered as useful additional information for students, parents, and educators using these sites. Such websites are frequently hosted by high school guidance offices, college financial aid offices, or associations and foundations involved with educating young people.

How do you find these secondary sites? All it takes is a simple, yet effective, Guerrilla Tactic: Type the official name of a scholarship program you already know into your favorite search engine. (If you don't have the name of a scholarship on the tip of your tongue, simply pick one out of this book.) Perform this task whether or not you already know the address of the scholarship's primary website.

Why should you search for scholarships you already know about? The reason is simple: Your search engine will come back with additional secondary sites that include this named scholarship in their listings. You can search these additional sites for information on scholarships that previously you didn't know anything about. Repeat the exercise by typing in the name of another scholarship that you are already familiar with. This, in turn, will lead you to other sites and listings, which will subsequently lead you to still others. Happy hunting!

GUERRILLA TACTIC

Follow the Internet Bread Crumb Trail

■ Type the names of scholarships you already know of into Internet search engines to turn up websites that also list additional scholarships you didn't know about.

This Internet search technique has a hidden bonus: Because secondary websites frequently specialize in listing certain types of scholarships, typing in the names of specific categories of scholarships will tend to lead you to listings for other scholarships in this same category. If you type into a search engine the name of a specific art scholarship, for instance, you are likely to find secondary websites that also tend to list art-oriented scholarships. Likewise, if you type in the name of a scholarship for nursing school, you will tend to turn up sites that have additional information about scholarship awards for nursing students. You can use this technique to locate specific scholarships that fit your interests, goals, and needs.

ASK THE COACH #18

Are there special search strategies for adult returning students?

As I mentioned earlier, scholarships for students in high school tend to have age limitations (such as being age 18 or younger), while scholarships for those in college often do not. In this way, the same scholarship search techniques used by 18- to 22-year-old college students work for the 25-year-old or older adult/nontraditional returning student.

In addition, many excellent scholarships have been crafted for the needs and accomplishments of this group. This is especially true at colleges and universities that have a substantial population of older learners or have special "extension" or "continuing education" schools. In general, seeking out scholarships at the colleges themselves—focusing on ones that have commuter campuses, distance education programs, or a large proportion of students over age 25—is a good approach for finding scholarships designated for adult students. For example, according to Penn State University's Commission for Adult Learners, the university offers about three dozen scholarships specifically for adult/nontraditional students. Some scholarships specified for adult students are targeted for those who have additional financial obligations. At the University of Louisville, for instance, the Beth K. Fields Scholarship—a full tuition award—is for students at least 25 years of age who provide financial support for at least one dependent. To find such scholarships, contact the office that administers adult and continuing education programs at colleges you hope to attend.

In general, seek out scholarships specifically for adult students, but don't neglect general scholarship programs open to *all* undergraduates. ■

UNCOVER SCHOOL-SPECIFIC AWARDS

Some colleges offer matching scholarships in which they provide you with an additional scholarship if you can bring in a comparable outside award. For more on this, visit ScholarshipCoach.com (keyword: MATCHMONEY).

Department-controlled scholarships are frequently available for such fields as art, drama, and music.

If you haven't yet enrolled in college or are a college student who is considering transferring to another school, you will definitely want to target scholarships sponsored directly by schools you are considering attending. You should start out by contacting both the admissions office and the financial aid office at these prospect schools. If you've already submitted an admissions application, inquire about scholarship possibilities with the admissions officer or recruiter assigned to your file. This person can be your ally, recommending you for any scholarships meant to entice students to enroll.

You should also contact any specific offices at the school relating to any special personal characteristics you possess. Minority students, for instance, should contact the college office responsible for minority affairs; they may be aware of specific college-sponsored scholarships for minority students at the school. The college's athletic office is a worthwhile resource for students with athletic ability, even if they are not necessarily planning to participate in formal college athletic programs.

Some school-specific scholarship awards may be controlled by individual academic departments. (The general admissions and financial aid offices may not even be aware of such awards.) For this reason, contact the heads of those departments *directly* for any academic disciplines you are interested in pursuing. Contacting individual academic departments is especially important for graduate students, since these departments typically control the bulk of scholarships, fellowships, teaching assistantships, and research grants at many schools.

If you're not sure about what school you'd like to attend, there are other methods for determining which schools have suitable scholarships. Searching the College Board's college database (available at http://apps.collegeboard.com/search/index.jsp) is one such way.

Using the "Advanced Search" feature and then proceeding to the "Cost & Financial Aid" section, you can search for colleges that have school-specific scholarships related to the following areas:

Academics
Art, Music and Drama
Athletics
Minority Status
ROTC
Religion Affiliation
State Residence

Because the matching system hunts for colleges that meet *all* of the criteria you specify, I recommend searching each of these areas one at a time. Search results indicate only whether a college awards a particular type of scholarship; you won't be able to use this database to find any specific information about the particular scholarship offered. (For that, you'll have to call or visit the school directly.)

Sometimes you can find the information by visiting the school's website—but realize that many awards never get posted in cyberspace. A sample search for merit scholarships related to art, music, and drama, for instance, yielded 779 colleges that offer these types of awards. Information on more than 3,500 schools is contained in the database (the source of which is the College Board's *Annual Survey of Colleges*).

You can also use the "College Quickfinder" function to determine if a specific college offers a particular type of scholarship (although this doesn't replace calling or visiting the specific school).

ASK THE COACH #19

What are some top school-specific scholarships for incoming freshmen?

Although Ivy League schools (along with schools like Stanford University and the Massachusetts Institute of Technology) don't award any merit scholarships, other top colleges do offer excellent merit-based funding opportunities. The following are ten of the most prestigious, lucrative, and sought-after school-specific scholarships for incoming freshmen:

California Institute of Technology: *Freshman Merit Awards*

The Freshman Admissions Committee chooses a limited number of admitted freshmen for these merit scholarships, which range up to full tuition. Selected students are notified at the time of admission.

University of Chicago: *College Honor Scholarships*

The University of Chicago awards scholarships to "distinguished scholars who are also leaders" and who exhibit "curiosity and passion for the life of the mind." Several hundred scholarships, ranging up to full tuition, are awarded each year.

Duke University: *Angier B. Duke Memorial Scholarships*

The scholarships provide free tuition at Duke, funding for a summer program in England at Oxford University, and further financial assistance for those demonstrating additional financial need. Approximately 15 recipients are chosen each year.

Emory University: *Emory Scholars Program*

Each year, Emory University awards about 70 students scholarships that range from full tuition to full tuition plus expenses.

Johns Hopkins University: *Hodson Scholarships*

The university awards 15 freshmen with scholarships that are worth up to $18,500 per year. The scholarships are renewable each year, and awards are based on academic and personal achievement and leadership.

University of North Carolina at Chapel Hill: *The Morehead Awards*

The Morehead Awards provide merit scholarships to approximately 60 lucky recipients each year. The scholarship covers the entire cost of four years at the university and funds a four-year summer enrichment program. Students must be nominated by a participating high school (all those in North Carolina and Canada, as well as 140 high schools throughout the U.S. and 32 in Great Britain).

Rice University: *Merit Scholarships*

Rice offers merit scholarships to its most outstanding applicants who demonstrate a wide variety of talents. Scholarships cover up to full tuition.

Swarthmore College: *McCabe Scholarships*

Swarthmore awards a very limited number of full-tuition merit scholarships. McCabe scholars are chosen during the admission process, and all admission applicants are considered.

University of Virginia: *Jefferson Scholars*

The Jefferson Scholars Program awards merit scholarships to 25 entering students who embody Jeffersonian ideals of leadership, scholarship, and citizenship. Recipients receive a scholarship that covers the entire cost of attending the University of Virginia for four years.

Washington University in St. Louis: *Academic Scholarship and Fellowship Programs*

Washington University offers merit scholarships through special competitions administered by individual academic departments—in such fields as physical sciences and mathematics, humanities, music, writing, and the social sciences. Available scholarships include annual awards of $2,500, half-tuition scholarships, and full-tuition scholarships with an additional $2,500 stipend.

Note that many of these schools have excellent merit scholarship programs for their rising sophomores, juniors, and seniors as well. ∎

SEEK OUT RELATED ORGANIZATIONS

Now that you know the basics of finding college scholarships, you're ready to explore an additional research technique that can broaden the reach of your scholarship net. This new technique opens an additional avenue for finding scholarship "diamonds"—the programs that are tailor-made for someone with your unique characteristics.

The key is to seek out a wide range of organizations, associations, foundations, societies, and other potential scholarship providers that are in some way related to your background, skills, ethnicity, interests, and goals—groups that are related to the information you provided on your Scholarship Coach Search Profile Worksheet. You can then contact these groups and inquire about scholarship prospects.

Not only should you inquire about any scholarships these organizations directly sponsor, but you should also ask individuals at the organization whether they know of any other organizations or groups in their field of expertise that may offer scholarship opportunities. To help locate groups that are relevant to you in the different ways mentioned above, check out the following resources.

Because contacting individual organizations can be time-consuming, hone in on those groups that are most relevant to you.

Encyclopedia of Associations

You should be able to find a copy of the *Encyclopedia of Associations* (published by Gale Research) in the reference section of your local public library. If your local library for some reason does not carry this mammoth three-volume directory, try the nearest college library.

The *Encyclopedia of Associations* is divided into a variety of categories according to the type of organization (such as commercial,

You can also look up organizations and associations in your home area–a good potential source of scholarships–by using the geographic index.

Some libraries may also subscribe to "Associations Unlimited," an electronic database drawn from the print version. Searching electronically for relevant groups can save you some time.

educational, or cultural). Go to the keyword menu and index to locate organizations and associations related to your interests and background—groups such as the Dance Educators of America, the National Society of Black Engineers, or even the National Ice Carving Association.

Each organization is described, and its major programs, publications, and membership are noted. In addition, many listings contain an "awards" section that details major scholarship, grant, and fellowship programs the organization runs. Don't rely on the information listed in the awards section, however, since it can be dated and not necessarily relevant to you.

Foundation Grants to Individuals and *The Foundation Directory*

Two other print resources that may prove useful to you are *Foundation Grants to Individuals* and *The Foundation Directory*. Both are published by The Foundation Center and are available in most libraries.

The *Foundation Grants to Individuals* directory identifies foundations that annually make grants of at least $2,000 to individuals. The directory is organized according to the types of grants awarded, and only a portion of the profiled grants are related to college scholarships.

The Foundation Directory is a broader work that lists all types of foundations—many of which make awards to agencies and institutions rather than individuals. Contacting foundations that don't offer awards to individuals can still be useful, because they may make grants to other groups that, in turn, may use the money to award scholarships. Use the contact information provided to further investigate any relevant scholarship leads.

Web Resources

In addition, several websites can also help you locate associations, foundations, societies, organizations, and groups of interest to you. Web resources include AssociationCentral.com (www.associationcentral.com), the Scholarly Societies Project (www.scholarly-societies.org), Associations on the Net (www.ipl.org/ref/AON), and The Foundation Center's "Foundation Finder" and "Grantmaker Websites" search tools (www.fdncenter.org/funders/grantmaker/index.html). You also can use the Internet search engines discussed in Action Step #8 to locate some of these special organizations.

International

ASK THE COACH #20

How can international students find scholarships to study in the U.S.?

Although many scholarship programs in the U.S. are open only to U.S. citizens, a substantial number of scholarship programs are targeted for international students or allow international students to apply. In general, there tend to be more scholarship options available for international students pursuing graduate studies in the U.S. than for those seeking an undergraduate degree.

One scholarship database for international students worth searching is located at the International Education Financial Aid Website (www.iefa.org/public/search.html). The database is fairly small, but searching it couldn't be easier: You simply select a field of study from a drop-down menu and enter a country of origin.

International students should also use the strategies in Action Step #10 to seek out associations, organizations, foundations, societies, and other groups that are likely to have an interest in international relations, cultural affairs, or students from a particular ethnic background. International organizations that frequently sponsor scholarships for international students include the United Nations, the Organization of American States, AMIDEAST, the International Telecommunications Union, the League of

Red Cross Societies, the International Maritime Organization, the World Health Organization, the Soros Foundation, and the World Council of Churches. Multinational corporations with an interest both in your home country and in the U.S. are also good potential sources of scholarship funds.

The Bureau of Educational and Cultural Affairs of the U.S. State Department coordinates a variety of educational exchange programs for undergraduates, graduate students, and professionals from selected regions of the world. The particular regions of the world targeted by such programs vary according to U.S. diplomatic goals. Currently sponsored programs include scholarships, grants, and fellowships for both undergraduate and graduate students from Russia and the New Independent States. You should also contact government agencies in your home country to inquire about any government-sponsored funding options for study abroad.

U.S. colleges and universities that have large populations of international students are also strong possibilities for school-specific scholarship awards. Keep in mind that public colleges in the U.S. (ones funded by the state) are generally, but not always, less expensive than private colleges. On the flip side, private colleges may have fewer U.S. citizen requirements for receiving their financial aid awards, and thus are typically more likely to have greater scholarships and grants for international students. For more information on colleges you are particularly interested in, contact the school's international student office and financial aid office.

If you already attend an institution of higher education in your home country, you should also look for formal exchange programs between your institution and a U.S. institution. Person-for-person exchanges can often reduce tuition costs and other expenses significantly. Full-fledged scholarship and fellowship programs for study in the U.S. may also be available from your home university. ∎

CHAPTER 4 SUMMARY AND KEYWORDS

Principles of Searching: The harder you have to dig to find a scholarship, the greater the chance that someone else won't, thereby tilting the odds of winning in your favor. Document all aspects of your (and your family's) background and affiliations to uncover additional scholarship possibilities. Cast a wide net by pursuing scholarships awards that most students can apply for, yet focus narrow by seeking scholarships open only to students with your unique personal characteristics. In addition to looking for scholarships that you can apply for right away, leverage your efforts by searching for scholarships for future years. Get organized from the beginning by immediately requesting and filing away scholarship information. ■

Useful Tools: Use scholarship search tools such as the Scholarship Coach Search Profile Worksheet, the ScholarshipCoach.com website, and *The Scholarship Scouting Report.* ■

Your School: Tap into the various scholarship resources available at your school. Many scholarship sponsors and administrators send applications, brochures, and other materials directly to high schools and colleges. Set up a meeting with a counselor, adviser, or financial aid officer at your school to discuss scholarship opportunities. ■

Scholarship Databases: A variety of scholarship databases are available as CD-ROMs online and as printed directories. The most widely used scholarship databases are available on the Internet and have either a matching or browsing search mechanism. A *source* database provides scholarship data that was gathered by the organization that provides access to the database. A licensed database is derived from someone else's database entries. Search a wide variety of databases, since they each provide access to different sets of scholarship information: Use source databases first, and then licensed databases.

For best results, consider the distinguishing features of a particular database before you search it. Special scholarship databases exist for grad students, Canadians, minority students, international students, and those wishing to study abroad. Scholarship databases should not be used to the exclusion of other search tools or methods, since they are not particularly comprehensive for local and state scholarships, newly created programs, or scholarships that are difficult to pigeon-hole in categories. ■

Visiting Other Schools: Scholarship information is not disseminated perfectly equally to each school. To uncover many scholarships you would otherwise miss, investigate scholarship resources at other schools in your area. Draw on the resources of distant schools—especially those with strong guidance and college planning programs—by visiting their websites. ■

Canvassing Your Community: Locating hard-to-find local scholarship programs—the contests that have the fewest entries—substantially increases your odds of winning. Search for local scholarships by querying community groups, local businesses, and chapters of national organizations. ■

Government Sources: Contact the government agencies in your state that are responsible for administering scholarship and financial aid programs (see the state listings in Appendix B). Such resources are especially useful if you are attending or are considering attending an in-state school. Federal agencies directly involved in your particular field of study can also provide helpful scholarship leads. Special government programs for high school students include the Robert C. Byrd Honors Scholarship and the President's Student Service Scholarships. ■

Personal and Family Affiliations: Use the information that you compile on your Scholarship Coach Search Profile Worksheet to locate scholarships with specialized requirements that fit your profile. Employers, job-related organizations and associations, and disability-related institutions are fertile ground. ■

Web Search Techniques: Use Internet search engines to locate primary websites (official sites from scholarship providers) and secondary websites (those that report scholarship opportunities). Input the names of scholarships you already know about into these search engines; this helps you locate websites that also list college cash opportunities you haven't heard about. ■

School-Specific Awards: Search for scholarships from the schools you are considering. Contact the general admissions and financial aid offices of these schools, any specific offices related to your personal characteristics (such as offices for students with disabilities, minority students, and athletes), as well as individual academic departments. Many top colleges offer excellent merit-based funding opportunities. ■

Approaching Organizations and Foundations: Search for scholarships and scholarship information at organizations, associations, foundations, and societies that are related to your background, skills, ethnicity, interests, and goals. You can efficiently locate such groups by using a variety of library and online resources. ■

SCHOLARSHIPCOACH.COM KEYWORDS

For more information on a scholarship or topic mentioned in this chapter, enter the associated keyword in the keyword link box located in the Coach's Locker Room section of ScholarshipCoach.com.

Scholarship/Topic	Keyword
Angier B. Duke Memorial Scholarships	DUKE
Beth K. Fields Scholarship	BFIELDS
California Institute of Technology Freshman Merit Awards	CALTECH
Canadian Scholarship Resources	CANADA
Dollars for Scholars Program	DOLSCHOL
Emory Scholars Program	EMORY
Hodson Scholarships	HODSON

Jefferson Scholars	JEFFERSON
Lilly for Learning Diabetes Scholarship Program	LILLY
Matching Scholarships	MATCHMONEY
McCabe Scholarships	MCCABE
Morehead Awards	MOREHEAD
Parke-Davis Epilepsy Scholarship Award	PDAVIS
President's Student Service Scholarships	PRESSERV
Rice University Merit Scholarships	RICE
Robert C. Byrd Honors Scholarship	BYRD
Rotary Foundation Ambassadorial Scholarships	ROTARY
Scholarship Coach Search Profile Worksheet	PROFSHEET
Scholarship Coach National Tour	TOUR
Scholarship Database Updates	DATABASE
Scholarship Search Case Studies	CASESTUDY
The Scholarship Scouting Report	SCOUTREP
U.S. Student Fulbright Grants	FULBRIGHT
University of Chicago College Honor Scholarships	UCHICAGO
Washington University in St. Louis Scholarships	WASHU
"Will to Win" Asthma Athlete Scholarship	ASTHMA

PART III

GAME PLAN: WIN

CODE RED 6

Strategies
That Give You the
Edge

Painting Your Own Portrait

INSIDE THIS CHAPTER

▌ Building a cohesive message

▌ Primary and secondary themes

▌ The keys to a persuasive application

▌ A sampler of winning thematic approaches

▍ KNOWING THE PERSON

Since becoming the Scholarship Coach, I've had the opportunity to inspect a variety of scholarship applications submitted by many different students—scholarship applications that brought home the scholarship bucks and plenty of others that didn't quite make it. What I learned from this process is that the winning scholarship applications don't look anything like the ones that aren't successful.

Unsuccessful scholarship applications, more often than not, resemble a laundry list of activities, awards, and accomplishments by the student. Although such credentials are often quite impressive, reading the application can feel like inhaling random conglomerations of facts. After I've skimmed just a few of these applications, I find everything starts to blend together; it's difficult to remember which accomplishments and credentials go with which applicant.

When reading a winning application, on the other hand, I usually feel as though I am actually getting to know the person who submitted it. The students behind these applications manage to communicate the underlying motivations behind all the facts and figures. I usually come away from each one feeling that I understand the person's core interests, skills, and values.

This assessment of winning scholarship applications is reinforced when I think back to conversations I've had with application judges at various scholarship award ceremonies. (If you win, you often get to meet those who evaluated your applications.) When chatting with these judges for the first time, I frequently heard comments such as, "I already feel as though I know you, Ben." They would then ask me how the tennis season was going, how this or that writing project was coming along, or how my documentary filmmaking apprenticeship had turned out—specifics that they remembered from my application. Sometimes, I would run into these same judges years later and they still would remember milestones of my teenage years.

Why do winning applications leave such strong impressions? Quite simply, great scholarship applications create vivid portraits of the applicants: They don't just recite accomplishments—they depict the person behind all the credentials, interests, and goals. After all, *judges award scholarships to people, not to résumés.* If a judge feels as though he or she knows you, it's much harder to pass you by when it's time to award the scholarship money.

Clearly defining who you are creates a powerful emotional connection with those who evaluate you. It makes your application memorable and your cause persuasive. Perhaps the best way to approach the process is to think of yourself as a Monet or Michelangelo (the Renaissance artist, not the Teenage Mutant Ninja Turtle) of scholarship applications: The written application form is your canvas, and your commission is to paint a vivid self-portrait.

▎The Painter's Touch

Of course, painting this self-portrait is easier said than done. The biggest obstacle is the physical limitation of the application itself: You're often trying to cram years of experiences, discoveries, and thoughts onto a couple sheets of paper. If application judges were to shadow your every move for a week, they could probably get a pretty good sense of who you are and what you're like. But because your evaluators are judges, not stalkers, you'll have to convey a great deal about yourself using just ink on a pristine white page.

So how do you paint a self-portrait? First, you must treat each component of the application (such as the essay, extracurricular activity list, and recommendation letter) as *part of a unified whole,* rather than as separate entities. Each essay, list, and letter contributes to the overall impression that you make, and each component makes this contribution in a different way. If you don't coordinate the message that each part sends in a harmonious and consistent way, the overall effect is unclear, jumbled, and chaotic.

The principle of painting a compelling self-portrait is crucial whether you're enrolled in high school, college, or grad school or planning to return to school.

A good way to understand the importance of coordinating all components of your application is to think of your favorite song. Don't the words and music seem to fit just perfectly? Doesn't the music seem to capture the spirit of the lyrics, and vice versa? Now suppose you took the hardcore lyrics of gangsta rap (think of a song by Snoop Dogg) and combined it with the syrupy melody of a romantic ballad (like one by Bryan Adams or Michael Bolton). The result would be utter musical chaos—neither rap fans nor ballad lovers would be pleased. To avoid performing this scary song within the auditorium of your application materials, strive to make each part of your application work together toward a common idea.

In my interviews with dozens of scholarship winners, the importance of having an application theme and painting a clear picture of it was repeated again and again.

Developing the specific idea you want to communicate is the second aspect of painting a self-portrait: You must decide on the message itself—what I call the **application theme**, the framework that puts all your activities, interests, and credentials in the proper context. Application themes are frequently created around particular activities that you're passionate about, particular interests that fascinate you, life experiences that you've faced, or career goals that you're striving toward.

No matter how complex you are as a human being, or how little space an application form gives you to explain yourself, your theme should convey something truly important about who you are and what you care about. The goal is not to explain all the facets of your life, but rather to focus on a couple of key areas.

Application themes for students going on to graduate school tend to be more focused on the reasons for pursuing a particular academic discipline or career path.

Which activities do you most enjoy? What types of disciplines and skills come naturally to you? What events have had the most impact on your life? What perspectives and opinions are distinctly your own? What do you dream of doing 20 years from now? These are a few of the underlying questions that help you to define a theme. Your goal should be to make this theme resonate throughout all parts of your application.

This is not to say that all your scholarship applications should have the same theme. Let's say, for instance, that a student has identified three potential application themes: (1) a fascination with science, (2) extensive participation in community service, and (3) a dream of one day dancing on Broadway. For applications focused on quantitative skills, her theme could be science related. For scholarships emphasizing contributions to society, the theme could be built around extensive community service experience. For awards based on artistic achievement, the hard work and sacrifice while developing dancing skills could be showcased.

In Chapter 6, I'll show you how to choose which of your personal themes to use in a given scholarship application, and how to best adapt your theme to fit the specific judging criteria.

PRIMARY AND SECONDARY THEMES

The typical application should have no more than one or two major themes. Any more than this dilutes the communicative power of your message. If you want an application to have two themes, make one of them the **primary theme** and the other the **secondary theme**. The primary theme should be the focal point of the application—the main message you are communicating. The secondary theme builds on the primary message by illustrating another important aspect of your life, your interests, and your personality. Your primary and secondary themes can be closely linked or entirely unrelated.

Even when your primary and secondary themes are seemingly unrelated, there may be ways to connect them together. A student interested in both science and community service, for instance, could highlight her participation in a service program that introduces young, disadvantaged children to the wonders of science.

Some adult returning students who have won scholarships have used their reasons for wanting to return to school as their primary theme and the time and energy they've invested into their children as a secondary theme. One scholarship winner I met tied the two themes together by describing how helping her daughter prepare for college (and realizing all that college had to offer) was the event that first sparked an intense desire to go back to school and prepare for the exciting second half of her life.

ENHANCING CREDIBILITY

"I tried to stick to a theme in my applications. This theme dealt with my involvement in peer education, sex education, and a lot of related issues. It became clear in my applications that this was something that I really cared about."

–*Alexandra DeLaite*
Scholarship Winner
Columbia, MO

Building a cohesive theme in an application serves another important purpose. Given the competitive nature of the merit-based scholarship application process, judges recognize that all applicants are more or less trying to say what they think the judges want to hear. This is understandable, but judges are on the lookout for applicants who aren't just paying lip service to lofty ideals.

Primary and secondary themes enhance an applicant's believability by communicating, and continually reinforcing, a consistent message. The applicants who seem the most credible are the ones who communicate the strongest themes.

■ EMPLOYING YOUR THEME

Perhaps the best way to understand how to use primary and secondary themes is to view them in action—as part of an actual scholarship application. The following excerpts are taken from my winning entry in the Discover Card Tribute Awards. My primary theme was my passion for writing and my deep appreciation for all forms of communication as tools for solving problems. My secondary theme focused on how I had already exhibited, and would continue to exhibit, a high level of leadership.

First, let's examine an excerpt from the "Goals Paragraph" that I submitted. The application materials requested that I submit a paragraph of no more than 200 words in which I was to describe my future career goals and discuss how continuing my education would help me achieve those goals:

> Because of a strong interest in writing and communication, an aptitude for analysis and problem-solving, and a fascination with the inner workings of government, I plan to pursue a career in print and broadcast journalism as a political columnist and commentator. A well-rounded education will unlock the gates of opportunity—not only helping to clarify complex issues and providing skills for becoming a more persuasive writer and effective speaker, but also preparing me to be a responsible contributor in this world of infinite possibilities. . . . As a well-educated journalist, I will strive to broaden minds and uncover truth—thus doing my part to make a difference in the world.

"You need a specific focus in your application to grab a judge's attention. For me, this strong selling point was my interest and involvement in politics and government."

–David Weiss
Scholarship Winner
Rockford, IL

Notice that both my primary and secondary themes are supported in this statement. My strong passion for writing and oral communication is reinforced both in my career goal itself and in how I describe that goal. My secondary theme of empowering leadership is demonstrated

Going over page changes with other members of my high school newspaper staff.

by the description of how I plan to contribute to society through my journalistic endeavors.

Next, let's examine an excerpt from the first section of a "criteria statement" that I also wrote for the Discover Card application. In this statement, among other things, I was asked to describe any special talents I possessed:

You have a limited amount of space to persuade the judges, so you want to prominently highlight your achievements and make them as compelling as possible (without seeming arrogant).

As far back as I can remember, a love for language and a passion for ideas have been integral parts of who I am. I have expressed this through the creation of poetry and short stories, active involvement in debate and public speaking, and by working in journalism and documentary filmmaking. . . . Eventually, my fascination with the power of words led to positions as editor-in-chief of my middle school newspaper; news editor of my high school newspaper, *The Axe*, as a sophomore; and presently, editor-in-chief of this nationally acclaimed publication. In these roles I have received recognition for both my writing and design and have had excerpts of my political commentary on the Senator Packwood sexual harassment scandal reprinted in my local newspaper, *The Register-Guard*.

Keep in mind that when it comes to application themes, there are no "right answers." A theme that works for me probably isn't right for you, and vice versa.

In the excerpt, I bolstered my primary theme by discussing different manifestations of my love of writing. I illustrated that this isn't just a transitory interest by showing how the interest can be traced back to my childhood. The description of the journalism-related leadership positions I have held strengthens my secondary theme.

In choosing letters of recommendation to include with these application materials, I picked recommendations that further enhanced my two main application themes. Shown below is an excerpt from a letter that was written by my faculty adviser on the school newspaper:

Conscientious, dedicated, and persistent, Ben is the kind of individual so greatly needed in journalism. He works equally well as part of a group or independently, he is concerned about others and his community, and he is keenly interested in current affairs. . . . In addition to being one of the top writers and analysts I have seen in 15 years of advising the journalism program, he is also an adept, articulate public speaker. Ben would make an outstanding journalist, a leader in his field.

A second letter of recommendation included in the application was written by my student government adviser and emphasized my leadership skills:

In Chapter 10, I'll show you how to cultivate recommendation letters that reinforce your application themes.

Ben has organized school elections, played a leading role in school-wide assemblies, is a part of the budgeting process for school clubs and activities, and has worked on projects to provide for indigent people in our community. . . . Ben is confident and comfortable in a small social group or speaking to a very large audience. He learns well from each situation in which he takes part.

The Discover Card application also allowed me to attach supplementary materials. To further bolster my primary theme (and to show that I had the necessary

One common application component that wasn't depicted in the above example was an extracurricular activity list. Activities that reinforce your primary and secondary themes should be at or near the top of your list. (We'll discuss this more in Chapter 11.)

skills to reach my career goals), I chose to include with the application some articles that I had written for my high school newspaper. Among them, I included my political column about the Senator Packwood scandal I had mentioned in my criteria statement. I also included an article on the pressing need for an important school reform; this reinforced my secondary theme by highlighting my "leadership through journalism" approach.

This example illustrates how a well-thought-out theme is implemented by reinforcing it in each component of an application. More specifically, this is done by placing activities, credentials, and ideas that support your theme in prominent places and addressing the theme in essays and personal statements.

STAYING BALANCED

As it turned out, this sports participation aspect of my portrait became a "balancing" factor that was important to the judging process.

Finally, I should mention that building a theme doesn't mean omitting areas of your record that don't fit neatly into it. I covered all these off-theme activities and achievements in my application, but I kept that material in the background. Case in point: In the Discover Card application, I included a third letter of recommendation, written by the co-principal of my school, that described in detail my involvement in activities, such as tennis, that didn't relate to my main themes.

You don't have to sacrifice a sense of well-roundedness to make room for your application theme. Activities that fit your theme should occupy center stage, but there's still plenty of room on the rest of the stage for all of your other credentials.

▮ NINE WINNING THEMES

Never blindly follow a theme if it doesn't feel right for you. Judges can tell if a theme isn't genuine.

In this section, I describe nine application themes that have been successfully employed by many scholarship winners. These descriptions are meant to stimulate your thinking and provide you with a sampling of the wide range of possible themes. Keep in mind that these themes represent only nine popular ones that I've chosen to profile: Winning scholarship themes come in all shapes and sizes, and yours should be specific to your unique qualities.

In each of the profiled themes, I discuss the characteristics of the typical student using the theme, as well as analyze the tactical advantages and disadvantages of that theme (every theme has its pluses and minuses). I describe strategies that scholarship winners have used to flesh out each theme and make their thematic portrait especially persuasive, compelling, and effective. Keep in mind that such strategies are designed to spark your own strategic thinking, not replace it altogether. If you can come up with your own creative ways to develop these themes, it will only help your scholarship chances.

Each of these nine examples is suitable for use as either a primary or secondary theme.

The Do-Gooder

CHARACTERISTICS: You volunteer for several community organizations. You may have even created your own service program. Community service is your passion; it dominates your extracurricular activities.

ADVANTAGES: Service to others is an important criterion in many scholarship programs. If scholarship money is awarded to you, society eventually receives a benefit many times greater than its investment. Your commitment to others is refreshing and admirable.

DISADVANTAGES: Service to others is a fine theme, but it's still a pretty broad one—and one that many competing applicants may use. If you don't develop your theme carefully, you could be overshadowed by applicants who have other areas of expertise but also fit in volunteer work on the side.

If you are interested in learning how I created my own homework-related community service program, go to ScholarshipCoach.com (keyword: HELPLINE).

The key for this type of applicant is to demonstrate a core purpose behind the services performed. Because you need to make your commitment to community service credible, your service theme needs to be specific. Do this by crafting your theme around particular types of service programs that you especially care about.

Whenever possible, use personal experiences to illustrate why you are so interested in and passionate about the particular type of service. Perhaps you are especially close to your grandmother and find it rewarding to volunteer to help the elderly through the Meals on Wheels program. Or maybe you helped raise your younger siblings and, as a result of that experience, enjoy working with young children.

This isn't to say that you shouldn't describe a broad range of community service efforts. Just try to focus a bit, making one type of service endeavor your special pet project. If you're really interested in community service, a personally rewarding way to build on your theme is to create your own community service program (that's what I did).

The Creative Talent

CHARACTERISTICS: You are unusually skilled in a particular creative discipline—visual arts, dance, music, drama, or some other field. You spend countless hours practicing the discipline, derive great enjoyment from it, and hope to pursue it in some capacity in the future.

ADVANTAGES: Your special talent helps make your scholarship applications stand out. Achieving distinction in a creative discipline illustrates that you possess many character traits (focus, determination, and work ethic) that are ingredients of success—and worthy of financial support.

DISADVANTAGES: Judges are looking for well-rounded applicants. The danger here is that you could appear too focused on your special talent to the exclusion of everything else. If application judges don't have much aesthetic appreciation for your particular discipline, they might not fully appreciate your talent.

Creativity is highly valued in scholarship applications. By passionately discussing significant milestones on the long road to proficiency and mastery, you can make your application memorable. But you don't want to look too one-dimensional, suggesting that the particular discipline you excel in is the *only* thing you do. Some applicants get around this by demonstrating that they are skilled in a wide range of creative disciplines; others balance their special talent with solid academics, community service involvement, or other extracurricular activities.

It is important to demonstrate your ability when employing a creative talent theme. If applications permit it, try to send a portfolio or samples of your work. Get professional artists and teachers in your field to comment on your work's quality, and enter various competitions in your field to establish evidence of distinction.

The Survivor

CHARACTERISTICS: You have overcome significant obstacles in your life—economic hardships, family problems, medical conditions, or personal issues. Overcoming such challenges has played an important role in shaping who you have become. Your favorite TV catch phrase is "The tribe has spoken."

ADVANTAGES: Stories of obstacles overcome can create applications of compelling human emotion and drama. Some of the most powerful scholarship applications I've seen have been submitted by students who have described, in dramatic fashion, how they triumphed over tough challenges through sheer will and determination.

DISADVANTAGES: Depending on the obstacle overcome, it could involve private matters that are difficult (or painful) to discuss in an application.

Merely describing a tough situation you've faced is not enough. Judges are more interested in how you've dealt with the challenge. The focus of your application should not be on the obstacle itself, but on how you have *responded* to it. As Booker T. Washington eloquently put it, "Success is to be measured not so much by the position one has reached in life as by the obstacles he has overcome trying to succeed."

Some types of obstacles (for example, drug abuse) may be things that initially put a negative image in the minds of judges. If the obstacle you've overcome is an obstacle created by your own doing, you'll want to clearly show how you've learned from your mistakes and now are an entirely different person. This is an effective strategy if there's a "black eye" on your record (such as a school disciplinary action). Such a theme can put the punishment in a more positive light.

The Brainiac

CHARACTERISTICS: You have a high GPA (3.8 or higher) and very strong standardized-test scores or are on the dean's list. You have taken a slew of Advanced Placement, honors, and other high-level classes or assisted your professors in their research. Your friends call you "Doogie."

ADVANTAGES: You're going to look great with any application that requires a transcript. Your success in school demonstrates your discipline and commitment. Your results in tough classes illustrate a drive to succeed in challenging environments.

DISADVANTAGES: Grades and high scores aren't everything. If you don't balance your academic prowess with success in other areas, you might come across as one-dimensional. And because it's impossible to garner a GPA of, like, 49.2 on a 4.0 scale, you need to find additional ways to distinguish yourself.

Some students believe that high grades and test scores alone will win them scholarships. Quantitative measurements, however, can't paint a full portrait.

Grades alone won't bring you scholarship success, but you are in an excellent position to build on your already solid academic record. There are a number of ways to do this: One way is to demonstrate that your good grades are, at a fundamental level, a result of your great curiosity and thirst for knowledge (in a wide range of fields, or one in particular). You could illustrate this thirst by explaining how much a particular in-school or out-of-school academic program, or independent study and research project, has meant to you. The strength of such an approach is that it presents you as someone who will get the most out of a collegiate academic environment or graduate program. Judges could feel that awarding you a scholarship would be money well spent.

Another approach is to emphasize that although schoolwork is primarily an individual task, you are interested in helping others get more out of their studies, too. Typical activities to support this theme might include tutoring other students in your school or starting an academic or mentoring program to encourage younger students.

The Activist

CHARACTERISTICS: You devote considerable time to supporting and promoting various social causes that you believe in. You have helped organize rallies, petition drives, awareness campaigns, and other projects. Your first words as a baby were, "Heck no, we won't go!"

ADVANTAGES: Your devotion to making society a better place is very admirable. Judges will like the fact that you are not content to just sit on your laurels, but rather are someone who takes action and has strong convictions.

DISADVANTAGES: Those who review your scholarship application might not be sympathetic to particular causes you support. You can alienate application judges by taking a controversial position. You don't want to come across as someone who takes on social causes just for the sake of being a protester.

These days we hear that fewer young people are active in social causes than in past generations. Since you work hard to better society, your efforts will definitely stand out from the scholarship application pack.

Students who use this theme should be cautious about too heavily emphasizing controversial opinions in an application. In general, a scholarship application is *not* the place to make bold political statements—especially ones that may alienate some of your readers. You should research potential political leanings of the organization sponsoring or administering the scholarship; you wouldn't want to focus on a cause that is adamantly opposed by the organization. In general, focusing on controversial topics (abortion, for instance) is always risky, unless the organization sponsoring the scholarship is clearly on your side of the issue.

That said, you still want to be true to your convictions. Just try to balance what you want to say within the pragmatic boundaries of a scholarship application. Remember to highlight the leadership, organizational, and communication skills that you exhibit in your activism work.

The Entrepreneur

CHARACTERISTICS: While in school, you started your own business. You're constantly coming up with ideas for products, value-added services, and other entrepreneurial projects. As a toddler, you franchised your lemonade stand to neighborhood kids and made a handsome profit.

ADVANTAGES: Starting your own business demonstrates a great deal of self-initiative and vision. If your business is a success, it's quite an achievement for a full-time student. The story of how you built your business—from idea to implementation—makes interesting essay fodder.

DISADVANTAGES: You could come across as overly concerned about making a quick buck. Given that scholarships fund education, you don't want to seem as though you've neglected your education to pursue your latest business plan.

Starting a business (especially a shoestring operation) requires that you wear many hats—those of innovator, problem solver, marketer, customer service representative, and manager. Because of this, entrepreneurial endeavors provide you with fertile ground to demonstrate your varied abilities.

What businesses have winning scholarship applicants started? Everything from Internet sales operations and web page design firms to jewelry-making outfits and investment advising companies. Really, anything is possible. Many students have assumed significant responsibilities in the family business (as in the particular business your family operates, rather than Tony Soprano's line of work).

Some applicants who have used this theme have stressed that they are saving money generated from their business to help pay for college. This underscores that they have taken the initiative to help pay for their own education and are worthy of scholarship aid.

The Leader

CHARACTERISTICS: You have been a driving force behind some type of project in which you have had to work well with others. You excel in the group environment and hold leadership positions in several organizations.

ADVANTAGES: Great leaders bring out the best from others, not just from themselves. This ability to positively influence others is an important aspect of many scholarship programs. The various titles and positions you have held contribute to your credentials and accomplishments.

DISADVANTAGES: Leaders are judged not by the positions they hold but by their *actions*. Your application could come across as less than compelling if it becomes merely a list of offices you have held. Titles backed up by minimal results or actual accomplishments can seem hollow.

Effectively demonstrating your leadership in a scholarship application takes more than just saying that you're a leader. As a result, students who use this theme often *have others communicate this message for them* through letters of recommendation that specifically comment on their leadership qualities.

Keep in mind that leadership, by definition, involves other people and groups of people. So the emphasis needs to be on activities you have participated in as part of a team. Interpersonal skills, such as your ability to get along with team members, work well in a group, gain the respect of others, and accept criticism, should be conveyed in an application.

Because leadership ability is really measured in terms of impact, it's important to be able to show tangible results. These results are often measured by what the overall group was able to accomplish and by how *you* helped bring about these results.

The Scientist

CHARACTERISTICS: You enjoy learning about science in your spare time—whether it's building model rockets, competing in science fairs, or conducting independent scientific research. You get excellent grades in science-related classes. You have a curious fondness for Bunsen burners.

ADVANTAGES: Quite a few scholarship programs are geared toward students who excel in science. Laboratory research can lead to impressive individual projects. Science projects outside the school curriculum demonstrate a commitment to learning and a fascination with knowledge.

DISADVANTAGES: Scientific jargon used too liberally can pass over the heads of application judges who don't have a strong background in science. Competition for science-related awards, credentials, and opportunities can be intense. Developing a quality science project is time-consuming, and can take years of hard work.

Scientific ability can be a powerful application theme, but it's also important to recognize that science-minded scholarship winners frequently have done significant research and study outside the normal classroom environment. If science is going to be the focal point of your application, be prepared to demonstrate your interest and ability through science contests, fairs, research projects, apprenticeships, and internships that extend beyond the classroom.

Working with a mentor has an added benefit: It typically yields outstanding letters of recommendation.

Good science research projects often depend on finding a mentor who is willing to take you under his or her wing. Scholarship winners have done this by seeking out local college professors and research scientists or by attending summer science programs on college campuses.

Because scientific research is, to a large extent, an individual endeavor, be sure to balance this out in an application by showing participation in activities that require interpersonal and teamwork skills.

THEME 9

The Athlete

CHARACTERISTICS: You have exceptional skill in a particular sport (good enough to play college athletics), or you have accumulated a solid record in several sports.

STRENGTHS: Describing athletic competition can add welcome drama to an otherwise average profile. Because sports represent a microcosm of life, recounting some poignant lessons learned on the court or playing field can make you stand out from the crowd.

WEAKNESSES: Many students are good at sports; it can be difficult to distinguish yourself. Some judges might not want to award high school athletes any money if the judges believe that such students will likely receive an athletic scholarship.

Being a good athlete is a nice attribute to have, but to translate this into a powerful theme, you need to extend what you've learned from your sport to other areas beyond the world of athletics. A good way to do this is to think about qualities and abilities you've developed on the court or playing field that have impacted other areas of your life—attitudes like determination, hard work, perseverance, grace under pressure, and teamwork.

The key to making this theme work is being able to show direct and tangible ways that the lessons of athletic participation have contributed to success in other realms. Perhaps the lessons you learned about teamwork on the basketball court have helped you manage your staff as sports editor on the school newspaper. Or maybe all those early morning swim practices taught you the importance of discipline—which, in turn, has helped you get better grades. There's a lot more to learn through sports than just how to catch a pass, sink a basketball, or run down a backhand.

▍ FINDING YOUR THEME

Now that you understand what themes are and how scholarship winners have employed them, it's time to think about developing your own. Keep in mind that even two applications with identical themes can have a different look and feel. The substance of a theme is derived from all the supporting details; the details are unique to *you*.

In any event, your job is to develop application themes that best reflect your individuality. If a theme doesn't come to mind immediately, that's perfectly fine. Part of this process involves taking a detailed look at your life and searching for subtle patterns that might be nurtured and developed.

CHAPTER 5 SUMMARY AND KEYWORDS

Winning Applications: Unsuccessful scholarship applications are laundry lists of credentials. Winning applications show judges the person behind the application. ■

Painting Your Self-Portrait: Treat each component of an application as part of a unified whole. Develop an application theme that permeates the entire application and communicates a cohesive message. Application themes are frequently based on extracurricular activities, longtime interests, seminal events, or future career goals. ■

Thematic Variety: All scholarship applications submitted by one student need not have the same theme. Certain themes may be better suited for particular types of scholarship programs and contests. ■

Primary and Secondary Themes: The typical application should have one or two major themes. Trying to fit in more themes than this devalues your thematic currency. If you feel that an application should have two themes, have one primary theme and one secondary theme. The primary theme should be the focal point of the application—the main message you're communicating. ■

Credibility: Cohesive application themes enhance credibility by providing a framework that gives meaning and purpose to activities, achievements, and experiences. ■

Employing Your Theme: Applicants create effective themes by consistently reinforcing the message in each component of their materials. This is often done by addressing the theme in essays and personal statements, choosing recommendations that highlight key thematic points, and by placing résumé items that support the theme in prominent places. ■

Application Balance: Building a theme doesn't mean that one should omit credentials that don't fit neatly into the thematic message. Applicants should still strive to appear well rounded. Although activities that fit one's theme should occupy the spotlight, there is plenty of room in the rest of the application for everything else. ■

Nine Winning Themes: Some popular themes employed by scholarship winners include: The Do-Gooder, The Creative Talent, The Survivor, The Brainiac, The Activist, The Entrepreneur, The Leader, The Scientist, and The Athlete. ■

SCHOLARSHIPCOACH.COM KEYWORDS

For more information on a scholarship or topic mentioned in this chapter, enter the associated keyword in the keyword link box located in the Coach's Locker Room section of ScholarshipCoach.com.

Scholarship/Topic	*Keyword*
Discover Card Tribute Awards	DISCOVER
Homework Helpline	HELPLINE

Positioning Strategies

INSIDE THIS CHAPTER

- ▌ Analyzing scholarship applications

- ▌ Conducting background research

- ▌ Custom-tailoring your materials

- ▌ Factoring in your competition

- ▌ Understanding the universal judging criteria

▌SCORING POINTS

In the previous chapter, we learned how to develop powerful application themes and how to use these themes to paint vivid portraits of ourselves. What we didn't yet take into account, however, was the preferences of our audience—the perspectives of the scholarship administrators, organizations, sponsors, and judges who are in charge of analyzing and evaluating these self-portraits we create.

In this chapter, we take these perspectives into account by examining how savvy scholarship winners highlight different aspects of their portraits—or choose among several thematic possibilities—for each scholarship application. The process of highlighting certain characteristics and de-emphasizing other ones is the essence of a **positioning strategy:** The portrait still reflects who you are, but we can strategically adjust your pose, attire, and demeanor to make your portrait most appealing to each specific scholarship awards program.

THE APPLICATION DETECTIVE

Move over, Sherlock Holmes. Take a seat, Sam Spade. In this section, you become an "application detective." Instead of investigating crime scenes, you will sift through scholarship applications. You'll learn how to search for clues about the selection process, dust for judges' fingerprints, and establish the motives of scholarship sponsors. By applying these techniques, you will gain a better understanding of each scholarship application and be able to custom-tailor your material to best fit the underlying emphasis, mission, and agenda—both the visible and the more hidden parts—of each scholarship program.

Collecting Your Clues

OK, so you're ready to become an application detective? Like any good detective, one of the first things you'll want to do is to gather a few clues. A good place to start is by carefully collecting and reading all the scholarship program materials—including ones that may be separate from the application form itself—as well as checking out the websites, newsletters, and descriptive literature of the organizations that administer or sponsor the scholarship program. You may then want to call, e-mail, or write the organizations' offices, and try to gather any additional information you can.

For important clues concerning the nation's top scholarship opportunities, check out my companion book, The Scholarship Scouting Report.

Ask for samples of past winning entries, as scholarship organizations will often release these examples upon request, especially for contest-type scholarships based around things like essays, orations, art, or science projects. If it's possible to ask some questions of the organization responsible for managing the scholarship program, seize the opportunity.

If there are students in your school or community who have experience with the particular scholarship program (such as past winners of the scholarship), ask them for their insights. Many times, past scholarship winners gain useful knowledge about a particular scholarship program that goes far beyond the published judging criteria. (I certainly did!)

Many scholarship administrators and sponsors will release the names and descriptions of past scholarship winners upon request or feature articles about the winners in organization publications. This is especially true of scholarships sponsored by organizations that wish to publicize the accomplishments of their recipients. Once you have obtained such a winners' list, it may be possible to locate e-mail addresses or Web pages for these scholarship recipients (especially for those you know are attending a particular college), and if you've got the

time and are feeling proactive, you may wish to contact them and tap their brains as well.

Getting an Overall Impression

After you have collected some of these clues, you will want to think strategically about the scholarship program in some key ways. The savvy scholarship seeker knows the importance of first taking a step back and assessing the overall tone of a scholarship program. Asking yourself the following questions about each scholarship program can help you to better gauge the award's central focus:

▌ What is the mission and agenda of the organization awarding the scholarship?

▌ What personal qualities or traits does the scholarship seem to value?

▌ Does the scholarship emphasize depth of involvement in a particular area or breadth of involvement in many areas?

▌ Do all activities and credentials appear to be weighted evenly, or are some emphasized more than others?

▌ Is the scholarship focused more on the future (what you want to do) or on the past (what you have done)?

▌ Does the program emphasize traditional achievement metrics (GPA, standardized tests, etc.) or nontraditional measures?

▌ Does the program categorize applicants in any special way (such as by career interest or geographic region)?

▌ Does the program's sponsor have any type of social agenda or political leanings?

▌ What are the common threads among past winners? Who will be your likely competition for the scholarship?

▌ Who will specifically evaluate your application? Do these judges have similar perspectives or views of the world?

Asking yourself, and trying to answer, questions such as these helps broaden your understanding of the type of applicant the scholarship (and its judges) seek to recognize. After doing this, you should have a much better feel for the scholarship program's "ideal applicant."

Paying Attention to the Details

The great Sherlock Holmes, of course, is renowned for his ability to notice, synthesize, and learn from seemingly insignificant details. Show good ol' Sherlock a morsel of dried dough, a lock of gray hair, and a pair of suspicious-looking oven mitts, and he'll show you the balding pastry chef who committed the dastardly deed.

Likewise, when investigating a scholarship application for clues, it's essential to pay attention to all the details. Here's a case in point from my own scholarship quest: At first glance, the judging criteria for the Milky Way/AAU High-School All-American scholarship appeared to be fairly straightforward. The application materials stated that judging would be based on "academic, athletic, and community service achievements." A closer examination of official rules (shown in eye-straining type on the back of the application form), however, revealed additional details. Specifically, it stated the following:

Academic excellence is not always reflected by such objective measures as grades, test scores, or class rankings. . . . School activities considered in this area [academic achievement] include such things as band, debate, and student government.

What this passage told me was that the scholarship program was employing a very broad definition of "academics," one that included many types of extracurricular activities. This suggested to me that I should make sure to include descriptions of my extracurricular endeavors in the application and that in such descriptions I should take special care to highlight the academic value and educational benefit of each activity (because the academic component was the fundamental criterion I was being judged upon). Because of this observation, I expanded my discussion of extracurricular activities and emphasized the academic lessons being learned through them—something I wouldn't have done if I literally hadn't read the fine print. Paying attention to these details helped me net a $10,000 scholarship from the program. Score!

This particular scholarship was recently phased out. Other scholarships, however—such as the ESPN SportsFigures Scholarship—are similar in scope.

Looking for the Unusual

Another investigative technique you will want to use is the practice of looking for anything in an application that strikes you as out of the ordinary. Because most scholarship applications are created from similar molds, any deviations from the usual boilerplate requirements provide you with valuable information about the objectives of particular scholarship programs.

Start your detective work with the published judging criteria listed in any application. If a particular scholarship contains a judging criterion that seems especially personal, specific, or unconventional, you should take special notice: It can provide valuable insights about how the judging works.

For instance, in the Discover Card Tribute Awards, students were asked to have their applications address four out of five categories: special talents, leadership, obstacles overcome, community service, and unique endeavors. In the preceding list, the category that seems to stand out from the rest is "obstacles overcome." Although we've discussed overcoming obstacles in the context of an application theme, it's somewhat unusual that a scholarship program of this type would single out this particular character trait as an entire judging category.

I was actually the only national winner that year who didn't choose the "obstacles overcome" category. It just wasn't one of my strongest areas. While you should factor in the inclinations of a scholarship program, don't try to be someone you're not.

Whereas the other four categories deal with traditional areas such as extracurricular activities, hobbies, and individual projects, this out-of-the-ordinary category is much more personal and specific. Discover Card's decision to highlight this aspect of a student's background demonstrated its importance to the scholarship application process. Sure enough, when the national winners of the Discover Card awards were announced, nearly all the winners had chosen to write about some key obstacles they had overcome in their lives.

Another place to look for the unusual is in the application requirements. In the Century III Leaders scholarship contest, for example, all applicants were required to take a school-administered examination on current events. Such a requirement highlighted the organization's emphasis on societal issues. Students who demonstrated a broad awareness of social problems and showed how, in their small way, they had tried to find solutions to such problems generally did well in the overall competition.

An unusual essay question can also help you understand the type of winner a scholarship program is seeking. On the application form of the National Honor Society Scholarship, for instance, I was asked to respond to a hypothetical situation in which I observed a classmate cheating. The inclusion of such an unconventional essay question suggested the program's emphasis on character, integrity, and other personal qualities. As a result, I tried to emphasize those character traits in other portions of my application, as well as in the essay itself. When the dust settled, I had again taken home the scholarship prize.

CUSTOMIZING YOUR MATERIALS

> "When you're awarded a scholarship, the sponsor is accepting you as one of their own. Try to come across as someone they would find interesting and be proud of."
>
> *–George Hicks*
> *Scholarship Winner*
> *Indianapolis, IN*

Using these application detective techniques will help you to clearly define each scholarship program's ideal applicant. Once you've come up with this definition, it's simply a matter of positioning and packaging your record in such a way as to emphasize personal attributes consistent with this definition.

GUERRILLA TACTIC

Tailor Your Materials for a Perfect Fit

■ Define each scholarship's ideal applicant, and emphasize personal attributes matching this definition.

In my three-dozen scholarship applications, I employed five or six major themes; this process of analyzing each specific scholarship program helped me choose which themes to use.

If, for example, your detective work tells you that a scholarship program places a high premium on community service, then bring any service activities you've done to the forefront of your application—highlighting any specific service projects that might fit especially well with the mission and goals of the sponsoring organization.

If community service happens to be a potential application theme that fits you well, then consider choosing service as a primary or secondary theme for this particular application. If service isn't a theme that's really appropriate to you, stick with one of your other themes, but raise the profile of service to the extent that you can within the context of that theme.

Keep in mind that the impact of such packaging strategies need not be limited to applications that evaluate your overall record. Speaking on the topic of "My Service to America," a recent first-place orator (and $20,000 scholarship winner) in the Voice of Democracy scholarship contest wove throughout her speech a vivid description of her grandfather's struggle for survival in the waters of the Pacific Ocean during World War II (see excerpt in box). Whether intentional or intuitive, her decision to define service in the context of wartime sacrifice makes good strategic sense in a program sponsored by the Veterans of Foreign Wars.

EXCERPT FROM A WINNING SCHOLARSHIP ORATION

Dazed and confused, with no time for a life jacket, he followed many dozens of his fellow shipmates into the black abyss of the Pacific Ocean. Within minutes his ship had vanished beneath the rolling sea. . . . My service to America can never come close to the drama of my Poppy's experience in the South Pacific, but it gives me reason to keep plugging away at the small things. The small things, that's what my Poppy taught me. I know these things will make things just a little better for America. As for me, it just makes me feel good. . . . Sometimes when I feel like I am bobbing aimlessly through the ocean of life, struggling to keep my head above water, I can feel the invisible hands of my grandfather lifting me up and giving me that strength and courage to be a proud part of what makes America strong and wonderful.

—*Heidi Holley*
Fair Oaks, CA

■ CONSIDERING YOUR COMPETITORS

Back in elementary school, when choosing kickball teams, the kid serving as team captain would look over the prospective players, consider their abilities at booting a red rubber ball, and make a selection. Likewise, part of how a scholarship judge evaluates you is based on how you compare to others in the application pile. For this reason, it can be useful to anticipate who your competitors will be and to consider what points they will emphasize, so that you can take steps to distinguish yourself.

If a scholarship is only for students interested in becoming lawyers, for instance, you might expect that a good number of applicants might have had some type of work or extracurricular experience in a law firm or courtroom, and they would likely include such credentials in their applications. If a scholarship targets members of an organization like the Future Farmers of America, you would expect applicants to highlight agriculture-related experiences.

Once you've anticipated what your competitors will highlight, there are two strategies you should follow. First, if you have activities and credentials in your record that others are likely to include, consider these areas as key battleground: Spend extra time on making sure that your descriptions of those activities and credentials are specific and detailed and that you present them in a way that helps you stand out from the pack. For the student interested in law school, for instance, she may wish to describe the specific case law research she helped conduct, the leadership role she played in helping direct other interns, and the impact of the research on the outcome of the case.

Second, make yourself stand out even further by playing up those aspects of your record that others in the application pool are *unlikely* to include, but that still fit in with the underlying mission of the scholarship program. The member of the Future Farmers of America may wish to highlight the laboratory research he did on seed cultivation techniques (probably not every FFA member has done independent scientific research) or give samples of the poetry he writes about nature and life on the farm (another more unusual agriculture-related activity).

The key is to forecast what your competitors will include, and figure out how you can go one or two steps beyond to distinguish yourself from everyone else.

TEN UNIVERSAL JUDGING CRITERIA

Although we've investigated the point of view of the scholarship providers and the impact of our competitors on the application process, there are additional judging factors that lie beneath the surface. To understand what I mean, consider the subjective element to scholarship judging—an evaluation process rooted in the biases, experiences, and values of each judge. In general, you would expect judges to be inclined to select students who possess personal qualities that they themselves value, admire, and respect.

Because it's usually impossible to precisely know the predispositions of the person or persons who will judge each of your applications, you have to resort to the next best thing. You can anticipate the personal qualities that judges are likely to respond well to (traits that aren't necessarily official judging criteria) by examining the qualities that our society as a whole respects and values. And you can look at the personal qualities that the most successful scholarship applicants have communicated in their applications.

Trying to communicate these qualities doesn't mean that you should emphasize traits you don't really have. The goal here is to take a deeper look at the things you've done and highlight the personal attributes you're most proud of.

When you combine these two approaches, what you have are ten universal judging criteria—the personal qualities that scholarship providers and judges commonly look for in their selected scholarship recipients. By illustrating in your application as many of these core qualities as you can, you gain the ability to communicate with your reader on an emotional level. So let's first discuss these ten personal qualities and then explore how students can use them in a traditional application format.

Hard Work

Farmers know that before you can reap a harvest, you have to sow your seeds. Likewise, before you can realize your hopes and dreams, you have to put in the necessary hard work.

Don't hide the fact that you've been putting in those extra hours of practice and training. If you happen to dream of becoming a concert pianist, letting judges know about all the effort you're investing into piano training and practice makes your dream seem substantially more attainable. Scholarships are awarded to students who invest their time and energy in things they care about and who demonstrate their dedication and commitment through this hard work.

Overcoming Obstacles

When I was younger, I had a fear of speaking in front of large groups. To conquer this fear, I forced myself to take the podium whenever possible. Eventually I came to love public speaking!

At the core of traditional American values is a "can-do" spirit—the notion that obstacles in our paths are challenges waiting to be surmounted. For some of us, over-coming obstacles may involve coming back from defeat, conquering that debilitating fear, or shoring up some of those personal weaknesses. For others, the obstacles may be something more dramatic: health conditions, unfortunate economic circumstances, or serious family problems.

Regardless of the obstacles to be faced (and we *all* face them), our culture respects those who tackle those obstacles head on. Such people are *not* defined by the obstacles they face, but rather by *how they respond to the roadblocks*. So if you have genuinely worked to conquer an obstacle in your life, communicate this in your scholarship application materials.

Teamwork

Why do sports like football, basketball, and baseball receive more national attention than athletic competitions like tennis, golf, or swimming? Perhaps it's because the former are all team sports. From the playing field to the workplace, and the schoolhouse to the statehouse, society places a premium on people working together in pursuit of a common goal.

So how can you illustrate your teamwork skills in a scholarship application? It's easy. Pick any activity in which you work with other people, and emphasize the team aspects. And if the group you're involved with has received some award or distinction, mention this in your application, too.

Perseverance

Gratification can't always be immediate. In fact, most things that are truly worthwhile take time. Usually before you can succeed at something, you have to pay your dues. And that's what perseverance is all about: sticking with a goal when others might quit or give up.

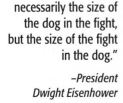

"What counts is not necessarily the size of the dog in the fight, but the size of the fight in the dog."

–President Dwight Eisenhower

In order to communicate perseverance in an application, discuss the journey you have undertaken to get where you are. Perhaps you didn't make the basketball team your freshman or sophomore year, but after putting in countless hours of extra practice, you now start for the varsity squad. Or perhaps you worked hard at your current job for many long years just to give yourself the opportunity and resources to attend nursing school. By illustrating how you have persevered, you can make your application more compelling.

Individual Initiative

Whether we're talking about a social worker who starts a shelter for the homeless, a teenager who decides to research her family tree, or a business-school graduate who creates an innovative Silicon Valley start-up company, we're illustrating the same core character trait: individual initiative.

Individual initiative means *taking action*. If something doesn't exist that should, *create it*. If opportunities and resources aren't immediately accessible, then *seek them out*.

How do you convey your initiative to scholarship judges? There are countless ways to do this. You can do so by describing a project that you helped initiate, either on your own or as part of a group. You can do it by discussing an interest that you went out of your way to pursue (such as by seeking out a mentor). Or try observing a problem in your community and proposing an innovative solution to fix it.

Passion and Enthusiasm

"Play up what you've done in terms of individual initiative. I had been in a math contest in elementary school, and I remembered how much I had enjoyed it. So I decided to re-create the experience for other elementary school kids."

–*Casey Cornwell*
Scholarship Winner
Henderson, NV

Many people in this world find themselves stuck doing things (often jobs) that they simply don't enjoy. So when scholarship judges come across applicants who truly love what they do, the judges sit up and take notice.

To convey this underlying passion and enthusiasm in an application, you need to describe your activities with a sense of excitement and wonder. For instance, in a scholarship essay that was excerpted in Chapter 5, I started with this sentence: "As far back as I can remember, a love for language and a passion for expressing ideas have been integral parts of who I am."

Such an opening sentence helped demonstrate how all the writing I did in high school was truly a labor of love. And phrases like "as far back as I can remember" communicated how this wasn't just a transitory interest that could change tomorrow, but something very important and deeply meaningful to me.

Responsibility

If you don't exhibit some of these qualities, then perhaps this highlights some areas of personal development to work on.

The essence of responsibility is accountability—being accountable for your own actions and the consequences of those actions. Demonstrating responsibility is important to scholarship judging because it is a sign of maturity, self-confidence, and trustworthiness: It is a sign of maturity because it shows that you acknowledge and accept ownership for your actions and the effects those actions have

You can demonstrate your level of responsibility in many different settings– including your home, school, and community.

upon others. It is a sign of self-confidence because taking responsibility for an outcome means being willing to put yourself on the line for its success or failure. Finally, it is a sign of trustworthiness when others (especially teachers, coaches, and parents) allow you to assume responsibility, illustrating their faith in your judgment and ability.

Civic Duty

In his inaugural address, President John F. Kennedy spoke these immortal words: "And so, my fellow Americans, ask not what your country can do for you—ask what you can do for your country." In this call for sacrifice, Kennedy's oratory rejuvenated the notion of civic duty: Each of us, he stressed, has a duty to give something back to the nation that has given us so much.

These days, however, people often forget or ignore their civic duties. That's why scholarship judges generally place substantial weight on such qualities. They want to leverage their scholarship dollars by granting college money to individuals who will pay back to society the amount of their scholarship award many times over. A common fault I have observed in unsuccessful scholarship applications is their one-way focus on *getting*, but not *giving*.

"A man wrapped up in himself makes a very small bundle."

–Benjamin Franklin

Successful scholarship applicants often demonstrate their sense of civic duty through participation in community service activities. In addition, applicants can communicate this through their expression of future goals that, regardless of the career path or line of work, involve making contributions to society.

Purpose

Perhaps the most challenging personal quality for a young person to develop is purpose—the inner compass that helps one define goals and gives life a sense of direction. Back in high school, I didn't know the purpose of my latest homework assignment, let alone the purpose of my life!

Now don't get me wrong—judges don't expect high school or college-aged students to have their lives already planned out. Indeed, even the best-laid plans of a very focused individual often get shaken up and rearranged. So when I talk about purpose, I'm not implying that you must devise a detailed road map for your entire future.

But you will want to demonstrate that you have taken the time to reflect on where you want to go and how you might get there. In my experience, the particular direction that your compass points at any one time does not really matter. The direction of your compass can indeed change (in fact, it almost always does), but the fact that you are aware of your life compass, and can communicate its importance to you, speaks volumes to scholarship judges. By describing the dreams that currently motivate your efforts, you convey that you are a person who is not afraid to voice your ambitions and set goals to reach them. Judges know that a student with a well-articulated purpose has a better chance than his or her counterparts of achieving goals and reaching dreams.

In many instances, conveying purpose in a scholarship application involves discussing a particular career interest (often in a personal essay). Purpose, however, is not limited to having a specific career goal in mind. Your purpose can be grounded in a desire to use your artistic ability and creativity in some exciting way. Or it can simply involve the need to make a positive difference in the lives of your family and friends, as well as others you come in contact with. Your individual purpose can be anything at all.

Character

Different people define personal "character" in different ways, but whatever your definition, the term deals with a person's core ethical and moral fabric. Character consists of qualities like integrity, honesty, loyalty, and courage. We often say that someone possesses *strong character*, as if it is a commodity that can be bought, sold, or stored in one's pocket. Character, however, is not so much a possession as it is a *state of being*. People with strong character don't possess it; they live it every day of their lives.

How do successful scholarship applicants typically demonstrate strong character in their applications? Applicants frequently do this by including letters of recommendation that comment on their personal qualities. It's often more effective to have someone else comment on your character than for you to do it yourself. You can, however, convey a sense of your character in an application by communicating your core values. Describing the qualities and values that you hold dearest can telegraph to a judge a great deal about your underlying character.

ADDRESSING THE CRITERIA

It's always a good idea to try and demonstrate additional traits that you find admirable—qualities such as creativity, open-mindedness, curiosity, or any others you wish to emulate.

Understanding the significance of these ten universal judging criteria has three main implications for the scholarship application process. First, it suggests that we should not only comb our records for activities that we have done, but also for instances in which we have exhibited outstanding personal qualities. Such qualities may be repeatedly exhibited in a given project or activity, or they may be associated with a particularly memorable one-time event.

Second, we should make a point of communicating these personal qualities in our scholarship materials. One useful approach that I have used is to make a checklist of these ten personal qualities and record next to each of them any activities, achievements, events, and experiences that demonstrate the specific quality. To make sure that I didn't forget to highlight these traits in a given application, I would then check each one off my list once I had done so. Perhaps some of these qualities may be alluded to in an extracurricular activity list. Others could be mentioned in a personal essay. Recommendation writers could comment upon still other qualities in their letters of support.

Remember, these references need not be blatant. (You *don't* have to explicitly say something like, "If you looked up hard work and civic duty in the dictionary, you'd find a picture of me.") It's usually more persuasive to demonstrate personal qualities by describing them in a situational context. For example, if a teenage Michael Jordan were filling out a merit scholarship application, he might communicate teamwork on an extracurricular activity form by emphasizing team dynamics in his descriptions of his basketball exploits.

GUERRILLA TACTIC

Work to Highlight Key Personal Qualities

■ Try to convey each of the ten universal judging criteria somewhere in your application.

For those of us who don't defy gravity, we can convey individual initiative in an essay by discussing some action we've taken on our own to help solve a problem. The ways to do this are endless.

Third, if you can't think how you have demonstrated a particular quality, try to find ways to exhibit it in future activities and endeavors. Perhaps you can't think of a time when you exhibited a strong sense of responsibility. Well then, be on the lookout for future opportunities for you to assume responsibility and successfully fulfill your obligations.

As an added bonus, this will help you grow as a person (it did for me). Remember, there's a reason why scholarship judges look for these types of personal qualities in applicants: Such qualities are important in life!

CHAPTER 6 SUMMARY AND KEYWORDS

Positioning Strategies: Savvy scholarship seekers "position" their applications by presenting themselves and their materials in a way that meshes well with the mission of the scholarship program and the fundamental judging criteria. ■

The Application Detective: Analyze scholarship applications, materials, and past winning entries—and talk to past winners—for clues about the selection process. Pay attention to application details, unusual judging criteria, and unique entry requirements that provide hints about the inclinations of the scholarship program. Ask questions that help define the scholarship's "ideal applicant." ■

Customizing Your Materials: Position your record and package your materials in such a way as to appeal to each scholarship provider's overall agenda, specific judging criteria, and general selection process. ■

Going Beyond Your Competitors: Determine what credentials your competitors will likely include in their applications. If you are including similar credentials, spend extra time making sure that you present them in a detailed and compelling way. Play up aspects of your record that make you stand out from the crowd. ■

Ten Universal Judging Criteria: Most scholarship judges look for evidence of certain personal qualities in their scholarship winners. These qualities include such things as hard work, overcoming obstacles, teamwork, perseverance, individual initiative, passion and enthusiasm, responsibility, civic duty, purpose, and character. Applicants should seek to communicate and demonstrate these personal qualities. ■

SCHOLARSHIPCOACH.COM KEYWORDS

For more information on a scholarship or topic mentioned in this chapter, enter the associated keyword in the keyword link box located in the Coach's Locker Room section of ScholarshipCoach.com. ■

Scholarship/Topic	Keyword
Century III Leaders	CENTURY
Discover Card Tribute Awards	DISCOVER
ESPN SportsFigures Scholarship	ESPN
Milky Way/AAU High School All-American	MILKYWAY
National Honor Society Scholarship	HONOR
The Scholarship Scouting Report	SCOUTREP
Voice of Democracy Contest	VOICE

Content Strategies

INSIDE THIS CHAPTER

▌ Analyzing width and depth in your profile

▌ How to build on your strengths

▌ Plugging up holes in your record

▌ A broader definition of academic achievement

▌ Nudging up your GPA

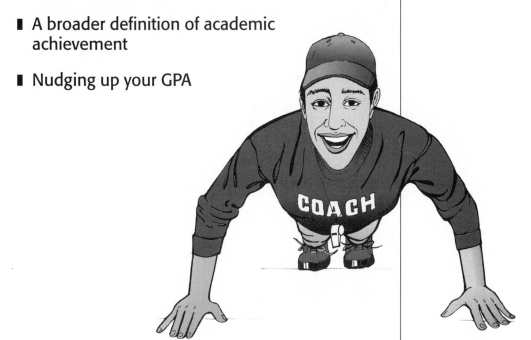

▌ SCHOLARSHIP BODYBUILDING

In Chapters 5 and 6, we examined how to paint your scholarship application portrait and explored how to take this portrait and strategically highlight components of it to appeal to particular scholarship programs. What most scholarship seekers discover, however, is that an application portrait is *less* a finished painting and *more* a work in progress. As you fill out scholarship applications, you will inevitably notice that certain aspects of your record are not as strong or as well developed as you would like. (We all have these "trouble areas.") You'll also observe that for many applications you will be lacking that perfect experience, activity, or anecdote needed to answer a particular type of question. In essence, you will want to do (just as I did) some *scholarship bodybuilding*—buffing up certain aspects of your profile, adding tone and definition to other areas, and increasing your fitness all around. You'll then be able to flex your scholarship muscles with the best of them.

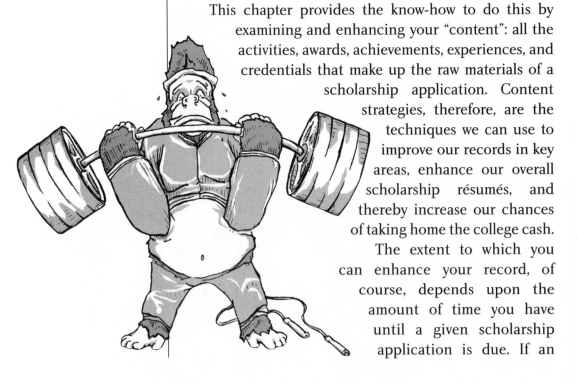

This chapter provides the know-how to do this by examining and enhancing your "content": all the activities, awards, achievements, experiences, and credentials that make up the raw materials of a scholarship application. Content strategies, therefore, are the techniques we can use to improve our records in key areas, enhance our overall scholarship résumés, and thereby increase our chances of taking home the college cash.

The extent to which you can enhance your record, of course, depends upon the amount of time you have until a given scholarship application is due. If an application is due tomorrow, there's not going to be a whole lot of content you can really add. If a scholarship deadline, however, is three to six months away—or even only a few weeks away—there is a great deal you can do to beef up your record.

What's the best way to begin? The first step is to think analytically about the content you have already accumulated.

ANALYZING DEPTH AND WIDTH

Evaluating your credentials in terms of *depth* and *width* helps you better comprehend and categorize the key leverage points of your existing record. Depth assesses the quality of your record in a particular area. Students with a great deal of depth in their record have made a strong commitment to a particular type of endeavor and have notable achievements in that area. Depth is evaluated in a scholarship application when you discuss things like awards and honors you have received, the time commitment you have invested, the leadership roles you have undertaken, and the impact of your involvement or participation in a particular activity. Depth can also be illustrated by participating in several different activities with a similar focus or emphasis.

Width, on the other hand, refers to the range and variety of your activities and credentials. Students with a lot of width in their record have had many different types of experiences and are quite well rounded. Width is commonly illustrated in a scholarship application through a list of your various types of activities, projects, jobs, and endeavors.

The key to effective content strategies is finding simple ways to increase *both* our width and depth. When we do this, we are able to create more multidimensional and fleshed-out personal application portraits that increase our chances of winning scholarship awards.

Which is more important to add—width or depth? That depends upon your unique situation. If you are a person who has always juggled a lot of different things, but who hasn't had the time to really pursue a particular area, then adding depth should be your focus. If, on the other hand, you are someone who has significantly developed your skills in one or two areas, then adding width may be key. Regardless of where you personally fall on this continuum, you can greatly benefit by finding simple ways to enhance both your width and depth.

THE ESSENTIAL CONTENT STRATEGIES

Now it's time to take what we've learned about width and depth and put it into action. In the section that follows, I describe three main content strategies and show how to implement these strategies in a way that's right for you—taking into account the time you have available.

EXPAND ON YOUR STRONG POINTS

At first glance, adding content in areas you are already good at may seem counterintuitive. If you already excel at something, why do you need to add to your record in this area? Fair question. The simple answer is that we want to take your strongest skills and transform them into truly standout talents—a sprucing up of your portrait that gets you noticed by application judges. Put another way, we want to add depth to the most critical areas of your record and use this depth to distinguish you from the crowd.

These content strategies are especially beneficial for younger students, particularly freshmen and sophomores in high school.

"I would ask myself, 'What am I most interested in? What types of things am I good at? How can I make what I'm interested in into a project?'"

–Tom Kuo
Scholarship Winner
Salt Lake City, UT

To illustrate this concept, I'd like to share with you a few examples from my own experience. As I described earlier, one of the areas I tried to highlight in my scholarship applications was my writing ability. I had spent considerable time as a writer and editor on the school newspaper, so I wanted to expand upon this strong point and add depth to my record in journalism. One way I did this was to submit a series of articles on pressing news items to various journalism competitions. Additionally, I sent off some of these articles to my local newspaper; I knew that getting them published in this larger, real-world venue would be an important mark of distinction.

Over time, I came up with more ways to expand my involvement in other activities that would showcase my writing skills in arenas a bit beyond my comfort zone. I approached KLCC, the National Public Radio affiliate in my hometown, with the idea of writing a series of radio commentaries on issues affecting young people. The radio station went for the concept, and in a matter of weeks I was on the air.

I also approached the owners of the tennis club where I practiced with an offer to write, design, and produce the club's monthly newsletter—thereby saving them significant money on contracting out the job to a local advertising agency. This project showcased a different side of my writing and provided me with additional clips to include as supplementary materials in scholarship applications.

Because I also earned some money for doing this work, I was able to communicate this activity as an entrepreneurial endeavor, further helping me in scholarships that recognized this type of self-initiative.

Now don't get me wrong: I didn't pursue these activities *solely* because they would enhance my scholarship chances. Writing was a field I loved, and such projects were exciting opportunities to grow. Working to enhance the depth of my writing activities, however, provided the spark that motivated me to find creative ways to express and improve my writing skills.

Adopting a similar strategy will help you enhance your skills in areas that are natural extensions of your interests and passions. You will be encouraged to dream up projects that you would have never considered and to do things that you've always wanted to do, but never got around to actually doing.

Time Juggling

If you don't have much time until a bunch of applications are due, adapt Strategy 1 to fit the time available. Perhaps this means simply joining and participating in that after-school club or college group you've been meaning to check out. Or maybe it means turning a class project into something that you can post on the Internet—informing and educating others. The possibilities are limitless.

Even if you're applying for scholarships right away, taking on longer-term projects now will still have an impact. Consider my radio commentary project as an example: For scholarship applications that came up 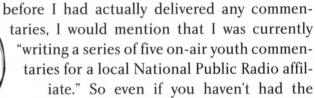 before I had actually delivered any commentaries, I would mention that I was currently "writing a series of five on-air youth commentaries for a local National Public Radio affiliate." So even if you haven't had the chance to complete a substantial portion of a project, just the fact that you are pursuing it can enhance the depth of your scholarship credentials.

ASK THE COACH #21

Do scholarship judges look at college students differently than high school students?

There are a few major differences. First, because college students are considerably older and more experienced than their high school counterparts, they are expected to have a clearer picture of fields and careers they want to pursue. Second, scholarship judges recognize that extracurricular activities at the college level are considerably more time consuming.

Undergrads are not expected to participate in as many types of extracurricular activities. They are, however, expected to have more notable accomplishments and achievements in these activities. Finally, once you are in college, there is a greater expectation of involvement in substantive internships, jobs, and work-study programs. ■

STRATEGY 2

SHORE UP YOUR WEAK AREAS

In addition to developing your strong points, it's important to come across as well rounded—thereby enhancing the width of your credentials. Although your application spotlight should shine on the major themes of your scholarship application, you will want to include activities, achievements, and other credentials that demonstrate a wider range of exploration.

To implement this strategy, try to participate in activities that fill in glaring holes in your record. To help you figure out the key areas in which you most need improvement (and we all could use improvement!), think about the academic subjects, extracurricular activities, or types of experiences you consistently avoid. Then try to find relatively painless ways to fill in these résumé gaps.

Participating in school clubs that extend the range of your involvement is a good way to shore up weak areas.

Don't be afraid to try activities that are a little outside of your comfort zone.

Improving my quantitative skills in this way provided me with a stronger foundation for handling the technical requirements of studying economics in college.

For example, in my high school record, a high percentage of my most compelling achievements and experiences were clearly in fields related to the arts and humanities. To emphasize that I wasn't just a one-dimensional student who wasn't interested in math and science, I joined my high school's science club and competed on the Science Olympics and math teams. This participation demonstrated my quantitative skills—a range of abilities that I didn't have the opportunity to exhibit in other extracurricular activities. Not only did this extra effort benefit my scholarship applications (and college applications, too), but I also improved my math and science skills on the side. Many students discover that subjects they didn't care for in a classroom environment suddenly become fun and interesting in a more hands-on setting.

GUERRILLA TACTIC

Patch Holes in Your Résumé

■ Determine the gaps in your record and find simple ways in the time available to address these weak areas.

CREATE OPPORTUNITIES

Some of the most rewarding experiences I had during my high school and college years were related to opportunities that I created for myself—whether it was my internship with a U.S. senator, a reporting job at the Democratic and Republican National Conventions, or starting my own Homework Helpline telephone tutoring service. I also discovered how each opportunity I created for myself kept propelling me forward to even more exciting opportunities—in effect creating a chain of life-changing events. In this way, the strategy of creating opportunities impacts both the width and depth of your credentials.

So what if your school doesn't sponsor a program in a particular activity that interests you? Try starting up your own club. What if you need guidance in a particular activity? Find a member of your community who can show you the ropes. What if you have a particular career interest that you'd like to explore? Then create your own internship or apprenticeship.

Winning scholarships can lead to many future opportunities. Some organizations recruit scholarship winners for special educational programs. Other winners have landed internships with the scholarship sponsor.

Likewise, if you are unable to get an appointment with certain influential people you want to speak with, don't just accept it. Instead, go to their office early in the morning, wait until they show up, and set an appointment in person. (I've had to do this. Believe me—it works!) If you are especially enjoying a subject in school, talk to the teacher or professor about how you can pursue it in more depth. In general, always go out of your way to talk to those who might be able to direct you toward intriguing future projects.

TRANSFORMING TRAGEDY INTO TRIUMPH

Scholarship winner Michelle Petrovic of Los Alamos, NM, is a wonderful example of the power of creating opportunities. As a high school student diagnosed with Hodgkin's disease, Michelle had to undergo chemotherapy treatment. Even in such circumstances, Michelle still had the vision to see opportunity. Using herself as a research subject, Michelle analyzed changes in the physical and chemical properties of her hair as she underwent chemotherapy. After she studied hair samples collected before, during, and after the treatment, her groundbreaking research showed that human hair is an effective vehicle to diagnose disease. In this way, Michelle courageously transformed a health tragedy into an intellectual triumph. In fact, she is currently attending medical school.

Remember to take advantage of all the special resources around you. If you live in a college town, look into special university programs or possible internships with professors. For those who live in more rural areas, take advantage of your proximity to things that your big-city counterparts might not have access to. One scholarship winner I met did agricultural research on her family farm. Another winner who lived in rural Alaska used his proximity to the *Exxon Valdez* oil spill to study the effects of the accident on the environment.

With this type of inquisitive mindset, you will undoubtedly find an abundance of exciting possibilities awaiting you. The key is to never just wait for opportunity to knock ... you do the knocking yourself!

ASK THE COACH #22

What can younger students do to prepare for winning scholarships?

In addition to a sizable array of scholarships you can apply for as a 6th through 10th grader, there are some important steps younger students can take to pave the way for future scholarship opportunities. As a general principle, participate in many different types of activities. Try all sorts of things, expose yourself to new ideas, and interact with all sorts of different 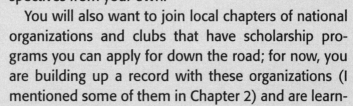 people, especially those who might have different perspectives from your own.

You will also want to join local chapters of national organizations and clubs that have scholarship programs you can apply for down the road; for now, you are building up a record with these organizations (I mentioned some of them in Chapter 2) and are learning and experiencing some neat things.

Next, be on the lookout for what I call stepping-stone programs. These include camps, summer learning programs, mentorship possibilities, and youth conferences. Such programs do not provide scholarships directly, but offer students a variety of other opportunities—many of which lead to later scholarship winning and stronger college applications.

You should start requesting scholarship applications for programs you hope to apply for in later years. Pay special attention to the kinds of questions that will be asked of you down the road. What can you do now to help you effectively answer those questions? The bottom line is that by starting early enough, you can affect almost any aspect of your record. If you work hard and start early, nothing can stand in the way of your eventual scholarship success. ∎

▌ ALL ABOUT ACADEMICS

As we've discussed in earlier chapters, numerous scholarship applications don't even request information about your academic record. To stake your claim to the ones that *do* consider academics, however, you will want to learn some simple content strategies for boosting the overall impression you make on application judges.

The first thing to recognize is that just because academics is a judging criteria for a given scholarship, it doesn't mean that the course grades or class rank are the only things considered. Academic achievement can be demonstrated outside the classroom through participation in academic-related clubs and teams, independent study, and individual research projects. For students who have blemishes in their grade transcripts or standardized-test results, developing content in these alternative academic arenas is a strategy that can help compensate.

The second point to note is that many scholarship judges will also consider the *difficulty* of the courses you've taken and the overall *trend* of your grades. So consider such things as being integral parts of your academic

record. Highlighting the grade trend is especially important if you've had rocky freshman and sophomore years, but have improved your performance since then. A strong grade trend can make up for sluggish grades early in a high school or college career, because you can demonstrate how you have learned from the experience and have made considerable progress. I've even encountered a few scholarships and fellowships that will not count your freshman year grades.

NUDGING UP YOUR GPA

If you already receive good grades, these methods will help you optimize your learning and minimize the time it takes to maintain these grades.

For most of this book, we've treated the grades on your transcript as being set in stone. In this section, however, I'll illustrate some simple principles and powerful techniques that can quickly nudge up your GPA. Nudging up your grades is an important way to increase your eligibility for scholarships that have GPA cutoffs (for instance, specifying that you must have a 2.75 GPA to apply). Such scholarships may not even look at your grades once you meet this minimum bar, so the key is to make these cutoffs. The common cutoff points, on a 4.0 scale, generally occur at increments of .25 (such as 2.5, 2.75, 3.0, 3.25, and 3.5). So if you have a 2.94 GPA, by nudging up your grades up to a 3.01, you can substantially increase the size of your scholarship universe.

The subject of how to do better in school, of course, could be a separate book in its own right. Instead, I've decided to focus on a few areas that can provide you with the most bang for your buck—simple, painless methods that can help you raise your performance in classes right away. In this section, I describe five simple, yet important, action steps to give a quick boost to your GPA.

Ask Questions and Question Everything

In the traditional school format, material is spoon-fed to you in different formats—including lectures, textbooks, and class assignments. But the problem with this approach is that *no one else but you knows how you learn best.* And since the material probably isn't tailored to your optimal learning style, it's likely to be presented in a way that isn't right for you.

Asking questions, however, leads to ownership of the subject matter. Questions allow you to translate the material into a framework that fits your style of learning. Not only does this help you understand the material better, but it improves your ability to recall information.

Asking questions doesn't just mean raising your hand in class. Even more important is developing an internal dialogue with the material you're studying. This dialogue signifies that you are continually questioning everything you read and asking questions *even when you think you understand the material.*

Especially powerful is the "what if" question. With this type of query, you test the margins of your understanding by applying your knowledge to a hypothetical situation. If you are studying economics (my college major), for instance, you might ask yourself, "What would happen to a market economy if supply didn't equal demand?" I've found that by constantly feeding myself these "what if" questions, I am able to predict and prepare for questions that actually end up on the exam.

The point of a question is *not* simply to answer it but to get you to think. In fact, *knowing what questions to ask is more important than knowing the answers.*

Make a good impression on your teacher or professor in the first few weeks of a class. Once you establish a reputation for good work, this can positively impact how your later assignments are graded.

"It's what you learn after you know it all that counts."

–John Wooden

Focus on the Most Important Material

2 ACTION STEP

It's important to recognize that not everything you are asked to read or do is of equal importance. Some assignments will contain meaty information requiring multiple readings to marinate the concepts in your mind. Other assignments may only necessitate a quick skim-read to pick out key themes.

Out of all of the action steps, this one took me the longest to perfect. If I wasn't doing well in a class, I'd try to sit down and go line by line through all the material. But by taking this approach, I would end up spending *too much* time on things that were not particularly important and *too little* time on the really critical subject matter. As a result, even though I had put in a lot of extra effort, I didn't see any substantial improvement in my school performance. Then I finally learned how to focus my energy on the most important areas and to avoid getting bogged down in the minutiae. My performance improved dramatically.

So how do you figure out what is the most important material? That's where Action Steps 3 and 4 come into play.

Try to do the assigned reading ahead of time. But if you haven't gotten around to it, make a comment or ask a question as soon as class begins. If you speak up early on, you'll lessen the chance of being called on later. File this under "Last Resort Strategies."

Put Yourself in the Teacher's Shoes

3 ACTION STEP

Everything that's assigned in a class is assigned to students for a reason. Savvy students recognize this and approach each assignment as if they themselves were teaching the class. Why was this reading passage assigned? What's the big picture here? How does this fit in with the rest of the course? By asking these questions, they are able to identify which materials and assignments are the most important to review and study and which ones they can breeze through.

If you're unsure about the answer to a test question, ask the teacher to clarify the question. Having a teacher rephrase a question can jog your memory or provide additional clues.

Thinking from the teacher's perspective is also a useful technique to employ when you're taking a test. I've often found that even though I don't know the answer to a test question, by thinking about the possible concepts that the teacher or professor must be trying to test, I can narrow down the possibilities until I figure it out .

Because grades are important (at least in the short term), it's also worthwhile to get to know the personal likes, dislikes, and biases of your teacher or professor. Use quizzes and little assignments to test out grading standards. Ascertain how much detail is required to get full credit on a question, so that you can estimate the amount of time you'll need to spend on a given answer before moving on.

Procure Course Overview Materials

In every course, there is a set of concepts and skills that students are supposed to master. Unfortunately, while we're in the midst of learning the material, we often don't have a good sense of the kind of things we'll be tested on at the conclusion of the course. If only we could take the course twice, then the second time around we'd already know which are the key concepts and skills to learn.

Teachers and professors may modify courses from year to year, so keep in mind that tests from previous years should be used only as study guides— not as substitutes for paying attention in class.

So how can we get a feel for where the course is headed without actually repeating the course? Try a technique that savvy students have used. Simply obtain unit and final exams from prior terms that the course has been offered—preferably when it was being taught by the same teacher. This way, as you're learning the material, you'll have a good idea about how you'll eventually be tested upon it. You can obtain old exams from students who have already taken the class or you can request them from your teacher directly. At some schools (such as Harvard), old exams are filed away in student-accessible binders or posted online.

Don't wait until the night before the final exam to do this. It would defeat the whole purpose. By having these exam references at the *beginning* of a course, you can figure out as you go along which is the critical material you must learn. In addition, I've often found that many teachers don't write entirely new exams from previous years. Because of this, you may have already prepared for specific questions (with only minor changes) that will appear on your exams.

Be Resourceful

Sometimes you will have to deal with a difficult teacher, a boring textbook, or a confusing assignment. But it's still up to you to find resourceful ways to learn the material.

> "I never let schooling interfere with my education."
>
> –Mark Twain

If your assigned textbook only adds to the confusion, stop by a library or bookstore to pick up a supplementary book or two. If your teacher isn't the easiest to understand, organize a study group (making sure to invite students who seem to know what they're doing, not just someone you'd like to date). To get a slightly different perspective on the material, try trading notes with classmates.

If you follow all these steps, not only will you nudge up your GPA when next term's transcripts come around, but you will get much more out of each course.

CHAPTER 7 SUMMARY AND KEYWORDS

Width and Depth: Depth assesses the quality of your record in a particular area. Width refers to the range and variety of your activities and credentials. Seek to enhance both width and depth. ∎

Content Strategies: Find ways to expand upon your strongest areas and turn them into standout talents. Shore up your weak areas by filling in résumé gaps with new types of participation. Take the initiative to create your own opportunities. Think both long term and short term and try to enhance your content in creative ways. ■

Younger Students: Those students in grades 6 to 10 can take several steps to prepare for later scholarship opportunities. Participate in all sorts of activities and join local chapters of national organizations and clubs that have scholarship programs. Seek out stepping-stone programs and request application materials now so that you can start preparing for future opportunities. ■

Alternative Academic Achievement: Academic achievement isn't just about your GPA. It can be demonstrated through participation in academic-related clubs and teams, independent study, and individual research projects. The overall difficulty of the courses you've taken and any grade improvement you've experienced may also be considered when assessing your GPA. If you have rough spots on your transcript, look to these alternative methods. ■

Grade Cutoffs: Common eligibility cutoff points for scholarships that do consider grades occur at increments of .25 on a 4.0 scale (2.5, 2.75, 3.0, and so forth). If your GPA is close to a cutoff point, boosting your grades slightly can open up additional scholarship possibilities. ■

Nudging Up Your Grades: Simple strategies for giving your grades a quick boost include asking a lot of questions, focusing on the most important material, thinking from the instructor's perspective, procuring course overview materials, and finding resourceful ways to learn outside of class. ■

SCHOLARSHIPCOACH.COM KEYWORDS

For more information on a scholarship or topic mentioned in this chapter, enter the associated keyword in the keyword link box located in the Coach's Locker Room section of ScholarshipCoach.com.

Scholarship/Topic	*Keyword*
Homework Helpline	HELPLINE

PART IV

When the Whistle Blows

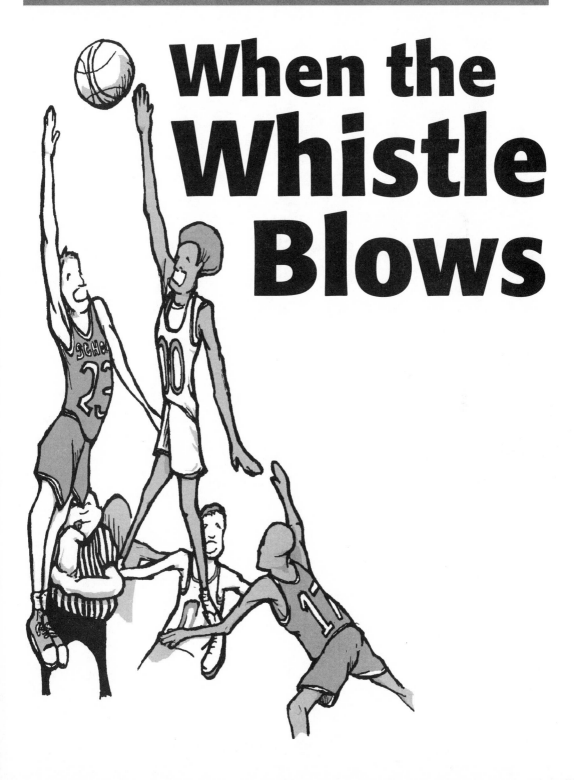

A Winning Game Plan

INSIDE THIS CHAPTER

- Keys for maximizing your odds of winning

- Strategies for managing the application process

- Techniques for leveraging past and future work

- The secrets of staying positive

EIGHT PRINCIPLES OF EFFECTIVE SCHOLARSHIP CAMPAIGNS

If you have followed the techniques outlined so far in this book, you are likely knee-deep in the scholarship hoopla, with applications up the wazoo. So now what? How do you develop a plan of attack that maximizes your chances of accumulating substantial winnings, while minimizing your investment of time and energy? The following eight principles have proven invaluable to serious scholarship applicants (including myself) and together form the basis of an effective scholarship campaign.

Apply for as Many Scholarships as Possible

Perhaps the best way to illustrate this important principle is by telling you a story about a kid I knew—named Froggy. (I don't think that was his real name, but that's what everyone called him.) Froggy was a small, run-of-the-mill kind of guy—the kind of kid who, for the most part, blends into the crowd. There was one characteristic about Froggy, however, that my fellow male classmates definitely noticed: He always seemed to date the most amazing, beautiful girls in the school! And all of us guys in the Dateless Friday Night Club—the club that nobody wants to join but one in which I found myself a charter member—were befuddled at how he did it.

Did those girls know something about Froggy that we didn't? Did he have a hidden stash of Love Potion #9? Had he taken courses at the James Bond School of Seduction? As you might imagine, we were determined to discover the secret of his dating success. And believe it or not, it turned out to be this: He continually asked out tons of girls! As simple as that. The guy had no fear of rejection whatsoever. He would ask out a girl, get turned down, and would just move on to another prospect. For Froggy, the secret to having amazing dates was to just play the numbers game: If he asked out enough girls, he was bound to get his share of rejections, but he was also bound to get his share of dates, too.

So when it comes to applying for scholarships, strive to be like Froggy. I've learned from experience that scholarship judging is far from an exact science. Although the strategies and techniques in this book dramatically increase your chances of winning numerous awards, your result on any one particular scholarship is unpredictable: A secretary could put your application in the wrong pile by mistake, or a particular judge could have some unusual bias that you couldn't have foreseen.

Because of the subjective nature of judging and the unpredictability of factors beyond your control, you'll

In several national scholarship contests that I thought I had no chance of winning, I somehow won. In others that seemed to be a sure thing, I didn't even receive an honorable mention. Virtually all the scholarship winners I interviewed have had similar experiences.

Apply for numerous awards, but also prioritize your scholarship opportunities. This way, if you ever face a time crunch, you can make sure you turn in applications for the scholarships on the top of your list.

If your objective is to go to college for free, the more scholarships you apply for, the better your chances of reaching your goal.

want to tilt the odds in your favor by applying for as many scholarships as you can. This way, you minimize the effects of any quirks in the judging process and leverage your chances to win sizable amounts of money.

Furthermore, applying for as many scholarships as you can makes good sense in light of the learning curve that is a part of submitting good scholarship applications. After you have completed your first few submissions, your ability to apply the techniques covered in this book will substantially improve. You'll simply get better with practice. But if you cut your scholarship season short, you won't get the chance to see this improvement—and could miss out on the big money that is only one application away.

STRIKING SCHOLARSHIP GOLD—A THREE-PEAT!

Jennifer Gray of Lebanon, NH, entered the ThinkQuest Internet Challenge—a scholarship contest in which student teams from around the world design educational websites—three separate times. As a high school sophomore, she took home a scholarship award worth $15,000. As a junior, she applied again and added a $9,000 scholarship to her growing scholarship fund. Finally, as a high school senior, she earned an additional $12,000 scholarship. Her scholarship winnings from the ThinkQuest program alone totaled $36,000! To top it all off, the administrators of the scholarship program decided to tap her considerable talents and offered Jennifer a summer internship during college.

Don't Neglect Smaller, Local Scholarships

Although the scholarships with the highest profiles tend to be national programs, don't overlook the multitudes of scholarships that exist on the local and state levels. Local programs are usually less competitive and sometimes have only a handful of entrants. There have even been cases where certain local scholarships have gone unclaimed!

One committee member of a local union-sponsored scholarship program called in to a radio program I was on to emphasize how difficult it was to actually get students to apply for their scholarship awards.

Although the money amounts, as one might expect, are often larger on the national level, scholarship winnings can also be lucrative in local competitions, too. Some local scholarship programs can fund the entire cost of attending a state college. Other ones provide sizable funds for use out of state. I won a portable $5,000 scholarship from the Georgia-Pacific Corporation that was earmarked only for students in my community.

But don't underestimate the value of local competitions with relatively small payouts. Your chances of winning these scholarships are often quite high, and the money can add up rather quickly. Even if the prize is only a couple of hundred dollars, I still recommend applying for the scholarship. This might not sound like much money in the context of an entire college tuition bill, but a couple of hundred bucks can cover the cost of books for a term (unfortunately, you have to buy your own textbooks in college) or help pay for that much-needed spring-break "research" trip to Cancun.

National companies with a business interest in a particular community frequently award some of the largest local scholarships.

Furthermore, winning smaller scholarship awards can help you win bigger ones. By highlighting your selection for smaller awards as important credentials on later applications (you need not mention the money amount), you can let the judging world know you are worthy of larger funding payouts. There tends to be a "snowball effect" with scholarship applications: *Once you've received one or two scholarships (even relatively small ones), it gets easier to win more.*

"Apply for all you can, especially all the small, local scholarships. Even if the prize is only a couple of hundred dollars, the little scholarships can really add up."

–Aileen Richmond
Scholarship Winner
Grand Forks, ND

ASK THE COACH #23

Should I still apply for scholarships that are very tough to win?

Although you want to be realistic about which scholarships are a good fit for you (you might not want to apply for a cooking-based scholarship if burnt toast is your culinary specialty), be very careful about assuming that you "don't have a chance" of winning a particular scholarship award. One mother I spoke with told me about how her son, who wanted  to pursue a career in aviation, had found a $5,000 in-state scholarship for those going on to pilot's school. But because he had didn't have the greatest academic record—and grades were considered in the judging—he assumed he didn't have a chance to win, and consequently, decided not to apply. He later discovered that *not a single person had applied* . . . the scholarship's sponsors had to give the generous prize to the person who won the year before!

In general, be wary of taking yourself out of the running for a scholarship by failing to apply. If you think the scholarship is even remotely appropriate for someone like you, then give yourself a chance to win it by completing the application. ∎

Bridge Multiple Applications

What if I told you I had a magic scholarship application machine that has the incredible ability to take one completed scholarship application and clone it into two? If I had such a machine, I'm guessing you'd be pretty excited, because it could potentially save you a great deal of time, energy, and anguish.

Unfortunately, I haven't invented that machine just yet (I'm working on it!), but you can still achieve the same results with a little advance planning of your own. Survey the landscape of upcoming scholarships, and isolate common questions and requirements (whether it is a similar essay, worksheet, form, etc.). With every sentence you write, form you create, and list you complete, attempt to bridge the requirements of multiple applications.

Some applications, for instance, will pose broad questions, such as asking you to propose a solution to a pressing societal problem. Although this type of question provides a framework, the specific essay topic is up to you. So if another application poses a more specific question—perhaps asking you to discuss illiteracy in America—you may want to make this the societal problem you discuss in the first scholarship entry.

The key to bridging multiple applications is to plan ahead. After you have identified and marked on your calendar the scholarships you want to apply for, carefully survey the requirements for each, noting any potential overlaps that might exist.

Recycle, Recycle, Recycle

Just as careful planning can help you bridge multiple scholarship applications with every sentence you write, an examination of your past work can help you isolate previously completed scholarship materials that can be rethought, reapplied, and reused. This is the essence of scholarship recycling.

See the next chapter for more details on how to best recycle scholarship essays.

When you are applying for large numbers of scholarships, recycling previously prepared materials saves you a great deal of time and energy. By drawing upon such materials, you will be able to spend *less* time completing application requirements and more time fine-tuning and customizing the materials you've already created. In addition, reusing and rethinking old materials can mean vast improvements in your work as you repeatedly refine and edit the same passages. By employing this strategy, you gain the opportunity to fine-tune your materials with every submission. And take it from someone who knows, your tenth draft will be far better than your first.

Not only does this entail recycling essays on recurring questions—such as ones on college and graduate school plans, career goals, and future contributions to society—but it also means trying to reuse imagery, quotes, structure, and other elements of your past work. Don't just recopy such passages verbatim. Rethink, improve, and custom-tailor your past work to fit the underlying mission and judging criteria of each new scholarship or fellowship.

To aid this recycling effort, make a habit of printing out and filing away all rough drafts of essays, forms, and other materials you are working on, even if the final version is very different from these earlier attempts. Because of essay word limits and other scholarship-specific factors, passages you discard in the editing process may still be recyclable in later scholarship applications.

PRINCIPLE 5

Keep a Written Personal Inventory

Without keeping a written record of everything you've done, a lot of potentially good scholarship fodder can become lost in the gray matter of your brain. So to remember all of the details of your life—the significant events and stats that you should include in various scholarship applications—you will want to keep a written personal inventory and update it on a regular basis. Taking a personal inventory means taking time to reflect on your interests, achievements and activities, as well as awards and honors. You take a personal inventory by compiling a bunch of personal lists in several key areas.

First, type or write "Extracurricular Activities" on the top of a page, and begin listing all the extracurricular activities in which you have participated during high school, college, and beyond, as the case may be. A good starting point for this new list is the Scholarship Coach Search Profile Worksheet you used in Chapter 4. This time around, however, include your years of participation, any leadership positions you have held, a brief description of the activity, and any admirable personal qualities you have demonstrated through the activity. Include in this listing literally everything you have done—even activities that may have lasted for only a weekend. In boldface or with a highlighter, identify those activities that were the most significant to you.

Next, using the same format, prepare a list of any awards or honors you have won or earned over the years. Some of these items may be repeats from your extracurricular activities list, but that's good. Because of the space limitations and formatting constraints on some scholarship applications, having these credentials on separate lists allows you to pick and choose the best spots to include the information.

When you make this list, it's also important to think of awards and honors in the broadest sense possible. Your list should include everything from that Employee of the Month award you received, to your election as sophomore class senator, to the ambassadorial role you assumed for your school at a special conference on cultural diversity. Remember, this list is for your personal review only. I'll show you in later chapters how to pick, choose, and rank the most compelling information to submit.

Third, complete separate lists for service activities you have been involved with. Community service warrants a list of its own because of its importance to many types of scholarship applications. If you don't have much to put down on this list, don't get stressed. Community service is one area of your record that can generally be quickly and painlessly enhanced.

Fourth, list any jobs you have held. A listing of jobs (both full-time and part-time) is especially useful if your extracurricular involvement or community service has been limited. Furthermore, substantial work experience,

Keep a record of the hours you spend on each service project. For some applications, I found it useful to include the time commitment devoted to each project and the total number of hours spent on community service during the year.

especially to save money for college, can help communicate to judges that you know the value of a dollar and actually need the scholarship funds (even when financial need isn't a specific judging criteria).

Finally, start a list for interests and hobbies that might not be reflected in the other lists. This includes the things you do outside of school-related activities—from piano playing and stamp collecting to break dancing and naked bungee jumping. Just because an activity isn't formalized within a school organization doesn't make it any less important. (Well, maybe you can leave out the naked bungee jumping.) Indeed, some of the most impressive types of activities that one can participate in are these individual, outside projects.

For all these lists, I recommend completing them on a computer so that you can easily modify and update the content with minimal additional work.

Leverage Schoolwork and Class Time

In a variety of school-related writing assignments, you may be able to choose your own topic. And even if this isn't the case, I've found that teachers and professors can often be persuaded to allow you to write on related subjects that are also applicable to particular scholarship applications. You have to do the schoolwork anyway, so why not make it count toward your scholarship quest?

The Ayn Rand Institute has separate essay contests for 9th and 10th graders, 11th and 12th graders, and college undergraduates.

For instance, if you're asked to write a paper on a work of literature of your choosing, you may find it advantageous to select books like *The Fountainhead* or *Atlas Shrugged* by Ayn Rand. That way, you will have a submission ready to go for the annual essay-based scholarship contests on these famous novels. If you're assigned a self-reflective essay, pick a personal topic that fits in well with scholarship applications that you are pursuing. As an added bonus, because it's part of a class assignment, you'll get a lot of feedback from your teacher or professor.

This feedback can help you hone and improve your work, thereby making it substantially better for scholarship submissions.

Papers and projects for classes related to history, social studies, and the humanities are often good sources of potential quotes, references, and metaphors that can be used to great effect in scholarship essays and short-answer statements.

The second way to leverage class time is to dig into the body of schoolwork you have accumulated over the years. During high school or college, you've undoubtedly completed notebooks full of writing assignments, essays, and papers. In completing my own scholarship applications, I found it very useful to search through this "junk pile" for hidden treasure. I rummaged through my old files for widely applicable topics, golden quotes, jeweled phrases, and sparkling metaphors. The treasure you dig up in this fashion can become an important contribution to your stash of reusable scholarship materials.

GUERRILLA TACTIC

Make Your Homework Count

■ Use course-related assignments and projects as an opportunity to flesh out materials for scholarship applications. Search old schoolwork for hidden scholarship treasure.

This technique isn't restricted merely to classroom assignments either. Most schools and colleges offer some type of independent-study class credit in which you pursue your own project under the guidance of an adviser. At many high schools, you are even allowed to use a class period during the day. So instead of added classroom time, you can spend the time on self-initiated projects that substantially improve your chances of scholarship (and college admission) success. Plus, it's a great way to learn more about really fascinating subjects.

At the time, I couldn't fit an English class into my term schedule, so naming my independent-study course "Advanced Expository Writing" filled a visible hole in my academic record.

Although your school probably won't permit an independent-study course on "Completing Scholarship Applications," you can use the time to pursue projects (such as an extended writing or science project) that enhance your record for scholarship applications. In high school, I created an independent-study course for myself entitled "Advanced Expository Writing." (Isn't it great when you get to name the course yourself!) In this course, I began writing a how-to manual about a service program I had founded. Another student I know used an independent-study course to conduct a survey on the attitudes of teenagers. You can also use independent study to pursue subject matter in an area of your academic record that might otherwise be light or deficient.

One added benefit of pursuing this independent-study option is the fact that it appears on your official transcript (as either graded or nongraded). And, of course, if the independent study is graded, it can be a relatively painless way to raise your GPA (advisers are known to be generous about grades when they see that you have seriously taken the initiative to pursue something on your own). Furthermore, cultivating this one-on-one relationship with an adviser will often lead to glowing recommendation letters down the road.

Learn by Example

Let's say that you have never shot a basketball in your life and suddenly you want to learn how to play. If you were serious about learning, would you lock yourself in a room all alone with a basketball trying to teach yourself how to shoot, pass, or dribble? Or would it be more effective to have people who have played a lot of basketball show you the ropes?

Well, if you really want to learn the game, you are much better off following the second approach—gleaning all you can from what others have already done and know how to do well. This approach of learning-by-example holds true in the scholarship game, too. In the chapters that follow, read, re-read, and refer back to the many examples from my own winning scholarship applications. Look at other past winning scholarship entries to truly internalize the key characteristics of well-painted application portraits, and learn what has worked for past scholarship applicants.

For America's top scholarship opportunities, a great source of sample winning entries and insights from past scholarship winners is my companion book, The Scholarship Scouting Report.

As we discussed in Chapter 6, a good number of scholarship programs post past winning entries on their websites or will send you past winning entries upon request. Track down a wide range of this type of material and study it closely.

ASK THE COACH #24

How much time must I invest to win scholarships?

Seeking scholarships isn't like buying a lottery ticket—the process does take substantial effort. It probably isn't, however, as much work as you think. By bridging multiple applications with each new sentence you write, and by recycling and rethinking old material, you can save countless hours. If you are smart about how you approach the process, once you have

applied for two scholarships, you've done 60 percent of the work to apply for ten! Mounting a major scholarship campaign should take about as much time as involvement in a typical extracurricular activity. And given the potential rewards—as well as all the important personal development and life lessons you learn along the way—it's definitely time well spent. ■

Stick with It

One student I met applied for seven scholarships and didn't win a single one. A lot of people, at this point, might have decided to call it quits. But this student didn't even think about giving up and applied for *ten more*. You know what happened? She ended up winning about $25,000 for college!

Many of the other scholarship winners I've interviewed related similar stories of determination and perseverance. In general, I've found that successful scholarship seekers:

▌ Stick with the process even in the face of adversity

▌ Never take the results of any given scholarship competition personally

▌ Realize that whether or not they are selected for the scholarship is never a measure of how good or talented they are

Deep thought of the day: It is better to apply for a scholarship and fail than to be eaten alive by a pack of ravenous wolves.

Receiving your fair share of "rejection" letters is part of the process (everyone gets them, me included). Unlike the game show *Jeopardy!* however, which penalizes you for your wrong answers, there is no penalty for failing to win a particular scholarship prize. Successful scholarship seekers further recognize that the more applications you fill out, the better you get at it, and the larger the suite of reusable materials you have to draw from—thereby increasing your odds of receiving the next scholarship that comes around. So take pride in completing a scholarship application to the best of your ability, but once you've given it your all, try to let go and allow the results take care of themselves.

No matter how closely you read and internalize the principles, strategies, and action steps of this book, if you don't stick with the process, you aren't giving yourself a chance to reap the rewards you deserve. *The common link among all scholarship winners is that they are the ones who actually APPLY for the awards.* And the common link among the most successful scholarship winners is that, regardless of the results, they keep applying again and again and again. . . .

CHAPTER 8 SUMMARY AND KEYWORDS

Numbers Game: Applying for as many scholarships as possible minimizes the effect of subjectivity in the judging process and maximizes learning curve effects. Applying for only a few scholarships is the best way to miss out on a lot of potential scholarship dollars. ■

Local Scholarships: Don't overlook smaller, local scholarships. Such awards are often less competitive and can still have sizable payouts. You should even apply for ones that may award only a few hundred dollars. Scholarships with smaller prizes can add up quickly and can be used as credentials to help you win bigger scholarship awards. ■

Spanning Multiple Applications: To save time and energy, survey the landscape of upcoming scholarships and try to create essays, forms, and lists that meet the requirements of multiple applications. ■

Recycling: Try to recycle past scholarship submissions. Rethink, refine, and custom-tailor old materials to make them better fit the underlying mission and judging criteria of each new scholarship. ■

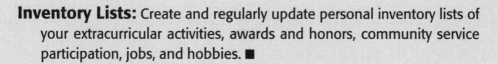

Inventory Lists: Create and regularly update personal inventory lists of your extracurricular activities, awards and honors, community service participation, jobs, and hobbies. ■

Leveraging Schoolwork: Use school writing assignments as opportunities to draft essays for scholarship applications. Search old schoolwork for potential ideas for scholarship submissions. Create independent study courses and pursue self-initiated projects that enhance your record. ■

Powerful Examples: Study past winning scholarship entries to understand how to craft winning scholarship applications. ■

The Right Attitude: Don't get discouraged if you aren't selected for a particular scholarship award. So-called rejections come with the territory. Stick with the process regardless of the short-term results, and keep on honing your applications. The common link among the most successful scholarship winners is that they keep applying no matter what. ■

SCHOLARSHIPCOACH.COM KEYWORDS

For more information on a scholarship or topic mentioned in this chapter, enter the associated keyword in the keyword link box located in the Coach's Locker Room section of ScholarshipCoach.com.

Scholarship/Topic	Keyword
Ayn Rand Scholarships	AYNRAND
Georgia-Pacific Foundation Community Scholarship	GEOPAC
ThinkQuest Internet Challenge	TQUEST

Essay Excellence

INSIDE THIS CHAPTER

- The principles of winning essays

- Techniques for choosing topics and recycling work

- Methods for finding your own writing voice

- Tips for overcoming writer's block

- How to revise your essays

- Strategies for answering the perennial essay questions

FIVE PRINCIPLES OF WINNING ESSAYS

What do hairy spiders, slithering snakes, and scholarship essays have in common? Quite simply, they are all things known for intimidating otherwise fearless students. In this section, however, I will show you how to put to rest any of your essay phobias and lay the smack down on even the toughest scholarship essay questions. (Sorry, you're on your own for the spiders and snakes. Yikes!)

Essays are critical components of many scholarship applications because they represent an applicant's best opportunity to directly communicate interests, passions, beliefs, and values. Essays may be the part of your application in which you have the greatest opportunity to paint a wonderfully vivid self-portrait.

One misconception about the scholarship essay is that you need to be a naturally gifted writer to craft a strong one. While writing skills can prove useful, you *don't* have to be a prolific writer to create an effective scholarship essay. More than writing ability, the key is understanding and properly applying a few simple, strategic principles.

Strong writing ability actually <u>harms</u> some scholarship applicants because they rely on this ability to mask a hastily thought through essay.

These principles are outlined below. As is the case with any set of rules, there are times when it may be appropriate to break them. But before we can even consider breaking the rules, we first need to thoroughly master them.

Show, Don't Tell

Here's the scenario: It's precisely 8:47 P.M. on a Saturday night, and you find yourself seated at a candlelit corner table at a pretentious French restaurant—one of those restaurants where there are more kinds of forks, knives, and spoons placed in front of you than any one human could possibly need. Your date sits across from you, looking especially inviting in the soft candle glow. It's safe to say you're eager to make a good impression. Being the dating maestro that you are, you know that a sense of humor is a personal quality that most people find attractive in a date. So here's the question: To convince your date that you are funny, which of the following do you do?

> Say something like, "You know, I am really, really, really funny. Some people even consider me hilarious, in a knee-slapping, sidesplitting sort of way. In fact, if you wanted to utter the words *comic genius,* I wouldn't stop you."

OR

> Crack a funny joke or two and make witty conversation.

Well, unless you happen to be Jim Carrey, you would probably do the latter. (If you actually *are* Jim Carrey, please skip to the next section.) You would choose the second option because you know instinctively that just *telling* your date that you are funny forces him or her to take your word for it. Why should anyone believe you? Chances are, instead of coming across as funny, you'll come across as a bit pompous and arrogant. But if you tell a few jokes and partake in witty conversation, you *show* your date your great sense of humor. He or she doesn't have to take your word for it because you've just demonstrated it to be true.

Just as in the realm of dating, one of the most prevalent mistakes committed in weak scholarship essays is that applicants *tell* rather than *show*. What's the distinction? *Telling* occurs when the applicant makes broad (often self-congratulatory) statements without backing them up with specific examples. *Showing,* on the other hand, involves describing a situation or activity or telling a story that powerfully illustrates your point.

So don't just *tell* application judges that you are "exceptionally trustworthy and responsible." Instead, *show* them your trustworthiness and sense of responsibility by describing an activity, event, or scene in which you demonstrated these admirable personal qualities. Don't just *tell* your readers that a particular reform will improve the educational system. *Show* them by describing the dramatic educational benefits of a pilot project you helped to initiate. Taking this approach captures the reader's attention and adds credibility to what you say.

This principle helps you avoid a common application pitfall: letting your scholarship essay become nothing more than a wordy résumé.

Keep Things Personal

Regardless of the specific question posed, most scholarship essays are designed to provide judges with a better sense of who you are, what you believe in, and how you think. As a result, making your essay intensely personal—by relating the essay question to your unique experiences and perspectives—goes a long way in making your composition more compelling.

Adding personal details to your scholarship essays also serves the important purpose of making your materials stand out from those of other applicants. When you add this personal touch—and truly *own* your essay—no one else in the state, nation, continent, world, galaxy, or universe (let alone, the application pile) could have written your words in quite the same way. This is the case because no one else has lived through your unique experiences and shared your personal feelings and perspectives.

"In my essays, I would include personal details that showed why I'm special, why I'm unique, why I'm an individual— unlike anyone else in the application pool."

–William Moss Scholarship Winner Brentwood, NY

Such a strategy is *not* limited to essay questions that are personal in nature. Some of the best essays I've seen on issue-oriented topics still relate the subject matter to personal experiences. A winning scholarship essay discussing the issue of homelessness was built around an applicant's eye-opening experiences working in a homeless shelter. In one of my own scholarship submissions, I connected an analysis of our public education system to my experiences in setting up a telephone-based peer-tutoring system called the Homework Helpline.

If the essay question deals with an area in which you don't have direct experience, try relating the topic to someone you know, such as a relative or family friend. If an essay question, for instance, asks you about cultures in other countries, you could discuss personal experiences your mom or dad had when traveling around the world after college. To frame the story in terms of your *own* experience, you could describe a memorable conversation you've had with your parents about their travel adventures.

Taking this approach also enhances the credibility and believability of your applications. As we discussed in Chapter 5, application judges view applications with a skeptical eye: They recognize that applicants have strong incentives to tell them what they want to hear. But essays deeply rooted in personal experience seem less likely to be contrived by the writer simply for the sake of appearances.

Use Effective Organization

Effective organization provides judges with a detailed road map that helps them navigate through the key points in your essay. Your organization demonstrates the thought you put into the essay and enhances the underlying logic of the main ideas you are trying to drive home.

A standard organizational framework for a scholarship essay—or *any* essay for that matter—is a three-part format. In the first part of the essay, the *introduction,* you frame the subject matter to be covered in the piece. In the introduction, you are trying to achieve two main goals. First, you want to give the reader some idea of where you're headed. This can be done formally with a thesis statement that summarizes the main point of the essay or more casually, by giving the reader a general sense of the terrain the essay will cover.

Second, your introduction should draw readers into the subject matter by grabbing their attention in an interesting way. Many scholarship winners have done this by telling an interesting story or anecdote or through vivid description. Whether the focus of your introduction should be more on summarizing the argument in the essay or grabbing the reader's attention depends upon the subject matter and the tone of your essay. Many issue-oriented essays focus more on summarizing the main argument, while many personal essays focus more on engaging the reader. Some of the best scholarship essays I've seen, however, utilize a two-paragraph introduction to emphasize both these elements in equal measure—with the first paragraph "hooking" the reader and the second providing a blueprint for the remainder of the essay.

The body of the essay is where the action happens, the place where you develop your main points and ideas. The body structure itself can vary significantly. The main effect you should be aiming for is a logical development of your points and a natural progression of thought, as if your ideas were moving along a clear path. To do this, it's often convenient to organize the body of your essay into a series of paragraphs, with each paragraph developing a major idea and building upon the previous one.

You might find it helpful to actually draw a blueprint of your essay structure. Using a pen or pencil, draw a series of labeled boxes with connecting lines or arrows indicating the flow of ideas.

You will hear from many people that the conclusion is the place to restate and summarize your main points. For me, however, merely revisiting ground you've already covered is a bit boring—and a waste of space in applications where each word is a precious commodity. I think of the conclusion as an opportunity to reference key points in an essay in an original way that extends the concepts even further. In a personal essay, for instance, you may want to comment upon how the personal qualities you've described will help you in your future career. In an essay focused on a particular societal problem, you may want to project your vision for what the world will look like once the problem is solved. If you've opened with a story, consider revisiting that story and extending the connections between the significance of the anecdote and the points you've covered.

The basic structure I've outlined, of course, is just one approach. I've seen many other organizational structures that work well, too. If you're struggling to come up with a good organizational format for your essay, however, the basic format described here is a proven way to go.

PRINCIPLE 4

Make Each Sentence Count

Because of word limits and space limitations, a big part of writing a strong scholarship essay is learning how to explain and fully develop all your points, ideas, and concepts in a limited amount of space. To do this, it's essential to make each sentence count toward the development of your main idea. You should be able to explain to yourself the purpose of every sentence you write. Avoid long transitional phrases and sentences that eat up space without accomplishing anything. Don't be redundant. Again, don't be redundant. Make your point and move on.

ASK THE COACH #25

Are word limits for essays strictly enforced?

Always adhere to the word limits. This demonstrates that you are capable of following directions. Besides, you don't want to give a scholarship judge or administrator any reason to disqualify you. Even if they don't disqualify you for going over the word limit, that could make the difference in determining who receives a scholarship award between two otherwise equal candidates. In general, try to keep your essays a few words *under* the limit just in case the reader makes a mistake in tallying up your word count. ∎

To keep your essay tight and to eliminate spots that drag, try the following technique: Write the first draft of your essay moderately long—perhaps 25 percent longer than the word limit. Then force yourself to pare down the verbiage. The best way to create concise, powerful writing is through careful editing.

Make Your Essay Unique and Memorable

For a moment, pretend you are judging a large scholarship program. As a judge, you may be responsible for reviewing hundreds of essays, and you're supposed to keep track of each applicant and rank him or her according to some objective criteria. A thick stack of applications sits on the desk in front of you, and because the each entry in the pile addresses the same set of questions over and over and over and over and over again (often in a similar manner to one another), it can indeed be a monotonous task.

To avoid having a judge just skim through your essay, you need to make it unique and memorable. The first way to do this is by taking to heart Principle #2 ("Keep Things Personal"). By adding vivid personal details to an essay, you make the essay uniquely yours. And by choosing details and stories that engage the reader, you make your essay memorable.

Using quotes in your scholarship essays can be effective, but don't overdo it. Excessive quoting makes you sound like a parrot that only repeats the opinions of others. Use quotes to reinforce your points, not to make them for you.

Second, you can make your essay unique and memorable through your intellectual approach. If you can, try to come up with your own original, unconventional, or thought-provoking idea on the topic. If you're stuck, try to redefine the question in an interesting way. For instance, if the question asks you the importance of art in our society, turn the question on its head by vividly describing a world completely devoid of art. You can make content memorable by including some interesting research, references, or facts that your readers aren't likely to already know or fully appreciate.

Third, you can take traditional ideas and express them in novel ways. One effective technique that I have employed on several occasions is the use of an *extended metaphor*—a metaphor that permeates your entire essay. The use of a metaphor is a powerful technique because it allows you to transform well-worn ideas into fresh-feeling concepts.

Metaphors allow you to simplify complex ideas and create vivid imagery in a judge's mind. Furthermore, a well-developed extended metaphor brings a sense of cohesion to a scholarship essay and can contribute to an attention-grabbing introduction and conclusion.

The types of metaphors are without limit. One winner of a prestigious national scholarship wrote an essay looking back at different points in American history as if they were different rooms in a house. In one of my own winning essays, I used a clipper ship to describe the importance of freedom to our nation:

> As a proud vessel of freedom, America has been crafted from the resilient planks of democracy. Our heritage of justice provides a firm rudder—holding this Yankee clipper on a steady course, while allowing for necessary corrections at critical way points on our voyage. . . . But no matter how seaworthy the craft, how adept the captain, or how friendly the waters, even a great sailing ship can become paralyzed: Without the winds of freedom to drive her forward, America would find herself shackled in irons.

■ SPANNING TOPICS AND RECYCLING ESSAYS

In Chapter 8, we discussed the importance of bridging multiple applications with each sentence you write and recycling prior materials whenever possible. In this section, we examine the subject in greater depth and explore specific techniques for employing these principles in the scholarship essay format.

Let's start by examining how one carefully chosen essay topic can span multiple applications and seemingly unrelated essay questions. For instance, suppose a scholarship application asks you to do the following:

Name an individual who has had a significant impact on your life, and discuss what you've learned from that person.

Meanwhile, a different scholarship application requests an essay on a seemingly unrelated topic:

Describe an important conversation you've had in the past year.

Even though these two questions are very different, it is still possible to write an essay that spans both topics. Why not write an essay about an important conversation you've had in the past year with someone who has had a profound impact on your life? By taking this approach, you would have to write only one core essay. Then you could customize it for each application by making small changes to the introduction, body, and conclusion—changes that would emphasize the *person* for the first scholarship and the *conversation* itself for the second.

Let's look at another example. Here's the topic presented in our fictional application #1:

Discuss and describe an extracurricular activity that has special meaning to you.

Application #2, on the other hand, asks you:

What do you hope to get out of college?

Because grad school scholarship essays often focus on why you are pursuing a particular field of study, in many instances it is a simple matter to recycle these essays.

Even in this setting, there are potential ways to span both topics. When asked to describe an extracurricular activity important to you, pick something that you plan to continue with in college—say, a certain type of community service work. In the essay on an extracurricular activity, you could include a discussion of how a particular community service project has been so important to your life that you plan to explore it even further as a college student. For the essay on your college hopes, you could work in a paragraph or two on how college offers a great opportunity to develop your service project to a greater degree.

Now that we've established how to use advance planning to bridge multiple essay topics, let's delve into the art of scholarship essay recycling. As you'll recall from our Chapter 8 discussion, recycling old material not only saves you time and energy, but also improves the quality of the work, as you repeatedly rethink and rewrite the same passages. When you get good at recycling, it's amazing what results you can achieve in minimal time: A nip here, a tuck there, a bit more reworking, then presto—your old essay has been magically recycled into a shiny new one.

As I rethought and refined old essays, they improved by leaps and bounds—as did my essay-writing skills. This skills enhancement proved useful when it came time to fill out college applications or apply for internships and jobs.

One approach for recycling essays is to combine elements of two or more essays you've already written to create a new essay that merges the best parts of both. To witness this technique in action, let's first examine an excerpt from an essay I wrote for a scholarship sponsored by the Portland Trailblazers basketball team:

As a sapling pushes its limbs skyward, its roots burrow deeper into the dark, moist sanctuary of soil. It is here, where the foundation lies—at the source of stability and strength—where probing tentacles soak up the very sustenance of life. And just as the young tree draws its strength from this underlying foundation, a college education empowers its graduates with the strong roots of lifelong learning: the impetus for intellectual growth, work-skills enhancement, and personality development.

Through this solid educational base, youth is instilled with the discipline and perseverance to stand tall in a world permeated with the winds of challenge and storms of adversity. Providing both stability and nourishment, a college education excites the mind and spirit—drawing out the inner faculties, as personality, convictions, perspectives, and attitudes blossom. To educate, after all, is to develop from within. . . .

I combined the above essay with another I wrote for the Discover Card Tribute Awards, an essay we first discussed in Chapter 5:

Because of a strong interest in writing and communication, an aptitude for analysis and problem-solving, and a fascination with the inner workings of government, I plan to pursue a career in print and broadcast journalism as a political columnist and commentator. A well-rounded education will unlock the gates of opportunity—not only helping to clarify complex issues and providing skills for becoming a more persuasive writer and effective speaker, but also preparing me to be a responsible contributor in this world of infinite possibilities. . . . As a well-educated journalist, I will strive to broaden minds and uncover truth—thus doing my part to make a difference in the world.

Merging together the Portland Trailblazers Scholarship essay and the Discover Card Tribute Awards essay, I created a new essay for the Georgia-Pacific Foundation Community Scholarship that analyzed the benefits of college for all students, discussed what I personally hoped to gain from the experience, and commented upon my career plans after graduating from college:

A college education empowers one with the robust skills of lifelong learning: the impetus for intellectual growth, work-skills enhancement, and personality

You can see that I've changed some words around and reduced the flowery content, but this essay is still a recycled combination of my previous two entries.

development. Through this solid educational base, I expect to have the discipline and perseverance to stand tall in a world permeated with the winds of challenge and storms of adversity. Providing both stability and nourishment, my college education will, I hope, excite both mind and spirit—drawing out my inner faculties, as personality, convictions, perspectives, and attitudes blossom. To educate, after all, is to develop from within.

The well-rounded college education that I am seeking should unlock the gates of opportunity— helping me become a more persuasive writer and effective speaker, as well as an adept analyst and problem-solver. . . .

Because of a strong interest in communication, an aptitude for analysis and problem solving, and a fascination with the inner workings of government, I plan to pursue a career in print and broadcast journalism as a political columnist and commentator. As a well-educated journalist, I will strive to broaden minds and uncover truth—thus doing my part to make a difference in the world. . . .

I won $5,000 from this scholarship, and a judge later told me that out of all the students who won scholarships through the program, my application stood out because of the care and thought that went into it.

The act of recycling essays, however, doesn't have to be limited just to the *content* of your essays. Recycling might also involve a specific way you express ideas, such as through a vivid metaphor. To understand this point, refer back to an essay I excerpted earlier in this chapter (at the end of Principle #5) in which I used a clipper ship to describe the nation, with freedom representing the winds driving us forward. I was able to successfully recycle this clipper ship metaphor in several scholarship essays on a variety of diverse and seemingly unrelated subjects. Here's an example from an essay on an entirely different topic—the importance of stock markets:

Stock markets harness winds of capital to help propel our nation's most promising—and often most fragile—entrepreneurial vessels. But more than passive sails that just capture these powerful winds, stock markets actually help summon them. . . . While the companies themselves must provide product and know-how—the hull and rudder of any corporate vessel—markets transform the raw power of investment capital into propulsion for our nation's best business ventures. After all, no matter how seaworthy the craft, how adept the captain, or how friendly the waters, even a great sailing ship becomes paralyzed without this driving force.

If you've come up with a good metaphor or a particularly poignant or creative way of expressing an idea, try to reuse it in different settings. Keep in the back of your mind as you recycle, however, that you don't want to force a passage into reuse that really isn't a good fit for the new essay question. Constantly ask yourself if the recycled passage is truly answering the question posed.

▮ FINDING YOUR OWN VOICE

Although winning scholarship essays have certain common characteristics—namely, the principles we discussed earlier in this chapter—unlike a multiple-choice exam, there is no such thing as a "right" answer to a scholarship essay question. In fact, two winning essays for the *same* scholarship program may very well approach the subject matter in entirely different ways. To see this in action, let's examine two winning essays from the prestigious Optimist International Essay Contest. In this scholarship program, students wrote on the topic "If I Could Give Freedom Away" and were asked to respond in an essay of no more than 500 words.

Winning Essay #1

If I could give freedom away, I would have to be a god for it is impossible to freely distribute liberty as one would a gift. Freedom lies in every individual, whether it only dwells in the solemn soul or is exercised daily in an open-minded society. One cannot give freedom away for the simple reason that every human being cannot merely receive such an intangibly magnificent gift, rather each must find this liberty inside himself or herself.

Each man and woman possesses freedom to a certain degree. While some enjoy more liberties than others such as the cherished rights to free speech or religion, every person does experience some level of freedom. John Milton once wrote, "Thou canst touch the freedom of my mind." Freedom of thought is often looked upon as insignificant, yet it is as precious a natural right as any.

Oftentimes, man finds that he must free himself from an oppressive government, but even this freedom could not possibly be a present hastily bestowed. It must be fought for, believed in, and supported to be prized. As Thomas Paine masterfully concluded in *The Crisis, Number One,* "What we obtain too cheaply, we esteem too lightly: it is dearness only that gives everything its value." Yes, the blessings of life such as liberty are much more treasured and appreciated when they are obtained through one's personal hard work, commitment, and dedication.

Any physical suppression is often viewed as the depletion of all liberty, yet is it not an axiomatic right of man to be free? During the time of tyranny by Great Britain, the American colonies were incessantly taxed and deprived of legal freedom. However, in actuality, these colonies could have rebelled at any time and followed their own will as they finally realized and strongly declared in the seditious Boston Tea Party.

They had freedom all along, maybe not legally, but they did own the liberty of choice, which was a "gift" they had to find the strength to exercise.

Perhaps the gift of freedom cannot be found by solely lifting political oppression. Are not the chains of society and its priorities just as heavy and enslaving? Is not the pursuit of money, success, fame, and glory equally oppressing? Just as in political suppression, freedom cannot be dealt to deliver one from the clutches of these worldly, oppressive desires. One must personally liberate oneself from these societal values, and how much more exhilarating it is to discover individual independence rather than receiving it, were it possible, on a silver platter.

Liberty must be realized and applied so that it may be cherished and truly appreciated. Each individual possesses this freedom to some extent, and for some, it is only a matter of discovering this inner quality. Liberty and independence are axiomatic rights that free one from political as well as societal oppression, and they are much more treasured when they are personally discovered instead of being simply given.

Winning Essay #2

I came to this country when I was eight or nine years old. I'm Hispanic and now I am 17 years old. I was living in a small city full of gangs, violence, drugs, and prostitution before I got arrested.

After seeing all this for a long time, I got used to it; I even got involved with it and liked it. I did not see that I was not free at all; I was in slavery to my surroundings. I didn't have the freedom that a gangster is supposed to have. I was a follower of people who did not have any future and were in the same low place as I was. I didn't realize that or I just didn't care. Everything was fun for me and that was all

I lived for. I thought freedom was just like that, but I was dead wrong. Nothing I was involved in freed me.

Being foolish and not wanting to accept the reality of my captivity cost me much of my life and I'm still paying. In March, 1998, I committed a crime for reasons that I could easily forget, put them aside, and keep on going with my life. But I didn't. I plunged ahead in my crazy life. I got caught, and I lost what I once considered freedom.

I never thought people could take my freedom away in just a few minutes. I'm not talking about the freedom to get drunk or high; what I lost was much more valuable than that. Now I am incarcerated and can never forget how much I have lost that I never paid attention to in the past. Real, authentic freedom was taken from me and I didn't even know I had it.

I see now that genuine freedom has to do with making your own decisions—good decisions. It's practicing your own religion and letting God have His way in your life. It is going where you choose and doing it when you feel it is right. Most importantly, freedom that I lost was all about not being controlled by anything or anybody. I knew that drugs once controlled me, but I didn't realize how all the gang members and wrong attitudes also had a grip on my soul.

Now I'm locked up and I can only plan for a free future; but if I could give my potential freedom to a group of people, I would try to find those who could appreciate what a gift it is, people who were truly alive in their hearts and would use their freedom to help heal a sick society.

I believe that all the people in the world were born with the potential to love freedom. Unfortunately, few of them ever find it. Shame on individuals like me who had it and threw it away so carelessly. Please don't throw your freedom away; it's a piece of your life.

Wow, what a difference. While the first essay was written from an intellectual and philosophical perspective, the second essay was actually written from behind bars!

The first essay is interesting because of its unique intellectual approach: The writer takes issue with the very essay topic itself and turns the topic on its head by challenging the notion that freedom can be given away at all. She argues that freedom, at its core, must come from within. The writer develops this argument with a thoughtful and organized progression of ideas.

The second essay is compelling in its intensely personal nature. The writer describes quite a few negative things from his past (including the fact that he's in jail), but skillfully keeps the focus on what these experiences have taught him about the meaning of true freedom. The writer is credible and the essay powerful because of the heartfelt way he approaches the topic.

These two examples illustrate how even among winning submissions, essay questions and topics can be interpreted and answered in very different ways. Imagine, however, if the first essay writer had tried to write in the style of the second essay, or if the second writer (the one in prison) had tried to write in a more academic style. Neither essay probably would have been successful.

The key, therefore, is not to waste time searching for that mythical perfect essay answer or copying someone else's writing style. Instead focus your efforts on developing your own unique voice, the one that's right for you.

GETTING IN THE FLOW

When I sat down to write this paragraph, I was fully prepared to tell you that writer's block is just a figment of the imagination—an idea conjured up by the same people behind the "Pet Rock" or the *Psychic Friends Network*. But then I jumbled my ideas, lost my train of thought, and couldn't write a single word!

So let me start again: Writer's block sucks. And for most scholarship applicants, it sucks most frequently when staring at a blank page. The intimidation of starting from scratch can cause even the most talented writers to feel paralyzed. In this section, I describe techniques that I have found useful to jump-start the writing process and cure even the most persistent case of writer's block.

The Free Write

In many instances an internal editing process stops us from making progress in our writing. It's as though a little, mean-spirited editor dude sits on our shoulders making sarcastic comments such as, "You call that a sentence, Shakespeare?" As a result, we're afraid to leave alone anything that doesn't already make us sound like the reincarnation of John Steinbeck. We start editing every other word, deconstructing every *the* and *it*, and before we know it, all we have to show for hours of work are two recycling bins full of crumpled paper.

What we should be trying to do, however, is to get as much as we can down on the page, so that we can edit and reedit it later. We need to give ourselves one simple freedom: the freedom to write *badly*. Instead of shackling this freedom, celebrate it. How badly can you write? Not as badly as I! Here's one way to reinstate this freedom in your life: Set a timer for 20 minutes, and force yourself to sit down and write nonstop for the entire time about anything that happens to jump into your head—even something barely related to the essay topic. The key here is to keep the ideas moving freely and to keep writing, no matter what.

Consult Other Essays

Sometimes to get us going, all we need is a little inspiration. Often you can get this inspiration by rereading other scholarship essays you've written or by reading winning essays written by others. Sometimes it helps to copy down or type some random text off a cereal box or from the newspaper, just to get the juices flowing. Just immersing yourself in language for a few minutes can spark a whole new range of ideas.

Talk It Over

Sometimes the cause of writer's block is a difficulty in organizing the jumble of thoughts running through your head. A simple solution to this is just to talk over your essay topic with someone else—a parent, sibling, or friend. Having this dialogue often helps you make sense of abstract concepts and see patterns that you missed before.

Record Yourself

There are times when the very act of writing can get in the way of idea creation. If you happen to be a particularly verbal person, try tape-recording yourself as you talk about the topic. Sometimes when I've done this, I merely transcribe what I said and wind up with part of a first draft.

Move Locations

If one place seems to be draining your creative juices, change your setting. If you've been writing on the computer, grab a pen and paper and go write elsewhere. Try writing in parks, coffee shops, or anywhere you're at ease. If you need to clear your mind, try going for a walk or a drive.

Zoom In

There have been occasions when I've felt overwhelmed by the essay topic and didn't have the faintest idea how to organize all the thoughts running through my head. At such times, I *zoom in*—focusing on some detail, description, or point that I do feel comfortable writing about. There's no law saying that you have to write in any particular sequence, so pick some aspect of the essay that you have a firmer grasp on and start writing.

■ Honing Your Essay

The process of rewriting your essay helps you hone your core message until your ideas can't miss the target.

There's a saying that some of the best writers are, in fact, not particularly great at writing—they're just good at *rewriting*. In my experience, a good scholarship essay is usually drawn out from a process of first reevaluating your concepts and ideas, then reassessing how to communicate those points. To illustrate how to do this, I've included an excerpt from an intermediate draft of an essay I wrote for the Century III Leaders scholarship program. The application materials requested that I propose a solution to a problem facing America. I chose the topic of reforming our public education system:

> Current solutions often throw money at problems in education, but don't look to harness already-present resources. In looking to the future, we must find solutions to this educational crisis in three steps. First, we need to make a strong commitment to deliver a quality product. School must make sure that basic areas are covered before expanding the curriculum. We first need to improve the building blocks of learning—reading, writing, and math. Next, we must

This excerpt is from the middle of the essay. I've chosen to focus on this section because it illustrates some important rewriting principles.

motivate and inspire students to go far beyond minimum expectations. America was built on the principle that with hard work and perseverance, anything is possible. We need to reaffirm this belief by encouraging students to pursue learning outside what is spoon-fed in class. Last, we must find new ways to customize education to help students adapt to the rapidly changing world of the future. We need to train students how to maximize resources, share information, and work cooperatively. These abilities will be the new measure of success.

This draft wasn't bad, but the passage still had some glaring weaknesses. It mentioned some important reform concepts, but didn't really take the time to fully develop the ideas. As a result, it seemed to be more a conglomeration of catch phrases for educational reform than something that had a lot of real substance. The passage made only passing reference to alternatives to my point of view. Failing to recognize and make my case against differing views was a big omission.

For additional scholarship essay critiques, visit ScholarshipCoach.com (Keyword: ESSAY).

The passage also lacked a sound organizational structure; all my ideas had been lumped into one big paragraph, even though each idea merited its own organizational unit. Furthermore, I wasn't making every sentence count. The second sentence of the passage was largely a transitional one that didn't accomplish much of anything. The sentence beginning "America was built on the principle" was tangential to the topic at hand. In short, both my ideas and my expression of those ideas had to be fleshed out further. I tried to address these weak points in a subsequent version:

Lowering standards so as to get more high school students through the system and into college each year is *not* the panacea for this debilitation in learning. Today, businesses rightly complain that they must reeducate even *college* graduates in basic academic skills. Some policy makers would have us believe that simply bolstering programs with more money will solve our problems. Unfortunately, money isn't the panacea either: Positive change demands wisdom and discipline, and a lack of money often becomes a convenient scapegoat for failure. In fact, as an active student government member, I've learned how workable solutions are achievable without always allocating new funds—by harnessing underutilized resources, such as the students themselves.

Educators must make the commitment to deliver a quality product. Schools must refocus their energies to ensure that basic core subjects are adequately covered before expanding content. By minimizing distractions, we can increase the critical time allotted to developing the building blocks of learning—reading, writing, and math.

Next, we must motivate and inspire students to go far beyond minimum expectations. And in the process, we must *raise* the expectations of students as well as their parents. Furthermore, we need to emphasize and teach *how* to learn, not merely *what* to learn. We should encourage students to pursue learning outside of what is covered in class.

Last, we must find new ways to customize education to help students better prepare for the 21st century. The communications and computer revolutions have forever changed our lives. We need to train students and teachers to maximize resources by sharing information over electronic networks. We should create lower-tech programs that will act as supplementary "training wheels" for the interactive, multimedia resources of tomorrow. The difference between present practicalities and future possibilities is only a matter of the technological level of the networking links.

In this revision, I developed each of my points more fully and revised my organizational structure to put each point in its own paragraph. The passage begins by addressing two alternative ways of addressing the problem and showing why such "solutions" won't work.

At the end of the first paragraph, I've made the essay more personal by referencing a lesson learned from my own student government experience. The phrase I used at the end of the paragraph—"the students themselves"—was meant to foreshadow a discussion of a service program I created called the Homework Helpline. I fully described this project in a later section of the essay. In addition, notice that I was more careful with my word choice and sentence structure. Overall, the persuasiveness of this essay was enhanced significantly.

I would have liked to revise the passage even further, but alas, I ran out of time. It didn't seem to matter, however, since I was the national winner in the competition.

TIPS FOR REVISING ESSAYS

Before revising an essay, try to distance yourself somewhat from the material. If possible, take a day or two off from working on the essay and allow the material to simmer in the back of your mind. You'll come back to the essay after your brief sabbatical with a fresher perspective.

When revising your own work, get in the habit of reading your essay out loud. Essay writers frequently skip over trouble areas when reading silently, because their minds fill in gaps in the text and gloss over confusing areas: They read more into the words than what is actually there. Reading aloud, however, gives your ears a chance to catch what your eyes miss. If something is awkwardly phrased or out of place, you'll hear it right away. As an added measure, you can tape-record yourself reading the essay, so that you can play back the tape and focus exclusively on listening to the words.

Better yet, have a friend or family member read your essay out loud. When we read our own writing, we have a tendency to think, "Man, that sounds a lot like Ernest Hemingway!" When others read the same passages to us, however, we can tell that the passage is more reminiscent of the movie *Ernest Goes to Camp*.

GUERRILLA TACTIC

Trust Your Ear to Help You Edit

■ Get others to read your essay drafts to you out loud and listen closely for trouble areas that need reworking.

When others read your work, keep a notepad in front of you and listen for places in which phrases are out of sequence, confusing, or poorly worded. Take note of where the reader fumbles over words, has to reread sentences, or seems to get lost. Such occurrences can clue you in to sections that may need more work.

In general, never craft your scholarship essays in a vacuum. Instead, ask teachers and peers whose opinions you value to analyze the strengths and weaknesses of what you've written. Ask family members to contribute their ideas. Spending hours revising the same essay can cloud your eyes to mistakes that others won't miss. Listen to what they say and heed their advice as best you can. Recognize that even though your editors might not know how to *solve* a problem in your essay, they will likely be able to red-flag areas that are problematic or confusing. And remember: Never take criticism personally.

Always spell-check your essays, but don't rely on this process; the computer won't be able to detect words that are spelled correctly but used improperly.

▮ ADVICE FOR SPECIFIC TOPICS

In scholarship applications, a handful of essay topics are enduring favorites. In this section, I describe some common strategies that scholarship winners use to shine in these types of essays.

FUTURE CAREER ASPIRATIONS

In career aspiration essays, seek to demonstrate four main points. First, you want to show *why* you're interested in a particular career. For the most part, it doesn't matter which career you choose; scholarship judges want to know what is motivating you to follow this path. Next, you want to demonstrate that you've taken the time to consider *how* you're going to reach this career goal. Building a successful career takes patience and hard work. Judges want to see that you understand what's involved in accomplishing your goals.

A nice touch in career aspiration essays is to discuss how you plan to contribute or give something back to society through your future career.

Third, you should demonstrate any steps you've already taken to pursue the particular career. This provides added credibility to your career aspirations and shows that the interest is more than just a passing fad. Finally, you want to illustrate your potential to excel in the field. Demonstrating this potential often involves showing that you have already begun to exhibit the skills and abilities necessary to succeed in that specific field.

YOUR GREATEST ACHIEVEMENT

When scholarship judges ask you to discuss something that you have accomplished, the particulars of the accomplishment are only *half* the story they are interested in. They also want to know how *you* view your own achievements and what types of accomplishments are important to you.

Seek to explain not only *what* you did, but *why* you did it. Relate a sense of passion and enthusiasm to the application judges, and illustrate how this has fueled your impressive results. Be proud of your accomplishment, but avoid congratulating yourself repeatedly.

A PERSON YOU ADMIRE

Contrary to popular belief, this type of essay is really *not* about the person you happen to admire. It's actually about *you*. The type of person you admire is really a mirror reflection of the personal qualities and characteristics that you value most.

So don't just produce a report on a particular person. Explain why you think the individual's contributions are important. Discuss the qualities of the person that make him or her admirable, and show how you've have tried to emulate those qualities in your own life.

Be aware that historical figures like Gandhi, Martin Luther King Jr., and Abraham Lincoln are frequent choices. So if you choose a well-known figure, try to approach the essay in a creative way. Otherwise, pick someone specific to your own life—someone you know others won't choose.

SOLVING A PRESSING ISSUE

Issue-oriented questions often focus on current events, policy debates, and ethical questions. Write about an issue you care about. It's much easier to be persuasive when you're passionate about the topic.

Do outside research in newspapers, magazines, books, and websites, and demonstrate that you are knowledgeable about the subject and have more than a superficial understanding of the issue. In making your argument, don't oversimplify the debate. Even if you advocate one position, discuss other viewpoints and then show why your perspective makes more sense. Issues are rarely black and white, so be sure to acknowledge the gray areas, too.

If you have the option of choosing an issue, try to find subjects that you have some personal experience with, which will provide you with more personal ammunition for your argument. Avoid controversial issues (such as abortion) that could alienate a scholarship judge.

GROWTH EXPERIENCES

Essay questions focused on growth experiences ask you to write about an episode or event that has had a significant influence on the type of person you've become. The experience itself can be either positive or negative, but the key factor is describing what you've learned from the situation.

A particular experience need not necessarily be dramatic to be an effective growth experience. Don't make the mistake of trying to attach some huge symbolic significance to everyday events that seem pretty mundane. (Avoid sentences like "By eating that ham sandwich, I suddenly felt a heartfelt need to explore my spirituality.") Growth experiences, by their very nature, deal with personal qualities and characteristics, so try to work in references to some of the universal judging criteria we discussed in Chapter 6.

Growth-experience essays are good opportunities to explain any blemishes in your record, without having to do so directly. Show how past mistakes have been catalysts for personal growth, and avoid making excuses.

If your growth experience is an obstacle you've overcome, don't dwell on the obstacle itself for too long. The focus should not be on the problem you faced, but on the steps you have taken to overcome it.

■ SHORT ANSWER QUESTIONS

To respond to short answer questions (usually 150 words or less), your essay approach needs to be modified to take into account the very compact space you have to make your case. Although the general principles of *showing rather than telling* and *focusing on personal details* still apply, you have to use them in a modified organizational format.

When you write responses to short answer questions, there is rarely enough space to develop an introductory paragraph, as you would in a normal essay. Make your opening sentence more of a thesis statement that declares the main point of your response. Don't overload your response to a short answer question with too many major points. Prioritize your potential points, stick to one or two of the most important, and make sure you develop them adequately.

After presenting your main point, back it up with a couple of examples. You won't have space for an actual conclusion, but try to end on a poignant thought that supports or extends your main point. To give you an idea of what a solid organizational structure for a short answer question looks like, here's one of my winning responses from the semifinalist round of the Coca-Cola Scholars Program.

Question: Coca-Cola Scholars have been representative of the diverse economic, ethnic, and occupational backgrounds of families in the United States. Please describe any personal characteristics about yourself or your family that have been important to your development.

Growing up as a child of mixed descent, with an American father and a Thai mother, I have learned that this difference is more significant than its "face value." Given the privilege of seeing life through this

Notice how this short answer response highlights many of the personal qualities judges look for in scholarship winners. Rather than immodestly stating that I embody such qualities, I softened the tone by talking about how I came to learn such virtues and values.

dual-focus lens, I have been exposed to views and am able to formulate ideas from two distinct perspectives. Because Western and Asian cultures have different things to offer me—for example, the patience, perseverance, and strong work ethic from the East; and the creativity, pioneering attitude, and spirit of volunteerism from the West—I have tried hard to combine the best from both worlds. My parents have demonstrated to me the benefits of this special East-West synergy when analyzing complex situations, solving problems, and exchanging ideas. I have been taught how courage, faith, concentration, and determination—in combination with high ethical and moral values—can help me achieve my goals and realize my dreams.

CHAPTER 9 SUMMARY AND KEYWORDS

Show, Don't Tell: Instead of merely telling judges how good you are, show them with stories and anecdotes. This makes your essays more credible and memorable. ■

Personal Details: Relate the essay question to personal experiences and unique perspectives. Choose appropriate topics that facilitate this. ■

Organization: Structure essays for clarity and logic. If needed, fall back on the standard three-part organizational format (introduction, body, and conclusion). ■

Conciseness: Each sentence in an essay should serve an important purpose. Eliminate long transitional phrases and redundancy. Write first drafts 25 percent over the word limit, and then pare down the verbiage, while keeping main ideas intact. ■

Unique and Memorable: Craft each essay to stand out by including personal details and notable content or by expressing ideas in novel ways (such as the use of an extended metaphor). ■

Spanning Topics and Recycling Essays: Pick essay topics that bridge multiple essay questions. Combine elements from two or more essays to create a new essay. Recycle well-phrased passages, metaphors, and other creative expressions of your ideas. ■

Developing Your Voice: When it comes to scholarship essays, there is no such thing as a "right" answer. Find the answer and writing style that is right for you. ■

Writer's Block: Don't let a blank page intimidate you. To get in the flow, write nonstop for 20 minutes, consult other essays, converse with a friend, tape-record yourself speaking, change locations, or focus on manageable details. ■

Honing Your Essay: Rewriting is even more important than writing. Reassess ideas, and reevaluate how you communicate these points. Taking some time off after writing a first draft is helpful. Read essays out loud, and get others to do so. Ask friends, family, and teachers for critiques. ■

Advice on Specific Topics: Scholarship winners often employ common strategies for essays dealing with career aspirations, outstanding achievements, role models, solving problems, and growth experiences. Learn from what others have done.

Short Answer Questions: When required to respond in 150 words or less, follow a compact organizational format. Focus on one or two main points. ■

SCHOLARSHIPCOACH.COM KEYWORDS

For more information on a scholarship or topic mentioned in this chapter, enter the associated keyword in the keyword link box located in the Coach's Locker Room section of ScholarshipCoach.com.

Scholarship/Topic	Keyword
Century III Leaders Scholarship	CENTURY
Coca-Cola Scholars Program	COKE
Discover Card Tribute Awards	DISCOVER
Essay Critiques	ESSAY
Georgia-Pacific Foundation Community Scholarship	GEOPAC
Homework Helpline	HELPLINE
Optimist International Essay Contest	OPESSAY
Portland Trailblazers Scholarship	BLAZERS

Glowing Recommendation Letters

INSIDE THIS CHAPTER

▮ Developing a menu of recommendation letters

▮ How to cultivate a great recommendation

▮ Working with your recommendation writers

▮ Streamlining the workload

▮ What to look for in a top-notch letter

▮ In Search of Perfect Recommendations

Not many people know this, but my own search for the perfect scholarship recommendation letter led me on a journey to the far reaches of the globe. On one such occasion, I found myself among the towering peaks of the Himalayas, where I asked for advice from an old Tibetan wise man:

> *Me:* Excuse me, sir. Do you know where I can find the perfect recommendation letter?
>
> *Wise man:* Ah, my son, the first step of any journey is to find inner peace.
>
> *Me:* Well, can you tell me the way to inner peace, then?
>
> *Wise man:* Head down the mountain and take a right at the second traffic light. Keep going until you see a gas station on your right and a Starbucks on your left. You can't miss it. . . .

After thanking the wise man for his sage counsel, I tried to follow his directions, but unfortunately got lost along the way. Somewhere along my trip down the mountain, it occurred to me that perhaps a recommendation letter wasn't something that you find by the side of the road, but rather was a scholarship application component that required cultivating and nurturing, just like other parts of your application. I'm obviously no Tibetan wise man, but here are some insights that I've picked up on my own journey, as well as from the collective experience of many other scholarship winners.

▮ STAR WITNESSES

Think of the people who write your letters of recommendation as your star witnesses—very much like the ones in a courtroom trial. They are the folks who corroborate your story, testify on behalf of your character, and offer supporting evidence as to why you are worthy of each scholarship award.

Obtaining letters from these character witnesses can be either an extremely satisfying or a totally frustrating experience. It's a positive experience when recommenders say such glowing things about you that the words just seem to radiate off the page. But when you're handed recommendations that don't exactly put you in a good light or weren't crafted with much care, you can wind up in a dark mood indeed.

The crux of the problem is this: Letters of recommendation are the one element of your application that *you* don't fully control. You are dependent on others—people who may or may not have the time, energy, or skills to craft the support letters you need.

And make no mistake about it, *the quality of your letters of recommendation can make or break your chances of winning scholarships.* They carry such weight because they provide another magnifying glass for examining your personality, skills, and character. It's not that judges don't trust what *you* say. They just want more objective evidence that you are really as wonderful as you say you are.

▮ FIVE "GREAT RECOMMENDATION" ACTION STEPS

Although you don't have *direct* control over what people write, there are powerful action steps you can employ to ensure that you receive recommendations placing you in the best possible light.

Develop a List of Potential Recommendation Writers

The first action step along the path to a great recommendation letter is to develop a list of people who potentially could write you such letters. On this list, record how well each person knows you, in what context he or she knows you, and the aspects of your life each letter writer could likely highlight. Teachers, professors, school administrators, counselors, employers, coaches, activity advisers, as well as ministers, rabbis, and priests, are good recommendation prospects to include on this list.

A good relationship with an English or journalism teacher can lead to especially powerful letters because such faculty members generally possess strong writing skills.

But don't limit yourself to traditional sources either. If you're planning to pursue a particular career or field of study, think of ways to get recommendations from people who work in this field (such as your family doctor, if you hope to pursue a medical career). Be creative in your list of potential recommendation writers in other ways: One scholarship winner I interviewed, who tutored a fifth-grade student as part of a community service project, actually managed to get a letter of recommendation from the fifth grader himself—written in pencil! (The fifth grader wrote about how much the tutoring had helped and about how mentorship from the applicant had made a tremendous difference in his life.)

Try to put as many people on the list as you can. For the time being, don't worry too much about whether a person will provide you with a strong recommendation. These are just *prospective* letter writers—putting them on the list does not mean that you will actually request a recommendation. Besides, even if you do get a letter of recommendation that isn't so great, there's no scholarship statute that mandates you have to use it.

Seek to Accumulate Numerous Recommendations

It's important to understand that the best recommendation letters for one scholarship application are not necessarily the best for another.

"I had something like 30 recommendation letters and would choose the ones to use based on the criteria of the scholarship I was applying for. For some scholarships, I used science-focused recommendations, while for others I picked ones that stressed community service."

–Will Carson
Scholarship Winner
Palmer, AK

For a variety of reasons, a particular recommendation letter may not be as strong as you had expected. The recommendation writer could have been juggling other projects and may not have devoted the time it takes to craft a quality letter. Or perhaps he or she was in a bad mood when sitting down to write your letter. In other instances, an individual who thinks very highly of you may not possess the writing skills to effectively communicate this sentiment on paper.

Because of these factors, seek to obtain as many letters of recommendation as possible. Procuring more than enough recommendations provides insurance against those that are less glowing than anticipated. And because most scholarship applications want you to include recommendation letters *with* your other application materials (as opposed to many college applications that require them to be sealed by the writer), you will be able to read the letters and evaluate their strengths *before* sending them off.

In this way, getting plenty of letters provides you with a virtual menu of recommendation entrées to choose from. People who know you in different contexts will have different perspectives, and the more perspectives you can accumulate, the better. Having this menu also provides you with the ability to choose the *most appropriate* recommendation letter when custom-tailoring each scholarship application. You will be able to select recommendations that best address a particular scholarship's judging criteria, best complement the other materials you've prepared for the application, and best reinforce your major application themes.

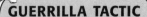

GUERRILLA TACTIC

Collect an Assortment of Recommendation Letters

■ Obtain more recommendations than you need, then pick and choose the best letters to include with each application.

If you don't have many individuals to ask for recommendations, don't worry: I'll show you how to cultivate new recommendation prospects in Action Step #3.

When choosing from this menu, I used certain recommendations over and over again, while others I included only in scholarship applications with specific types of judging criteria. Remember, it's always better to first request a recommendation letter, then decide later whether you want to submit it with a particular application. By doing this, you will be able to choose which letters are best to include with different scholarship packages. If you want to maximize your chances of winning, having this flexibility does make a difference.

ASK THE COACH #26

Can scholarship recommendation letters be used for college applications?

Absolutely. Developing this menu of scholarship recommendation letters becomes a big advantage for students who have not yet applied to college. Unlike submission guidelines for most scholarship recommendation letters (in which recommendations are generally submitted with the rest of the application materials), many college applications specify that recommendation letters be mailed separately by the recommendation writers (thereby decreasing your chances of reading them before they are sent off). Because your scholarship recommendation letters will likely become your college recommendation letters, however, developing a menu of scholarship recommendations provides you with the ability to pick and choose between letters you might not otherwise get to see. ■

Cultivate Relationships with Potential Recommenders

You will be able to request a recommendation letter right away from people who know you well in multiple contexts. For potential recommendation writers who don't know you as intimately, you will want to get to know them better before you ask them for a letter.

I call this process *cultivating* a recommendation, and it's important for several reasons: First, there's a big difference between a *passable* recommendation and a *great* one. As I explain later in this chapter, only people who know you well can write you great recommendation letters that are truthful. Because of this, cultivating a great recommendation is well worth the wait.

Second, once someone has written you a recommendation, it's more difficult to get him or her to update or enhance it. So you don't want to have someone write it too soon—before he or she has a chance to learn all the wonderful things about you. Of course, if you need a recommendation for an application right away, you won't have time to cultivate a new relationship with a potential letter writer. But if you work steadily at developing a menu of recommendation letters, your scholarship fate won't hang on the quality of a letter that is less complimentary than you would like.

The process of letter cultivation is especially important if you aren't able to list bunches of people who you're certain would write you strong recommendations. By following

Some applications give you the option of submitting additional recommendations, beyond the number required. If you have enough strong letters (don't settle for mediocre ones), then submit the extra letters.

some simple guidelines, however, you will be able to transform nonexistent recommendation letters into solid ones and mediocre recommendations into glowing testaments to your ability.

So how does one cultivate a great recommendation letter? You do it by getting to know a potential recommender in a more in-depth context. If you're seeking a letter from a particular teacher or professor, you might, for instance, participate in the extracurricular activities or school committees he or she advises or oversees. Or you could serve as a teaching assistant (which usually means helping grade papers) or lab aide for the teacher or professor. Or perhaps it's as simple as regularly asking questions and meeting after class or during office hours. There are countless possibilities.

For others in your school—principals, counselors, department heads, headmasters, or deans—make a point of getting to know them. Regularly ask for advice and sign up for appointments. Remember, these individuals are powerful allies to have in your quest for scholarship money.

For recommenders outside the school environment, the process is much the same. If you hope to get a recommendation letter from the coordinator of a community service program you volunteer for, perhaps you want to first take on added responsibilities for the program. If you plan to get a recommendation from an employer, go the extra mile to make sure that you perform your job above and beyond what is expected.

Cultivating a recommendation isn't about putting on a show so someone will write nice things about you. It's about giving someone the opportunity to learn more about you—thus gaining a better understanding of your personality, talents, skills, and character. And who knows, this might even lead to a mentoring relationship and other opportunities that can change your life.

In college, I served as a student representative on an academic committee made up of mostly history professors. My duties consisted of showing up at lunch meetings, eating excellent food, offering a few opinions, and getting to know the professors (and them to know me) much better.

Valuable by-products of this cultivation process are the new friends you make and all the interesting new things you learn.

Communicate Effectively with Letter Writers

For a moment, pretend that you are a trial lawyer in the midst of a big case. Your ace in the hole—a star witness—is scheduled to take the stand. Would you put this witness on the stand without prepping him first? Of course not.

And just as in this courtroom scenario, you wouldn't want your letter of recommendation writers to "testify" without preparing them first. No, you can't give them a script of exactly what to say. But you *can* give them some talking points to mention, and thus you can substantially influence what is written.

Savvy scholarship seekers help guide their recommendation writers by providing them with written summaries of their activities, achievements, awards and honors, and goals. A lot of this information can simply be copied from other components of the application or from other applications you've completed. In your summaries, only include résumé material that you want recommenders to address, since they may quote information directly from these sheets. Don't overwhelm your recommenders with pages and pages of information. As a rule, I always tried to keep these summaries to a maximum of three pages. Any more than this, and the recommender might opt not to read the material thoroughly.

Communicating to your recommenders the application themes developed in Chapter 5 is critical. That way they can mention points in their letters that will reinforce your theme.

To the front of this summary attach a cover letter. This letter is your opportunity to tell the recommendation writer about the focus of the scholarship program, the application theme you are developing (which you would like her to help reinforce), and any specific points you hope she will mention. Think of this cover letter as the equivalent of driving directions: You can give the recommendation writers a roadmap of where you need them to go, but the actual choice of how fast to go, where to take rest stops, and what radio station to listen to along the way is up to them.

The key is to do this *tactfully*. Express your deep gratitude for the help. Don't make it seem as though you're *telling* someone what to write. Instead, you're just trying to provide your recommendation writer with enough information to make the job easier and less time-consuming.

All the recommendation writers I have encountered were appreciative of the cover letters and summaries because the items helped jog their memories of what I had done, informed them of achievements they hadn't been aware of, gave them a better idea of what type of letters the scholarship judges were looking for, and made the process of writing a personalized recommendation much easier. (Recommendation writers find it intimidating, not to mention time-consuming, to stare at a blank page, too!) You should include information on:

Taking the time to write good cover letters demonstrates to your recommendation writers that you are putting a lot of time and care into your applications. And when they witness you treating your own materials with care, they will feel a responsibility to do the same.

▌ How to address the letter (if it's not simply, "To whom it may concern"),

▌ The date you need to receive the letter by,

▌ Any directions specified by the application (such as when a particular scholarship requests that the writer comment on "your ability to work with others").

To give you an idea of what this letter might look like, I've included a sample recommendation cover letter for a fictional scholarship on the following pages. If you're short on time, you can simply substitute your own personal information and scholarship-specific facts into this template.

SAMPLE RECOMMENDATION COVER LETTER

Dear Ms. Thompson,

Thank you again for agreeing to write me a recommendation letter. As I mentioned in our conversation, your recommendation letter is part of a scholarship application I'm submitting to the Student Excellence Scholarship Awards—a scholarship program that seems designed to recognize someone just like me. The program seeks to award scholarships of varying amounts to students who exhibit excellence in extracurricular activities.

In my application materials, one of the important areas I'm highlighting is my leadership responsibilities and skills and how such duties and abilities have had a positive impact on my school and community. As my student government adviser, I thought you would be an excellent person to comment on these aspects of my extracurricular involvement. Of special interest to the Student Excellence Scholarship Awards are activities and projects such as:

> *Separating out as bullet points the specific examples you want mentioned in the letter subtly communicates to the recommendation writer to pay special attention to these key points.*

- the community food and clothing drive I have helped organize for the past three years
- the student government fundraising program I recently initiated, which has already raised more than $9,000 for school-sponsored clubs
- my representation of our school on the city youth violence task force

The application materials also request that you comment upon the personal qualities I have exhibited through such projects.

> *To make sure that your recommendation writer hasn't forgotten about your letter, use the following memory jogger: About a week after you've submitted the cover letter, ask your recommender if he or she needs any additional information or has any questions for you.*

As additional background information, I've attached a list of my extracurricular projects, with the ones directly related to student government in boldface. Since the deadline for postmarking materials is December 5, it would be great if I could pick up your recommendation letter (for inclusion with the rest of my application) two weeks from this Wednesday. Your letter can be addressed to the "Student Excellence Scholarship Awards Judging Committee."

Once again, thank you so much for all your time and energy spent in writing me this recommendation. I really appreciate your efforts to help in my quest to secure much-needed scholarship funds, and I am especially grateful for all the help and guidance you have shown me during the year. If you have any questions, feel free to contact me at 555-1234.

Sincerely,

Ivana Winn

Communicating effectively with your recommendation writers enables you to take advantage of a loophole in the requirements of many scholarship applications. Letters of recommendation, unlike essays or extracurricular activity lists, rarely have length limitations. So if there wasn't any room elsewhere in an application to mention an activity or award, I would ask my recommendation writers to include these "selling points" in their letters. This allowed me to bypass application space limitations and work in an extra plug or two.

Minimize the Work for Recommendation Writers

When you are applying for many scholarships, it can create a lot of extra work for your recommendation writers. Let's say, for instance, that throughout the year you will be using a particular recommendation letter in about 10 to 15 different applications. This means that you're going to need to get 10 to 15 copies printed, with slight modifications made to each version to meet the specific demands and requirements of each scholarship. If specific references are made to the scholarship's name in the header or body of the letter, you'll need to get those changed, too. And all this has to get done in time to meet each scholarship's deadline.

As you can see, all these tasks would involve a lot of repetitive work for your recommendation writers. To minimize work for them, suggest to your recommendation writers that they give you an electronic copy of their letter on disk (and provide you with some letterhead or stationery, if they use it). Then *you* can be the one to print out each copy and make sure that references to the scholarship's name are correct. Once you've done this, you'll be able to hand the recommendation writer a printout of the customized letter, ready for a final look-over and signature. Doing this not only helps out your recommendation writers, but also serves the added function of giving *you* the control to make sure that new copies of letters are done properly and completed on time.

GUERRILLA TACTIC

Capture Recommendations on Disk

■ Get electronic copies of recommendation letters on disk to reduce the burden on recommendation writers and to gain more control over obtaining additional copies.

Try to anticipate in advance which applications are suitable for the reuse of a particular recommendation letter. That way you can include briefings on several upcoming scholarships in one cover letter, and have the recommendation writer include additional information that may not be needed for immediate applications, but that will be necessary for later ones.

Making small changes and additions to a recommendation letter to fit new applications actually helps to refine the letter—almost as if you were editing it. I discovered that after a few of these small alterations were made, good recommendations could become great ones.

When this isn't possible, you will need to get your recommendation writers to make small changes, additions, and adaptations to their basic letter to fit each scholarship. To do this, write another cover letter and ask them to add comments on a particular area requested by the new judging criteria. To make things even easier on your recommenders, attach a copy of their previous recommendation letter and suggest that they make changes and additions in red pen. Then you can be the one to type the changes into the letter, obtain a printout, and take it to them for a signature.

There may be times, however, when you need changes on such short notice that you may have to employ other quick-response strategies. In the case of one scholarship contest, for instance, I found out about it only the night before the application was due. I was scrambling to put together an application, and I wanted to use a particular recommendation letter, except that it didn't comment upon some key areas specifically requested by the application materials. So I called up the recommendation writer and politely informed him of the situation. He suggested that I ask him over the phone any additional questions the application posed, take down his responses, add them to recommendation letter myself, and bring him a copy to review and sign in the morning. (What a guy!) I took him up on the generous offer and ended up winning the scholarship. I later used this technique when rushing to meet impending deadlines of other scholarship programs.

If an upcoming application requires a nomination statement (generally 150 words or less), approach someone who has already written you a strong recommendation, and ask if you can assemble this statement by stringing together key passages from a previous letter.

So if you're rushing to meet a deadline and need modifications made to a recommendation letter on short notice, tactfully suggest to the recommendation writer that you interview him or her in person or over the phone. Explain that you could take down his or her answers verbatim and insert the comments in appropriate places in the existing letter. The recommendation writer then has an opportunity to read the changes (and make any additional modifications) before signing off on the copy.

The great thing about this approach is that it works whether or not your recommendation writers decide to go along with the interview method. Since you've tactfully informed them of the impending deadlines—while being considerate of the burden this places on their time—some of them may very well offer to make the necessary modifications themselves.

Keep in mind that mounting a major scholarship campaign means that you will need the help of your recommendation writers over and over again. The best way to garner this help is to be courteous and appreciative. Try to plan ahead and give your recommenders *at least two to three weeks' notice before you need the letters*. And just as your mother always told you, be sure to make a habit of writing thank-you notes. Writing recommendation letters isn't part of anyone's job description, and people are doing so out of the kindness of their hearts, their belief in your potential, and their desire to help.

▌ QUALITIES OF A GREAT LETTER

A fashionmonger knows the difference between secondhand clothing and an Armani suit. A sports-memorabilia collector knows the difference between a washed-out signature and a mint-condition autograph. Similarly, as a recommendation-letter aficionado, you need to be able to tell the difference between a run-of-the-mill recommendation letter and a truly outstanding one. Understanding what separates a glowing letter of recommendation from all the rest helps you to make better decisions when choosing which letter to include with a particular application. This understanding also assists you in cultivating recommendations and in communicating more effectively with your recommendation writers.

Too many students include in scholarship applications recommendations from individuals who don't know them well enough to comment in depth on their personal qualities. When a letter of recommendation is basically nothing more than a form letter, judges can see right through it. Statements like "Bob is a valued member of the class" or "Mary shows great promise"—without any specifics to back up these statements—come across as empty, shallow phrases.

Great recommendation letters, on the other hand, are so specific, detailed, and personal that they could be meant only for you. Often they include revealing stories or anecdotes that illustrate how you've exhibited certain positive qualities. References to specific incidents and occasions make your recommendations seem more genuine and memorable. To see this in action, let's examine an excerpt from a recommendation by my high school journalism adviser:

Merely stating that I was a good reporter would have had a limited effect on application judges. But my adviser backed up this statement by citing a specific example that illustrated the point.

As a reporter and editor, Ben continually took complicated, difficult issues, researched them thoroughly, interviewed numerous sources, and wrote clear articles appropriate for his readership. For example, Ben covered the school reorganization that has been mandated on the state level by House Bill 3565. Even educators had trouble understanding and analyzing the complex information and how it should be applied to their respective schools. Ben, after reading numerous documents most students would resist digging into, attended faculty information sessions after school, interviewed key people in the school and the district, and wrote a series of clear, comprehensive articles.

So that you can appreciate the power of anecdotes in another style of letter, I've reprinted part of a letter written by my longtime tennis coach, discussing an event that occurred when I first started playing tennis at age ten:

My tennis coach could have said simply that I have a strong work ethic on the court. This anecdote, however, illustrated the point much more vividly.

Ben had been playing tennis only for three months when he entered his first tournament. My employer warned me that Ben would lose handily in the tournament and advised me to prepare him for the worst. Throughout the tournament, I watched Ben run down hundreds of balls with unwavering concentration. When the smoke cleared, Ben took home the championship trophy. This accomplishment was incredible, but the thing that astonished me most was how this victory caused Ben to work harder, instead of being satisfied with his great accomplishment.

Finally, great recommendation letters distinguish themselves by making bold statements that application judges know are not written for just anyone. My student government adviser, for instance, wrote the following in a recommendation letter for a leadership-related scholarship program:

I also recycled this letter for the Washington Crossing Foundation Scholarship, a program focused on government service.

I have taught in Oregon's schools for more than thirty years and served a couple of terms in the Oregon legislature, and I can say unequivocally to you that I've not seen a better candidate for this type of scholarship.

Now contrast the above recommendations with an excerpt from another teacher's letter in my scholarship file that wasn't nearly as compelling:

Ben dutifully completes his homework, pays attention in class, and is an active participant in class discussions. He is an asset to the class and has a bright future ahead.

The difference is like night and day. The first three recommendations—the ones from my journalism adviser, tennis coach, and student government adviser—mention revealing examples or include high praise. The last one makes broad, general statements that could describe plenty of other students as well. When it came down to crunch time, I used the first three recommendations for numerous scholarship applications, but didn't use the last one at all.

FAMOUS ISN'T ALWAYS BETTER

Of course, you can always request these "big-name" support letters just to see how they turn out. But don't count on a great result.

Some scholarship applicants make the mistake of going out of their way to include recommendations from famous or well-known people. One scholarship applicant I know, for instance, pulled some strings to get a recommendation letter from the governor of his state! The letter he received, however, lacked specifics (as the governor hadn't spent much time with him) and was filled with political statements that seemed to better highlight the governor's campaign for reelection.

Don't fall into the trap of submitting impersonal recommendation letters. They won't help your scholarship cause. Your best bet for strong recommendation letters is people who know you well. The content of the letter itself is far more important than whose signature appears on the last line.

CHAPTER 10 SUMMARY AND KEYWORDS

Make a List: Develop a list of prospects to write recommendation letters. Teachers, professors, school administrators, counselors, employers, coaches, activity advisers, as well as ministers, rabbis, and priests, are good candidates. Try to think of creative and nontraditional sources for recommendation letters as well. ■

Compile a Menu of Letters: Obtain as many letters of recommendation as possible from individuals who know you in a wide range of contexts. Use this menu of letters to custom-tailor application support materials. ■

College Admissions: Recommendations gathered for scholarship applications may also be used for college applications. You can pick and choose your best letters. ■

Cultivate Relationships: Cultivate deeper relationships with potential recommendation writers. Allow them to learn more about your personality, talents, skills, and character. ■

Communicate Effectively: Provide a recommendation writer with a written summary of your activities, achievements, awards and honors, and goals. Attach a tactful cover letter that explains the focus of the scholarship application, your thematic approach, and any special points that should be mentioned. ■

Get Electronic Files: Obtain copies of recommendation letters on disk. Print out copies and obtain signatures as needed. ■

Ask for Modifications: To fit the demands of particular contests, ask your best recommenders for small modifications to their standard letters. Do whatever is necessary to minimize their increased work. ■

Recognize Outstanding Recommendations: The best recommendation letters include stories, anecdotes, bold statements, and other compelling details. Seek out and identify such letters to maximize your chances of winning scholarship awards. ■

SCHOLARSHIPCOACH.COM KEYWORDS

For more information on a scholarship or topic mentioned in this chapter, enter the associated keyword in the keyword link box located in the Coach's Locker Room section of ScholarshipCoach.com.

Scholarship/Topic	*Keyword*
Washington Crossing Foundation Scholarship	WASHCROSS

Filling in the Blanks

INSIDE THIS CHAPTER

▮ Tips for the application form

▮ Perfecting extracurricular activity lists

▮ Highlighting your awards and honors

▮ Working extra information into your transcript

▮ Submitting supplementary materials

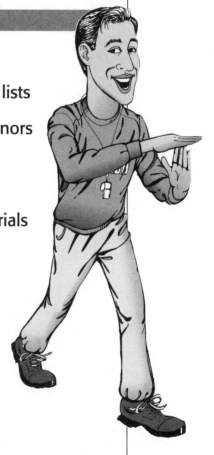

▮ PAPERWORK PROWESS

We've researched. We've strategized. We've got killer essays and glowing recommendation letters up our sleeves, too. Now it's time to actually fill out all those pesky scholarship application forms. This may sound like as much fun as having all your wisdom teeth pulled, but if you understand what you're doing, and why you're doing it, you'll pull through just fine.

The goal of this section is to show you how to whip all those questions, lines, boxes, and blanks into tip-top shape. In the section below, I discuss some practical considerations in filling out forms; later in the chapter you'll learn strategies and guerrilla tactics for submitting stat sheets, extracurricular activity lists, awards and honors summaries, transcripts, and supplementary materials.

Make Plenty of Copies

As a rule, the first thing you want to do is to make multiple copies of the original scholarship application form. You will want to keep at least one copy on hand for a practice run, in which you will fill in all the blanks in pencil, while planning your responses. Additional copies should be kept as backups for the inevitable tears, typos, smudging, and last-minute editing that always occur. So befriend your local Kinko's worker—this is definitely not the time to skimp on those seven-cent photocopies.

Type Your Application

Scholarship applications should be typed—whether on a computer or a typewriter. No matter how many gold stars you received in elementary school penmanship class, handwritten applications still look tacky and are hard to read.

For many scholarship applications, you'll have to fit at least some of the requested information in blanks on the preprinted application form itself, so you may want to drag that old typewriter out of the closet. If you decide to get a little high-tech, you can scan the form into the computer and then "type" into the blanks. Otherwise, enter your responses on a computer in your favorite word-processing program, print them out, then cut and paste them by hand into the proper spaces. Make a photocopy of the completed form to send off in the mail. (This makes the application look neat, keeps the glued responses from falling off, and most important, prevents your application from looking like a ransom note.)

Attach Additional Sheets When Possible

Like the board game Monopoly, scholarship application forms have a limited amount of real estate. Many applications do allow you to attach additional sheets of paper to the forms if the space provided is not adequate. If the scholarship administrators permit you to add additional sheets (you may have to ask), definitely take them up on the offer.

For lengthier application components like extracurricular activity lists, I would simply write "please see attached sheets" directly on the application form. Then I would include the lists exclusively on my own self-attached sheets.

Attaching additional sheets allows you to bypass the built-in limits and constraints of the forms themselves. Furthermore, because you complete and save these additional sheets on your own computer in a format that *you* (not the scholarship administrators) specify, you will easily be able to reuse, adapt, and print out old submissions from other applications, with minimal work.

Don't Leave Spaces Blank

On applications that require you to use the forms provided, you will be prompted to include lists of extracurricular activities, awards and honors, and other data in pre-formatted spaces. As a general rule, avoid leaving any spaces blank, if possible. Leaving spaces blank gives the impression that you don't have enough credentials to meet the demands of the form. Instead, you want to leave the impression that you have many more credentials than could possibly fit in the space provided.

What do you do if a form has spaces for a listing of ten activities, but you can think of only seven? And what if your seventh "activity" was such a s-t-r-e-t-c-h that it actually involved watching late-night reruns of *The Brady Bunch* while munching on potato-like snack foods? Try the following guerrilla tactic: Add more detail and significantly more description to *each* activity you have listed. (And drop the seventh activity altogether.) By doing this, you can get rid of the extra white space and expand upon your strongest areas.

GUERRILLA TACTIC

Expand Activity Descriptions to Fill Blank Space

■ If you don't have enough credentials to fill up a form, expand the descriptions of what you do have and add more detail to your most compelling achievements.

To see this technique in action, let's presume that you have the following activity listed on your preliminary activity list:

Volunteered for local congressional campaign.

To expand upon this item—and take up an extra line or two—you could write the following instead:

Volunteered for local congressional campaign. Spearheaded voter registration drive at five area college campuses and helped organize a team of four student volunteers.

This not only helps fill up some of the blank space, but it is also more unique and memorable. The key is that you *don't* want to add meaningless material just to fill in the blanks. Consider leftover space on an application form an opportunity to flesh out your existing credentials and make them more persuasive and compelling.

Trimming the Fat

Sometimes on a very compact application form, you have the opposite problem: If you're given only very limited space, it's hard to fit in a lot of compelling information. To combat this problem, you'll need to eliminate information that isn't 100 percent essential. You can do this by getting right to the meat of the information (or tofu, if you are a vegetarian) and getting rid of the fat. On an application with unlimited space, you might have written:

As vice president of the Service Club, I was in charge of organizing a special community auction to raise funds for the local Meals on Wheels program.

But on a compact application, instead write:

Service Club (vice president). Organized charity auction.

For especially compact spaces, try separating items in a list with semicolons and using parentheses to briefly mention important details:

Service Club (VP); JV Basketball (captain); Science Olympics (Physics Bowl winner); School Newspaper (sports editor).

Save Each Draft and Revision

Always save every draft and revision that you complete. When you are revising something on the computer, don't save on top of the old version. Instead, create a new file with a slightly modified name. It's also a good idea to include the date as part of the modified file name (such as "essay_may1") so that you can tell months later which version is the most recent. Be sure to file away old printouts, notes, and other printed or written material in an accessible place.

Taking these steps serves two important purposes. First, it provides a safety net in case you accidentally delete material or decide that you actually prefer an old revision of a piece to a rewritten version. Second, keeping all your intermediary work facilitates your reusability and recycling efforts. Some early draft that didn't quite work for a particular application might be a good starting point for a different scholarship program.

■ THE STAT SHEET

The "stat sheet" is the part of the application where you fill in basic information such as your name, address, graduation date, information about your school, names of recommendation writers, career interests, majors, degrees, and so on. For applications that take into account academics, you may also be asked to supply your GPA, class rank, or test scores.

Stat sheets are fairly self-explanatory, but I'll offer two quick tips, since I've filled out dozens of them. First, search through the stat sheet right away for any signatures that may be required. Some applications require signatures of recommendation writers, nominating teachers, principals, professors, or department heads; I can remember overlooking such details and having to run around trying to track down people the day before an application was due.

Second, make sure that all the information on the stat sheet matches or is consistent with what is contained in all the other application components (especially things like your career interest or grade-point average). This sounds simple enough, but it can get confusing when you're filling out multiple applications simultaneously and highlighting different aspects of your record for each application.

■ ACTIVITY LISTS

Compiling extracurricular activity lists represents a prime opportunity to reap the benefits of reusability and recycling. Because most scholarships generally expect these lists in the same general format, you'll be able to customize lists that you have already submitted elsewhere to fit the demands of new applications.

You can do this in one of two ways. You can choose the extracurricular list format of an upcoming scholarship application, and after completing this submission, modify the format to fit the requirements of subsequent applications. The method that saves more time in the long run, however, is to create your own master extracurricular activities list that contains the full range of information any scholarship application is likely to request.

To create your master list, I suggest developing a format that includes the following categories: activity name, brief activity description (including your specific contribution to the activity), activity-related awards and honors, offices or positions held in the activity, and hours per week spent on the extracurricular endeavor. You can format this list in a word processor like Microsoft Word or in a graphics layout program like Adobe Pagemaker.

After creating the basic format, it's time to start filling in the information. Begin by pulling out information from the personal inventory lists you created in Chapter 8. When you created these lists, however, the goal was just to keep track of all of your potential scholarship résumé items. To add them to the master extracurricular activity list, you need to convert these notes into "résumé speak." To do this, use words that convey action, responsibility, and leadership—words like *organized, managed, coordinated, led, founded, recruited, achieved, spearheaded,* and *represented.* You don't want to say something that isn't true, but like with any résumé, you want to put your record in the best possible light.

For students already in college or graduate school, the demands of your current coursework exceed what was expected of you during high school. You may be doing important class-related projects that can be included on these activity lists. For instance, as part of my statistics class in college, I did an independent statistical analysis of professional basketball. As a bonus, I won an award from the professor for my analytical report. This project and award could be included as an activity in its own right on scholarship application forms.

Look for simple ways to expand a paper or research project that you did for class into a full-fledged activity that can be included on scholarship application activity lists.

If you have accumulated a long string of activities on your master list, you may want to group particular types of activities together to make it easier for the judges to make sense of all the information. On my own high school extracurricular activity lists, I grouped together, in separate categories, the types of activities I wanted to emphasize most: the ones related to journalism, leadership, and community service.

Ranking Your Activities

While the phrase "save the best for last" has become a clichéd expression, this is definitely a sentiment that does *not* apply to scholarship application activity lists. The spot of highest visibility in an activity list is at the *top of the list.* Since application judges review piles of submissions, there is no guarantee that they will thoroughly read all your meticulously crafted listings. They will, however, read the items that come first.

Because of this, you should rank your activities in order of importance, with the top of the list reserved for activities you definitely want judges to notice. What criteria should you use to determine what's most important? Here are the characteristics of activities that should be highlighted near the top of your list:

▮ Activities that are directly related to application themes you frequently use,

▮ Activities that you initiated or founded,

▮ Activities in which you hold a title or position of responsibility, and

▮ Activities in which you have made a special contribution (be sure to note this contribution in a few words).

Keep in mind that this pecking order on your master list is not an absolute one—just your best guess on where your activities stack up against one another. You'll modify the order of extracurricular activities to fit the strategic considerations of each scholarship program.

Customizing Your Master List

Once you've created your master list of activities, an ongoing task will be to customize this list to fit each new contest. This means re-ranking and reordering the listings, modifying the format to fit each application's guidelines, and eliminating some listings to fit the space limitations.

First, you need to take into account your application theme and place activities that mesh well with this theme at or near the top of your extracurricular list. Second, after using the "application detective" packaging techniques described in Chapter 6, you will want to place certain activities higher in your list—activities that have special relevance to the scholarship's definition of the ideal applicant. Finally, make a decision to highlight or eliminate any category of information that isn't specifically requested by the scholarship program. For instance, if an application doesn't request information on how many hours per week you devoted to an activity, include it only if it helps your cause.

If you need to trim your list to fit space requirements, start by eliminating activities near the bottom of your master list. Be sure, however, to leave in enough variety of activities to illustrate your general well-roundedness.

■ Awards and Honors Lists

In putting together awards and honors lists, many of the same strategies used in compiling extracurricular activities apply. Start out by using the personal inventory information you've been collecting to create a master list. Some of these items can be culled from the awards and honors segment of your master activity list. Be aware, however, that when awards and honors are treated as a separate component, you should also include awards and honors that aren't associated with any particular activity (such as if you're selected for the honor roll or dean's list).

To rank your awards and honors, first list those that are most impressive. How do you decide what's most impressive? Just try to imagine which awards and honors your mother and grandmother would be likely to brag about to their friends. (Note: The so-called "Clean Underwear Award" doesn't count.) Typically the most prestigious awards would be ones that involve national or state recognition. Follow that up with any local or regional awards that are prized in your community or academic/professional environment.

If you're short on awards that you can cite, remember that an award doesn't have to mean that you received a shiny gold-colored trophy or wood-like wall plaque. Try thinking of recognition in broader terms—such as if your fellow Investment Club members "honored" you by selecting you to be vice president. Just being *nominated* for an award or scholarship can be considered an honor. Even if you didn't win a U.S. Senate Youth Program Scholarship or Harry S. Truman Scholarship, for instance, you could write that your school nominated you as a candidate for the award.

Sometimes there are awards for "most improved student" that can cancel out less-than-stellar grades early on in your high school or college career.

Include details about the selectivity and significance of the award if it puts the award in a more impressive context. For instance, if your high school or college selects only one individual to receive its "outstanding student award," make the judges aware of that fact. However, if practically everyone with a pulse (and a few people without one) gets the award, keep this information to yourself. You should also add explanations for any awards and honors that will not be clearly understood from the titles alone.

Once again, when customizing this information for particular scholarships, take into account any packaging considerations as you decide what awards and honors to highlight. Any awards in areas dealing directly with the particular judging criteria should be placed at or near the top of your list.

If a scholarship requests *both* an extracurricular activity list and an awards and honors list, there are a few additional considerations. To sidestep any space limitations in the awards-and-honors section, you could include activity-related awards with your extracurricular activity list. You should avoid too much redundancy between the two lists, except in those areas that you want to stress (such as areas dealing with your theme).

■ THE TRANSCRIPT

Many scholarship seekers assume that a school transcript is an application component that one can't affect or shape, short of getting better grades. I've discovered, however, that this is far from the truth. You *can* impact your transcript because transcripts contain—or potentially can contain—more than just a record of your grades.

Here's how to do it: At some high schools and colleges, students are allowed to include lists of their awards and honors within the official transcript. (Sometimes a brief extracurricular activity summary can be included, too.) Usually, this information is included on a secondary page of the transcript, apart from the standard course and grades summary. In most cases, however, this information doesn't just get automatically listed there as your grades do; you typically have to submit the information yourself. Most students aren't aware that this is possible. So inquire with your registrar about whether there is anything like this included in your school's transcript. Request a sample official transcript to see for yourself.

Even if it isn't standard policy at your school (it wasn't at mine), you can still use this strategy—you just need to get permission to include the extra information from the powers that be. My high school principal gave me permission to have listed as part of my official transcript a special two-page addendum describing honors and awards I had received in both school- and community-related activities. Moreover, I was allowed to format this list of awards and honors, print out a copy, and provide a copy to the registrar. As the year progressed and I accumulated some additional awards and honors (especially scholarships I won), I updated my awards list and submitted the latest version for inclusion with my transcript. It gave me a big advantage.

The inclusion of this addendum allows scholarship applicants to circumvent space limitations imposed on the rest of the application and places special emphasis on their most compelling achievements. Even in applications that don't specifically request this kind of information, you can't be faulted for including it—after all, *it is part of your school's official transcript*. In applications that limit you to compact spaces for awards-and-honors information, you're not accountable for your addendum's length or detail because each school has its unique transcript format. Because the entire transcript is authenticated with the school seal, having it included in your transcript serves the added purpose of reinforcing the credibility of what you say.

GUERRILLA TACTIC

Append School Transcripts with Extra Information

■ To sidestep space limitations and highlight your most compelling achievements, include an awards-and-honors addendum as part of your school transcript.

So take the initiative to ask your principal and registrar about the possibility of including some support information as an addendum to your transcript. Explain in a tactful way that students at some schools are allowed to do this, and that it provides them with strategic advantages. Remember, in the eyes of your school administrators, you are one of *their* students; they want to do what they can to help *you* succeed and make your school look good in the process.

Home School

ASK THE COACH #27

How can homeschoolers submit grade transcripts to scholarship contests?

Your mission—should you choose to accept it—is to communicate your *nontraditional* education and level of achievement in *traditional* terms that the rest of the world can use to compare you with other students. In short, you must become a master linguist of "educationese" by creating your own transcript.

As a homeschooler, you should start your transcript with the equivalent of first-year high school courses. Keep in mind that a transcript is not limited to rigid textbook learning. You can adapt it to whatever method you and your parents have been using—but your parents face the task of attaching credits and grades to your work, as well as calculating GPAs. Can it be done in a way that doesn't look biased? That is your greatest challenge.

One thing that should make the task easier is the knowledge that there is no standard look to this quasi-official document. There are so many different ways that public and private high schools design a transcript that your homemade work of educational art (if done with care) can look appropriate and impressive. To produce your own transcript, obtain sample transcripts from as many traditional schools as you can in your area (you can get them from the schools themselves or from students who attend them), and use these transcripts as models to design your form. You will want to think up a name for your school (one that identifies it as a home school, of course), and create, if you have artistic talents, a school seal or logo.

When you are preparing the content for your transcript, keep in mind that it needs to list your courses under names that are acceptable for high school classes in your state. Try your state's Board of Education to get an official list. Make sure that the front page of your transcript is easy to read and that the name of the parent who is serving as principal or primary teacher is printed (since the transcript will have to be signed). You may also want to consider placing greater attention on course descriptions than the average school transcript, because descriptions can add credibility to the specific things you are learning or projects that you are completing as a homeschooled student. ■

Are Test Scores Included?

You can exert some influence over another aspect of your transcript, too. To do this, choose whether to include any standardized-test scores that you have taken. This information may be kept as part of your school's official records, but it is often segmented into a separate section of the transcript that may or may not be included when you request a transcript for scholarship organizations or college applications. So the first step is to find out whether your school specifically includes these types of test scores on a secondary page of your transcript.

Keep in mind that such test scores aren't limited to just PSATs, SATs, ACTs, GREs (graduate school), LSATs (law school), or the like. Schools generally keep records on how you have performed on SAT II subject tests, Advanced Placement (AP) exams, and state assessment tests. My high school automatically included all these scores on page two of my transcript.

Once you know whether test information is included, you can lobby your principal or registrar to include or not include this information in your transcripts for scholarships. If you have received stellar scores, you'll obviously want this information included. Then even when scholarships don't request test score information, the judges will still see your high marks.

On the other hand, if your scores are nothing to write home about, you'll want to keep this information out of your transcript. Be aware that some high schools have more rigid policies when transcripts are mailed directly to colleges as part of admissions applications. You can, of course, argue that a particular scholarship organization requesting a transcript is only interested in your grade information and isn't entitled to see your test scores. So explain your particular situation, and school officials may give you more leeway.

■ ADDITIONAL MATERIALS

If a scholarship application allows you the option of sending additional supplementary materials, then do so—assuming you have something worthwhile to send. Many students can substantially strengthen their applications by including writing samples, artwork portfolios, music recordings, and other examples of their work. This is especially useful if your application theme specifically deals with your talent in one of these areas. If you have any, you might also consider sending news clippings about yourself (even if they are just from the school newspaper).

If you do submit something, however, make sure that whatever it is has relevance to the scholarship you're applying for and is indeed impressive. (Scholarship application judges don't need to see your baby pictures, no matter how cute or cuddly you may have been.) Talk to your teachers, coaches, or instructors in specific areas to help you pick which samples to include, and don't go overboard with pages and pages of extra stuff. Instead, pick a few exemplary samples of your work. In general, refrain from including things like photocopies of award certificates. These only take up space and can annoy some application judges.

Some scholarship programs—especially smaller, local ones—might not specifically state that you can submit samples of your work, but if you call and ask, they may permit you to do so. If a scholarship form exhibits flexible rules and formatting guidelines, then it may be acceptable to include a few pages of supplementary material, even without specifically asking permission. You'll have to evaluate each situation carefully.

▌ MAILING YOUR APPLICATION

If you have enough time to mail out your scholarship application well in advance of the deadline, you can send it regular U.S. mail and follow up to make sure that it was received. If you are short on time or there's no other way to verify the package's arrival before the deadline has passed, you may want to send your materials with "built-in" verification that they have arrived safe and sound. When you invest a lot of work into an application, it's often worth a couple of extra bucks to guarantee that your materials have arrived at their destination.

In this case, opt for delivery by U.S. Postal Service "Certified Mail" with a Return Receipt Requested card, or "Priority Mail with an Acknowledgment Receipt." If your deadline requires only that you postmark it by a particular date, then it's usually not necessary to use an overnight or second-day delivery service. If the scholarship application has to be received by the following day (or day after), you might have to depend on overnight services such as Express Mail, FedEx, UPS NextDay, or other couriers. Remember, too, that if you are mailing to a post office box, you are required to "go postal"—this means using the good ol' U.S. Postal Service.

CHAPTER 11 SUMMARY AND KEYWORDS

Paperwork: Make multiple copies of original application forms, and type your application. Attaching additional sheets (if allowed) is preferable to cramming information on the form. Save all intermediate work—both on the computer and as printed copies. ■

No Blanks: Fill in all blanks when scholarship application forms request lists of activities or awards. If necessary, expand the descriptions of your credentials to fill up the space, and expand upon your strong points. ■

The Stat Sheet: Scan forms for required signatures. Make sure that information on the stat sheet matches the rest of the application. ■

Activity Lists: Create a master extracurricular activities list that includes the following categories: activity name, brief activity description, related awards and honors, offices or positions held, and time commitment. Rank activities on the list in a systematic fashion—with activities of great strategic importance at the top of the list. Customize this master list to fit the strategic considerations of each scholarship application. ■

Awards and Honors Lists: Create a master list, rank your most impressive awards first, and customize this ranking to fit each scholarship program. Include added details about the selectivity and significance of the award if it helps your cause. ■

The Transcript: Obtain permission to include an awards-and-honors addendum as part of your school transcript. Find out if standardized-test scores are included, and lobby your school if this policy isn't optimal for you. If you are a homeschooled student, you may need to create your own transcript, so use the transcripts of other schools in your area as model forms. ■

Additional Materials: Send samples or portfolios of your work if permitted by application guidelines. Don't pad applications with excess material; pick and choose your highest-quality work. ■

Mail Service: For added peace of mind, send completed scholarship applications using a mail or delivery service that verifies its safe arrival. ■

SCHOLARSHIPCOACH.COM KEYWORDS

For more information on a scholarship or topic mentioned in this chapter, enter the associated keyword in the keyword link box located in the Coach's Locker Room section of ScholarshipCoach.com.

Scholarship/Topic	*Keyword*
Harry S. Truman Scholarship	TRUMAN
U.S. Senate Youth Program Scholarship	SENATE

Acing the Interview

INSIDE THIS CHAPTER

▌ Preparing key points and anecdotes

▌ Practicing your interview skills

▌ Achieving a two-way conversation

▌ Staying relaxed and focused

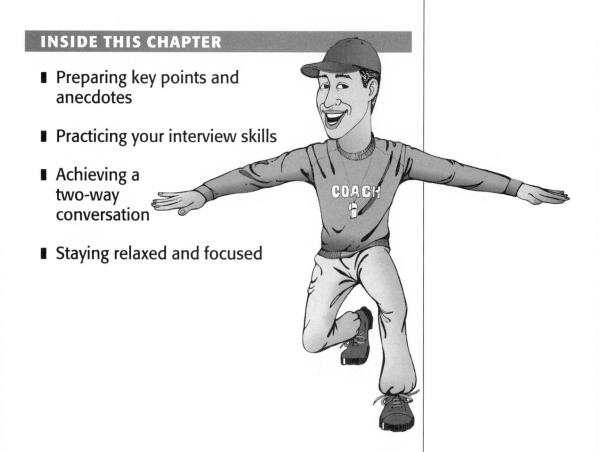

INTERVIEW MASTERY

Ever wonder how certain entertainers, journalists, and politicians seem so poised and well-spoken in television interviews? Well, here's a little secret: For most, it's not because they've got natural on-screen talent exuding from their pores. Rather, it's that they are so familiar with the interview format, and what to say in any given situation, that their performance becomes second nature.

In this chapter, I'll illustrate some proven strategies and tips that will help you achieve similar results in your scholarship interviews. You'll discover that an interview need not be a dreaded event. In fact, scholarship interviews can actually be *fun*.

Before we begin, I should note that the majority of scholarship programs do *not* require applicant interviews. This doesn't mean, however, that knowing how to handle yourself in interviews isn't important: When judges do conduct interviews, your performance usually carries considerable weight in the overall evaluation process. That's because the interview allows scholarship judges the ability to get to know you better than they can on a written page.

Because of the importance of the interview when it is used, take the time to learn and employ the techniques outlined in this chapter. Strong skills in this area of interpersonal communication will serve you well during your entire life—whether you're applying to college or graduate school, trying to land that dream job, or undergoing the informal "interviewing" of a first date.

PREPARING FOR THE INTERVIEW

What you do before you even show up for an interview *contributes to more than 50 percent of your overall performance*. How can this be? How can what you do *before* you even show up, shake hands with the interviewer, or utter your first word have that much to do with the ultimate success of the interview?

Quite simply, it's because preparation and practice are the keys to feeling comfortable and confident in the interview setting. Preparation and practice give you the ability to relax at the interview, respond effortlessly and naturally to questions, and add some spontaneity with ease. How do you prepare for a scholarship interview? Try the following action steps:

Do Your Homework

An important precursor to performing well in an interview is to understand the perspective of the interviewer. If you understand where the interviewer is coming from, you'll be able to anticipate where he or she will go with questions—allowing you to formulate answers that are likely to be well received by your audience.

To prepare, research the organization or organizations sponsoring, administering, and judging the scholarship program. The Internet, with its powerful search engines, has made this job much easier in recent years. Make sure you clearly understand (and can state in a few sentences) the purpose of the scholarship program, the judging criteria for scholarship selection, and the underlying missions of the organizations involved.

If you've used the "application detective" strategies outlined in Chapter 6, you've already completed a lot of this work. Taking the time to research and understand this also demonstrates something else to your interviewer: The scholarship is important enough to you that you were willing to put in some extra effort. (Remember, hard work is one of the universal judging criteria we examined in Chapter 6.)

To the extent possible, find out what you can about the person or people who will be interviewing you. Are they affiliated with the sponsoring or administering organization? Are they educators? Are they business-

Ideally you should start preparing for an interview three to five days in advance. Yeah, I've done my share of last-minute preparation, but it's better when you have more time.

On one occasion, I knew that I was to be interviewed by a particular college professor. So in advance, I dug up some papers and articles he had written. The professor seemed impressed by how much I knew about his work.

people? Or are they members of the Fraternal Brother-hood of Fervent Aardvark Lovers? Uncovering snippets of background information gives you some idea about the types of questions to expect and the types of preferences your interviewers might have.

Prepare a Few Key Points

Don't respond only to what an interviewer tosses your way. That's like being on a basketball team that only plays defense. Instead, play offense as well: Go into an interview prepared to make several key points of your own—selling points that demonstrate *you* are deserving of the scholarship award. At least one of these points should emphasize your application themes (the same ones developed in Chapter 5). Communicate your themes with passion and enthusiasm, and never assume that interviewers have read your application word for word (they probably haven't).

You may want to prepare key points that appeal to the ten universal judging criteria discussed in Chapter 6.

At the same time, don't dwell on your themes to the exclusion of everything else. Interviews allow judges to discover more dimensions of you than they can on the written page, so prepare at least one key point that goes beyond anything mentioned in the written application. Use the opportunity of meeting the scholarship judges in person to show them something fresh, new, and even surprising about yourself that they might not have considered before.

Prepare Anecdotes to Illustrate Your Points

What's the cure for a dull interview? Quite simply, *an anecdote is the antidote*. Telling stories and giving examples keeps the interviewer interested and engaged. Don't just recite a list of your key personal "selling" points; take the time to communicate interesting anecdotes and stories that illustrate each point. Rather than communicate these points as a laundry list of credentials, approach the process as though you're putting together a descriptive clothing catalog: Take the time to describe the quality of the material, the style of the fit, and the vibrancy of the colors.

To emphasize my love of writing, I would often tell stories about all the books my mom read to me as a child and about how my dad and I would spend Sunday afternoons analyzing the writing of leading newspaper columnists.

For instance, if your application theme centers on community service, don't just summarize all the service activities you've done. Talk about a specific community service project and a particularly memorable occasion when you felt your efforts made a big difference. Tell an interesting story about a person you helped and how that made you feel. In the end, this conveys much more about your service efforts than just reciting a list of credentials or facts.

Use the opportunity of an in-person interview to delve into particular experiences in a more in-depth way than you could in the written application. And when it comes time to make the cut for the scholarship awards, it will likely be your anecdote that a judge remembers— your interesting, humorous, funny, sad, or poignant story that sets you apart and calls attention to your merits.

Anticipate Interview Questions

The specific questions you'll be asked in any given interview are generally no big secret. With a little forethought, you can usually predict at least some of them. So take the time to come up with a list of potential questions. Don't just review the questions in your mind; write them down on index cards.

Interviews for graduate school scholarships and fellowships are often highly focused on your knowledge of the academic field you wish to pursue.

The specific questions, of course, depend on the emphasis of the particular scholarship. You'll be able to anticipate questions by drawing on the research you did in Action Step #1. For instance, in my interview for the U.S. Senate Youth Program Scholarship—an awards program with a focus on government and politics— I anticipated interview questions on current events and

Scholarship interviews for adult returning students tend to focus on life experiences, changing goals, and your reasons for wanting to return to school.

It's no surprise that many of these questions are similar to standard scholarship essay questions.

my state's political leaders. Sure enough, the questions materialized.

For scholarships aimed at students interested in a certain field of study, expect questions about your career goals and your experience with the subject matter. If the scholarship program is sponsored by an organization that highly values patriotism, expect questions asking about your citizenship duties as an American. To get you started, I've listed some common scholarship interview questions.

General Questions

▌ How would you describe yourself?

▌ Where do you see yourself in 20 years?

▌ What are your greatest strengths and weaknesses?

▌ What is your favorite book, and why do you like it?

▌ Who is someone you admire, and why?

▌ How would you like to be remembered?

▌ What has been your greatest accomplishment?

▌ What was an occasion when you overcame adversity?

▌ What is your family like?

▌ How might you contribute to society in the future?

Activity-Oriented Questions

▌ What are your favorite extracurricular activities?

▌ What are some activities in which you've shown leadership?

▌ What types of things have you done to help others?

Course-Related Questions

▌ What courses most interest you?

▌ Why did you choose your specific major?

▌ Do you plan to continue your studies in graduate school?

▌ Who are your role models in your field of interest?

College-Related Questions

▌ Why do you want to go to college?

▌ What do you hope to gain from college?

▌ Why did you choose to attend your particular college?

Closing Questions

▌ Is there anything else you'd like to add?

▌ Why should we award you this scholarship?

▌ Are there any questions you'd like to ask us?

Prepare Responses

Once you've come up with a pile of questions on index cards, write out answers to the questions on the reverse side of the cards. Don't bother writing out actual sentences; just jot down a few notes that will remind you what you want to talk about. Never try to memorize actual responses verbatim. After all, you want to seem relaxed and natural.

Realize that there are two parts to every interview answer: (1) the answer itself and (2) the personal qualities and attributes you communicate by how you approach the question.

The key to preparing your responses is to try to be specific, to focus on personal experiences and perspectives, to take into account the mission and judging criteria of the scholarship, and to avoid generic-sounding answers. What you don't want to do is prepare a response that sounds like ones given all too often by beauty pageant contestants—responses that are perceived as little more than lip service to what the judges want to hear. ("My goal for the future is to single-handedly bring about world peace!") It's perfectly fine to give idealistic, optimistic, and even clichéd answers, but the key is backing up these statements with concrete and specific examples that demonstrate you truly mean what you say and have thoughtfully considered the statement you are making.

Prepare Questions to Ask the Interviewer

Standard questions for scholarship interviewers include "How did you get involved with this organization?" or "Do you have any advice for someone with my interests and background?"

During a scholarship interview, you often get the opportunity to pose questions to the interviewer. Your interviewers may ask you directly if you have any questions for them, or a less deliberate moment may arise when the flow of the conversation suggests that you should pose a question. So be prepared for such a moment. A well-thought-out and articulate question can tell the interviewer a lot about you. Questions are also an opportunity to convey your knowledge of the sponsoring organization and of subject matter relevant to the scholarship. It's nice to be able to give the interviewer a chance to talk as well.

"Pepper" Yourself

Put these index cards in a box or favorite hat, and draw out random questions to practice your interview responses. To view yourself from the interviewer's perspective, videotape your responses, then review and study

Fill in your mock interviewer on the goals, mission, and judging criteria of the particular scholarship so that he or she can evaluate you from this perspective.

those videotapes. Conduct the practice sessions as if they are a rehearsal or a scrimmage. When you feel comfortable with your responses, do a mock interview with a parent, friend, family member, teacher, or school counselor. Provide them with your list of questions, but also allow them to ad-lib as well. If at all possible, videotape your mock interviews.

After the mock interview is complete, get as much feedback as you can. Find out what you did well and what you need to work on. What were the strongest aspects of your interview? What parts of the interview could use a little more practice? Did you sound natural and relaxed? Use their comments and suggestions as stepping-stones for improvement.

Prepare Samples of Your Work

With certain scholarships, samples and portfolios that illustrate your talents can leave a strong impression with interviewers. Bring copies of your sample work that you can leave behind. The sample work will emphasize your strengths and will remind the interviewer to consider you when it's time to decide who wins the scholarship money. This strategy is especially important if a focal point of your application is your artistic or writing ability—talents that are best demonstrated through sample work.

Never force these sample materials on the interviewer. Tactfully mention that you have brought along some examples of your work, and feel out whether the interviewer is interested in perusing them.

In addition, it never hurts to bring informative material that was not contained in the written application. If, for example, the written application provided you with only limited space to list and discuss your extracurricular activities, bring expanded listings and descriptions to possibly leave with the interviewer.

Place Supplementary Materials with Interviewers

■ Leave sample work and other compelling materials with scholarship interviewers to highlight your talents and remind them to consider you when it's selection time.

ACTION STEP 9

Reread and Review Your Written Application

In most instances, you will have submitted a written application before undergoing a scholarship interview. Given the time it takes to evaluate scholarship candidates, your interview may take place weeks or months after you have submitted the written application. Because of this, it's important to refresh your memory about everything that was contained in the written form. During interviews, judges often ask you specific questions about things you've included on the form. So review your application, and be prepared to talk intelligently about any information you have submitted.

Incidentally, all these tips are also good advice for college admissions interviews, internship interviews, and job interviews.

▍ THE BIG DAY

It's the morning of the big interview. You're feeling prepared and confident, but the butterflies in your stomach are doing the mambo. To do your best, you will want everything to be in order the moment you walk into the interview room. To ensure this result, employ the following suggestions:

DRESS FOR SUCCESS. Make a dramatic impression on the judges by wearing a lime green jumpsuit with a pink feather boa . . . just kidding. In general, you should make a bold statement with what you say, *not* with how you dress. Men should wear either a business suit or else a dress shirt, nice sports coat, and tie. Women might go with a dress, pantsuit, or dressy skirt/pants and blouse. Cover up any obtrusive tattoos, and avoid ostentatious jewelry (especially things like nose or eyebrow rings) that could distract an interviewer's attention from what you have to say. The time to make an individual fashion statement is not during the scholarship interview.

As the old adage (and shampoo commercial) goes, "You never get a second chance to make a first impression."

AVOID STRESS. Before your interview, stay away from people or activities that easily irritate you. Think happy, happy thoughts.

PACK YOUR GROOMING SUPPLIES. Bring a hairbrush, makeup, deodorant, lip balm, mouthwash, or any other last-minute supplies you may need.

REFRESH YOUR MEMORY. An hour or so before your interview, review your key points, anecdotes, and practice questions and answers.

ARRIVE AT LEAST 15 MINUTES EARLY. It's always better to arrive early and get settled. The interviewers could be ahead of schedule, and you wouldn't want to make them wait. If you're unfamiliar with the location of the interview, make sure ahead of time that you know how to get there.

▌ THE MAIN EVENT

Finally, it's time for the main event: the interview itself. The following tips are a few tricks that scholarship winners have employed to win interviewers over to their worthy corners. Practice these techniques in your mock interviews until they are second nature.

USE A FIRM HANDSHAKE AND MAKE EYE CONTACT. Sure, it's old-fashioned, but it still works. Make a mental note of the interviewer's name when he or she tells it to you. Burn the name (with the correct pronunciation) into your brain cells.

LISTEN. No one likes to be ignored. Look attentive when the interviewer is talking to you—even if he's expounding on a subject about as interesting as the history of butter lettuce in the 20th century. Resist the temptation to "tune out" the interviewer in preparation for what you want to say next. Failing to show attentive listening communicates to interviewers that they don't matter. Remember—attentive listening is one of the highest compliments you can pay anyone. Show genuine interest in what an interviewer is saying, and you'll create a strong impression.

DON'T PERFORM A MONOLOGUE. It's easy in an interview to start reciting your opinions and accomplishments to the point where the interviewer isn't able to get a word in edgewise. Resist the urge to start talking and never stop. Be careful to not get lost in the minutiae of every activity so that you wind up giving a ten-minute discourse on the finer points of your city dump cleanup project.

To the extent that you can, strive to create a two-way dialogue—a real interactive conversation. If your interviewer comments on something you say by talking about his or her experience and background, ask a follow-up

Interviewers never, as a general rule, remember specific facts and figures. They do, however, take with them a general impression of you based upon how you made them feel.

question. Most people enjoy talking about themselves and will appreciate the opportunity and attention.

FIND COMMON GROUND. Each interviewer will respond to your various activities, experiences, credentials, and goals differently. This is understandable. Interviewers are viewing *your* life through *their* eyes. For this reason, observe when interviewers are especially interested in something you say (made obvious by body language and verbal clues), and talk about this in more depth; don't forget to ask them questions, too.

If you're talking about how much you love painting, for instance, and the interviewer comments, "Oh, I enjoy painting as well," seize the opportunity to ask her a question (such as "What type of painting do you do?"). I know of one student who spent nearly an entire interview conversing with the scholarship interviewer about their shared interest in volleyball—a topic that had nothing to do with the scholarship's judging criteria. What happened as a result? The student took home the scholarship prize.

BE FLUENT IN BODY LANGUAGE. Researchers at UCLA tell us that an astounding *93 percent of communication is nonverbal.* So use body language to your advantage. Remember, you're not on trial here. It's not an interrogation. An interview should be a friendly conversation, and you hope an interesting one because, after all, it's all about *you.* When you speak, don't hold back: Use natural hand gestures, keep your face animated, and project your voice with energy and enthusiasm. Refrain from slouching the way you probably do when hanging out with your friends or watching television. By sitting up straight, you communicate confidence and assertiveness.

MAKE YOUR POINTS . . . BUT DON'T FORCE THEM. Try to communicate the points and anecdotes you have prepared by working them into your answers. But if you

When interviewed by a panel of judges, make eye contact with each person and seek to include everyone in the conversation. Treat each person equally, but give added deference to the individual leading the interview (such as the committee chair).

"No one likes to interview someone who looks really uncomfortable. So you want to look calm and relaxed and make the interviewer feel at ease."

–Mattias Geise
Scholarship Winner
Northumberland, PA

aren't asked about something you wanted to talk about, don't completely digress from the interviewer's questions and attempt to force it into the conversation. In other words, don't respond like the stereotypical politician; you should actually answer the question asked.

LEAVE YOUR ANNOYING HABITS AT HOME. We all have our share of annoying habits, but in an interview you want to look mature and composed. Avoid tapping your foot, shaking your leg, or doing any type of fidgeting. Try to cut down on using "um," "like," and "you know" when you talk. Do not, under any circumstances, ask the interviewer to "pull your finger."

Remember, no matter how formal the interview situation, scholarship interviewers are just people. They like to have fun and would rather have an enjoyable interview experience than a boring one.

BE ENTHUSIASTIC, SMILE, AND HAVE FUN. During the interview, try to be enthusiastic and cheerful. Don't be afraid to show off your pearly whites. A smile puts the interviewer at ease, dissipates the tension inside you, and conveys confidence. Besides, interviews should be fun. If you've practiced enough, all the other points I've mentioned should already be second nature to you, and you'll be able to relax and go with the flow.

It's natural to second-guess yourself after an interview, but don't beat yourself up over something you didn't say or do. You did your best at the time, and that's what counts. Besides, you are generally your own harshest critic: You probably did much better than you think.

WRAP UP WITH STYLE. At the end of the interview, express your gratitude for the opportunity to interview, and communicate how much you enjoyed the discussion. In addition, try to repeat the interviewer's name in your closing remarks. (Remember, to the person you are talking to, his or her name is the sweetest sound in the world.) Your interview duties, however, don't end when you walk out the door. If possible, send your interviewer a handwritten thank-you note to express your gratitude for his or her time and the chance to meet in person.

ASK THE COACH #28

What should I do differently in a scholarship interview conducted by phone?

The key to making a long-distance scholarship interview work is to treat it just like an in-person interview, albeit one that has a few extra challenges standing in the way of effective communication. First, you need to take extra care to know who's on the other end of the line. Jot down the person's name and position, if he or she offers it, as well as any other bits  of information you uncover. Listen closely to verbal clues to figure out whether the interviewer is interested in what you are saying (snoring is definitely one of these clues).

Next, pretend that the interviewer is actually in the room with you. Use the same gestures and facial expressions you would for a face-to-face interview. In my experience, it's actually possible to "hear" some of your body language (such as whether or not you are smiling). You can, however, use the fact that no one can see you to your advantage: Lay out your prepared points and answers to anticipated questions on a table near the phone so you can reference the materials during the interview. Resist the urge, however, to read the notes verbatim over the phone (that sounds stuffy and fake), and instead just use them merely as talking points and conversation reminders. In addition, try to avoid using a speakerphone, cordless phone, cell phone, or any other phone that can distort your voice, pick up surrounding noise, or make it difficult to hear the question.

Finally, be sure to find a quiet place for the interview, turn off your call-waiting (so you're not distracted by the beep), and alert everyone in the vicinity that you're about to take an important call. ∎

CHAPTER 12 SUMMARY AND KEYWORDS

Early Preparation: Find out what you can about the person or people who will be interviewing you. Prepare some key points and anecdotes to illustrate the theme of your application and other pertinent information. Anticipate potential interview questions, and jot down notes about how to answer them.

Practice your responses by yourself, with a friend, or in front of a video camera. Brainstorm some questions to ask your interviewer. Prepare samples of your work to bring to the interview, and reread your written application. ∎

Before the Interview: Dress appropriately for the occasion. Avoid stressful activities before the interview, and bring needed grooming supplies. Review key points, anecdotes, and practice questions. Arrive at the interview early to allow for time to get settled. ∎

Face to Face: Upon meeting the interviewer, give a firm handshake and make eye contact. Be attentive when the interviewer talks, and listen carefully. Refrain from talking endlessly; give the interviewer a chance to comment on what you say. Seek to find common ground and shared experiences with the interviewer. Make your prepared points and anecdotes when appropriate, but don't force the issue.

Act mature and composed, and leave your annoying habits at home. Remember to be enthusiastic, smile frequently, and enjoy the experience. When the interview is wrapping up, express your gratitude to the interviewer, try to repeat the interviewer's name in conversation, and follow up with a thank-you note. ∎

Phone Interviews: Use the same strategies as in face-to-face interviews, but take extra care to know who's on the other end of the line, and whether or not they are responding well to what you are saying. Keep important notes and information for the interview in front of you, but don't rely on them. Select phone equipment and find a location that minimizes distractions. ■

SCHOLARSHIPCOACH.COM KEYWORDS

For more information on a scholarship or topic mentioned in this chapter, enter the associated keyword in the keyword link box located in the Coach's Locker Room section of ScholarshipCoach.com.

Scholarship/Topic	*Keyword*
U.S. Senate Youth Program Scholarship	SENATE

PART V

When the
Buzzer
Sounds

Parting Shots

INSIDE THIS CHAPTER

▌ Tracking your scholarship winnings

▌ Tuition reductions through AP and CLEP testing

▌ What winning scholarships is really about

THE HOME STRETCH

Well, you've made it! I'm exhausted just thinking about all we've been through together. (And you've been the one doing all the work!) You now know the hidden rules, proven strategies, insider secrets, and guerrilla tactics of winning the scholarship game. If you've internalized the information in this book and have invested the necessary time and energy into applying the principles and following the action steps, you're well on your way to staking your scholarship claim. Before we call this a done deal, however, there are a few issues to consider in the game's aftermath. In this chapter, I'll give you some key tips for managing your winnings, describe a powerful method for reducing your tuition bill, and reflect on what winning scholarships is *really* about.

KEEPING TRACK OF YOUR WINNINGS

When you get that congratulatory letter or phone call informing you of your latest scholarship triumph, I suggest doing one or more of the following three things: screaming at the top of your lungs, scarfing down a mountainous ice cream sundae, or running 3.6 miles . . . buck naked. Once you've gotten that out of your system, you can begin to ponder the nitty-gritty details of how you actually get paid your scholarship money. (Hint: Don't expect a brightly painted sweepstakes van to roll up to your door with Ed McMahon in the front seat holding a big fat check.)

SCHOLARSHIP PAYMENT PLANS

Through the process of managing my own scholarship funds, I've encountered several distinct variations of scholarship payment plans. To give you an idea of what to expect, I'll describe them below:

These variations in payment plans arise, in part, because scholarship administrators have standardized logistical systems for transferring money, disbursing it to students, and accounting for these transactions.

- a one-time, lump-sum payment to you,
- a one-time, lump-sum payment to your school,
- term-by-term fixed payments to you,
- term-by-term fixed payments to your school,
- unscheduled variable-sum payments to you,
- unscheduled variable-sum payments to your school.

To make it even more confusing, the sponsors and administrators of scholarship awards often specify limited time frames in which you *must* use the funds. Common variations of these time-frame limitations include:

- four years from the time of your high school graduation,
- four years from the time of your first college enrollment,
- six years from the time of your high school graduation,
- 12 years from the time you receive the award,
- coincident with your enrollment in graduate school.

Some scholarships may be restricted for use at two- and four-year colleges, while others allow funds to be used also at trade and technical schools and for the pursuit of graduate-level studies.

In a nutshell, you will need to clearly understand who gets paid the scholarship check (you or your college), how this payment is made (in one big lump or in multiple installments), when you must use the funds (in four years or a longer time frame), and what schooling it covers (two- and four-year colleges, trade and technical schools, graduate school, or even post-doc studies). All this may give you a headache (unless you've won the Tylenol Scholarship), but hey, figuring out how to collect your money is a good problem to have!

Staying Flexible

The best scholarship payment plans provide you with *choice* and offer maximum flexibility in each of the above key areas. Such flexibility is important because it enables you to choose payment schedules that take into account changes in your family's income and expenses, your own income and expense fluctuations, college-funded financial-aid allotments, and any potential tax consequences. The best payment plans I've encountered allow you to draw on the scholarship money in chunks of any size, whenever you so choose.

Having this kind of flexibility in determining how much of your scholarship winnings to collect at any point in time can in many cases help you maximize the amount of need-based aid you receive each year from your school.

Getting to Know Your Friendly Scholarship Administrator

The scholarship administrator is the person in charge of handling the logistics of paying out your scholarship money. I've found it very helpful to start a dialogue with the administrator for each scholarship and to discuss payment options and procedures with these individuals. (It's fun talking about how to spend your hard-earned money!)

First, you want to be aware up front of any possible limitations, requirements, or restrictions on receiving the funds. For instance, some scholarships require that you submit an annual proof-of-registration form, official transcript, or fund-request letter. Other scholarships, such as the Coca-Cola Scholars Program, require that you submit a brief statement of your major activities and projects. Some of the more academically focused scholarships require that you maintain a GPA of, say, 2.5 or better.

Second, you need to be aware of the procedure for getting funds transferred to you. For scholarships administered by an organization different than the one putting up the money, the funds aren't just sitting in an account waiting for you. The administrator has to request funds from the sponsor, and there is often a strict, time-intensive procedure for doing so. This becomes important when you need scholarship payments immediately (which is often the case, so that you can register for classes), but face a lengthy delay for the money transfers to be processed.

Most important, the scholarship administrator often has the power to make special exceptions to payment rules to meet your needs. For instance, several scholarship administrators allowed me to determine withdrawal amounts, come up with my own payment schedule, and defer the balance of my winnings until later years—even though the official regulations didn't specifically permit this. In other instances, when I missed request deadlines or forgot to submit required documentation (oops!), those administrators helped me figure out a way around the red tape. Starting a friendly dialogue with your scholarship administrator can be very advantageous and puts a powerful ally in your corner.

Tracking the Details

My parents and I discovered that the more scholarships and money I won, the more we had to pay attention to all the different requirements and compliance forms for each organization administering the funds. Keeping all this straight will also be important for institutional financial aid and tax considerations that may be pertinent to your particular situation.

To stay organized, the first thing you'll want to do is to make a list of everything you've won, then set up a

If you don't have time to take care of all these details, having a parent who can help manage your award winnings is very useful.

summary chart of key information. On this chart, you will want to include:

▍ the name of the scholarship,

▍ the administrator's name and contact information,

▍ the total amount of the award,

▍ the payment schedule,

▍ the expiration date for final payout,

▍ any reporting and maintenance requirements,

▍ the allowed use of the funds.

Pay special attention to the reporting and maintenance requirements portion of the chart. This information tells you how frequently you must communicate with scholarship administrators (each term, annually, etc.) and what paperwork you must submit before receiving your money. If you neglect these simple tasks, you might not be able to get your scholarship money when you need it.

Some Additional Tips

I've learned from experience the importance of making sure that your scholarship checks actually do make it to your school's billing office *and* get entered into your account. In some cases, checks sent directly to your school's billing office might just sit there (meanwhile, no one has informed you), waiting for you to come in and sign your name, endorsing them over to the school. There might also be cases where a scholarship administrator has dropped the ball and has not sent out your check to your school when you requested it. So in the end, it's going to be *your* responsibility to track the money from point A to point B.

If you are planning to take time off from college, you will need to check with each scholarship administrator to inquire about the usage rules and make special provisions, if possible. If you're involved in a study-abroad program, for instance, some administrators allow you to forward the checks to the foreign school. In other cases, you're allowed to postpone payment until you re-enroll (if, for example, you're taking time off to pursue an internship opportunity). It all depends on the rules and flexibility of each scholarship's payout plan.

■ USING TESTING TO SLASH COLLEGE COSTS

Some colleges may also offer tuition-reduction possibilities for students who pass the International Baccalaureate (IB) exams.

One of the most underutilized methods for reducing the costs of an undergraduate education is taking standard tests that earn you college credit. In this bonus section, we'll look at two different types of tests for doing so: the Advanced Placement (AP) program for students in high school and the College-Level Examination Program (CLEP) for students of all ages.

ADVANCED PLACEMENT (AP) PROGRAM

Many students have encountered the term "AP" somewhere along their high school careers, but relatively few recognize the dramatic savings that are possible if you know how to use the program in the most beneficial way. In exchange for achieving passing scores on a specified number of tests (definitely doable), 1,400 colleges around the country will grant you up to one year's worth of college credit—thereby saving you 25 percent of the total cost of your four-year college education!

The College Board runs the AP testing program. Visit www.collegeboard.org/ap for more information and a complete list of current courses offered.

Here are the basics of how AP testing works. Throughout the country, in May of each year, students can take special exams that cover 23 subject areas, including American history, economics, physics, biology, Spanish, studio art, government, calculus, music theory, computer science, environmental science, and psychology. The tests are supposed to be equivalent to introductory college-level courses, but in actuality, passing many of these tests is considerably easier. Around the world, roughly 13,000 high schools offer AP classes that prepare you to take these exams. The cost of taking an AP exam is not cheap (the fee is currently $77), but the potential college savings make this price a bargain.

Colleges typically grant credit for passing individual AP tests and give considerably more credit for passing several of them. The latter case is where the dramatic savings can occur. At most colleges, if you achieve solid scores on a specified number of AP tests, you're granted sophomore standing! This means that when you first set foot on campus to register for classes, you already have the credits of a sophomore. Because you can graduate in three academic years (six semesters), the cost of your college diploma is reduced by one-fourth!

If you've heard that AP classes are only for brainiacs, you're mistaken. What determines AP success is whether you're willing to invest the time and energy necessary to learn the material.

In addition, the standard set by most colleges to receive one year's worth of credit is not particularly tough. At Harvard, where I applied this strategy, students are granted one year's worth of credit if they receive scores of 4 or 5 (passing is 3 on a 5-point scale) on only four AP exams. In the scheme of things, achieving those scores on four AP exams is definitely doable if you're willing to put in the effort to prepare for them. For instance, if you take two AP exams your junior year in high school and two more your senior year—a manageable number for any student—you've already made it.

If you're going to be in high school taking classes anyway, why not use the opportunity to take AP classes that prepare you to take AP tests that can ultimately save you a

Four AP exams may seem like a lot, but it's nothing for Diana Hong of North Hollywood, CA, who took 21 AP exams and received a score of 5 on 17 of them! (Did she ever sleep?)

ton of money? Because these classes are more demanding than your average high school course, you may want to arrange your schedule or pick classes so you can devote the majority of your homework time to these courses. Even if your high school doesn't offer AP classes, you still have several options. Talk to your principal about arranging to take or sit in on AP classes at other schools in your area. Some students (including yours truly) have studied for these exams on their own by using a variety of special test-prep books available in libraries and bookstores.

I'll also note that just because you use AP tests to gain sophomore standing, it *doesn't* mean that you have to graduate in three years. Many students choose to spread out their three academic years (six semesters) over four calendar years so that they graduate with their regular class (in fact, that's what I did). This is an especially good strategy if you're interested in taking a term or two off to study abroad, travel, work, take an internship, or conduct thesis research. By starting with sophomore standing, you can take a year off from classwork, not receive course credit for that year, and still graduate with your class. Some students who choose to stay in the area during their time off even live on campus—allowing them to participate in college life without having to go to classes. Furthermore, most colleges give you the option of staying for a fourth academic year, if you so choose.

Of course, if you choose to work during that year off, the money earned can go a long way toward paying for the rest of your education.

Using AP tests to gain a year of credit is like winning a scholarship that covers an entire year of college costs. For students attending some of the country's most expensive private colleges, this can mean more than $30,000 in savings!

COLLEGE-LEVEL EXAMINATION PROGRAM (CLEP)

The College-Level Examination Program is a widely accepted credit-by-examination program that helps students of all ages earn credit for what they have already learned through independent study, high school courses, noncredit adult courses, or professional development. Whether you are 16 or 61, you can take CLEP exams and earn 3 to 12 college credits for each exam you take and pass—saving hundreds to thousands of dollars in tuition costs in the process. Like AP testing, CLEP exams are powerful tools to accelerate your coursework and reduce the time it takes to graduate.

Currently, more than 2,900 colleges award credit for achieving satisfactory scores on CLEP exams, although many do not accept all the tests that CLEP offers. In addition, each college has its own requirements for a score or percentile rank that it considers to be a passing grade. Depending on a college's CLEP policy, a student can receive up to 60 credits by taking CLEP exams.

CLEP exams are an especially good option for students who have never taken Advanced Placement or honors courses.

Presently, there are a total of 32 CLEP exams on a wide range of subjects not covered in the AP program. Such subjects include accounting, sociology, marketing, introductory business law, human growth and development, and trigonometry. Each exam currently costs $46, but the potential savings are far greater. For more information on CLEP exams, visit the College Board website (www.collegeboard.org/clep).

LESS EXPENSIVE FIRST, THEN TRANSFER ELSEWHERE

An additional option that may be appropriate for some students is to pursue their first year or two at a less expensive college (often a state school, community college, or junior college), and then transfer to a more expensive (and often more prestigious) school that would be preferable to attend. By doing this, a student would pay significantly less for the first couple of years of college, but wind up with a degree from his or her first-choice institution.

If you are considering this option, the main thing you should avoid is choosing to attend an inexpensive college *solely* for the reason of its cheaper tuition. That's why I recommend such an option *only* if you can find a less expensive school that actually suits your needs and one you actually want to attend. It's not wise to sacrifice your first couple of college years while hoping to go elsewhere later on.

As a variation on this theme, American students may want to consider attending a Canadian college or university (which often have cheaper price tags than equivalent American schools) and then later attending grad school in the U.S.

▌ WHAT WE'VE LEARNED

Well, every book has to come to an end. And I suppose the best books do this sooner, rather than later. So before I've worn out my welcome, I'd like to offer a few reflections on what playing the scholarship game is really all about.

Although the need for money has motivated our quest, the scholarship game is not solely about winning college cash. The game is also about setting a goal and being willing to do whatever it takes to reach it. It's about not letting current financial circumstances dictate our destinies. It's about accepting risk and having faith: the risk of putting yourself on the line, and the faith that comes with believing in yourself.

To succeed in this game, we've had to expand our skills, talents, and abilities. We've had to think strategically. We've had to learn how to effectively promote ourselves. We've had to become more well-rounded. We've even had to reflect on our lives, and in the midst of the chaos, try to paint vivid portraits of who we really are.

And therein lies the beauty of it all: To win the scholarship money, we've had to become *worthy* of winning it. And win or lose, this may be the grandest prize of all.

In conclusion, I'd like to thank you for sticking it out with me to the end. Best of luck with your scholarship quest, and may all your educational dreams come true. Until the next time . . .

I'D LOVE TO HEAR FROM YOU . . .

How did your scholarship quest turn out? Was this book helpful to you? Any suggestions for future editions? Have any interesting scholarship stories to share?

In case I haven't already made it abundantly clear, I want to hear from you! Don't leave me hanging by my inbox and mailbox with nothing to do. When you get a free moment, jot me a quick note.

I might even take some of your comments and include them in future editions of this book or post them on ScholarshipCoach.com. (If you don't want me to include your name, just say so.)

The preferred way to contact me is via e-mail at:

Ben@ScholarshipCoach.com

Or if you're so inclined, you can snail-mail me at:

Ben Kaplan
c/o Waggle Dancer Media, Inc.
P.O. Box 860
Gleneden Beach, OR 97388

I look forward to hearing from you!

Scholarship Coach Search Profile Worksheet™

The Scholarship Coach Search Profile Worksheet™

(For High School, Undergraduate, Graduate & Non-Traditional Adult Returning Students)

Instructions: This worksheet will help you document and organize your personal information, credentials, interests, and affiliations. You will then be ready to employ ten powerful action steps (see *How to Go to College Almost for Free*) for finding all types of awards that are right for someone like you. This form will prove especially useful when utilizing Internet-accessible scholarship databases, in which you must input a substantial amount of personal information. Therefore, the more precisely you can profile yourself on this worksheet, the better your chances of discovering many "hidden" scholarships that *you* are uniquely qualified to apply for—and that others will not be able to find. For a printer-friendly version of this worksheet, visit Ben Kaplan's award-winning **ScholarshipCoach.com** website. For more information on scholarship searching, see Ben Kaplan's bestselling books, *How to Go to College Almost for Free* and *The Scholarship Scouting Report*.

Age:_____ **Gender:** _____ **Year in High School/College/Grad School:** _____

City/State/County/Country of Residence: _____

State(s)/Country of Intended Study: _____

Past/Current GPA & Class Rank: _____

Test Scores (PSAT, SAT, ACT, LSAT, GMAT, etc.): _____

Degrees Earned: _____

Advanced Credits (AP, IB, CLEP, etc.): _____

Awards/Honors Won (non-monetary including trips/internships/conferences, and monetary awards with amounts): _____

Focus of Present Studies and/or **Major Areas of Interest to Study/Pursue Career:** _____

_____

Interests/Hobbies/Activities/Abilities (e.g., school athletics; other sports (bowling, surfing, backpacking, etc.); arts & crafts, aviation, performing arts, band & songwriting, story writing, poetry & journalism, amateur radio and web programming; photography, playwriting & filmmaking; foreign languages; debate & oratory; radio/TV broadcasting; beauty pageants; dog & horse activities; science & research projects; etc.): _____

_____

_____

Work/Apprenticeships/Volunteer Experience/Community Service (e.g., food service & gasoline sales; golf caddying & newspaper delivery; church work; marketing & healthcare; teaching & tutoring; fundraising; social, environmental & political activism; journalism & broadcasting; Peace Corps/VISTA/Job Corps; military & law enforcement; coaching & mentoring; etc.): _____

_____

Your Student Affiliations & Other Groups Joined (e.g., student government, Boy/Girl Scouts; National Honor Society, Key/Beta/4H Clubs; Junior Achievement, Future Farmers/Future Homemakers; fraternities & sororities; Armed Forces & ROTC; sport/hobby leagues & political groups; etc.): _____

_____

Disabilities/Medical Conditions (e.g., visual/hearing impairments, asthma, dyslexia, etc.):

Your Current/Past Employer(s): _____

Parental Employer(s): _____

Ancestry, Nationality & Minority Status (e.g., ethnicity; family membership in ethnic organizations; orphan status; descendant of historical figures & groups; sexual-orientation minorities; etc.): _____

_____

Non-Ethnic Family Memberships, Military Affiliations & Religious Denomination (e.g., labor unions; credit unions; fraternal lodges & patriotic/civic organizations; business/trade/professional organizations; active, reserve & retired military; special military units/groups & veterans of specific campaigns; specific religious denominations; etc.): _____

_____

State Agency Contacts

STATE GOVERNMENT AGENCIES

The following are state agencies that administer government-funded scholarship programs. The agencies generally administer both federally funded scholarships (such as the Robert C. Byrd Scholarship) and state-funded programs. In selected states, such agencies may also be contracted out to administer privately funded scholarship programs. In states with more than one listing, administrative functions may be divided between both agencies.

ALABAMA

Alabama Commission on Higher Education
100 North Union St.
P.O. Box 302000
Montgomery, AL 36130
Tel: (334) 242-1998; (334) 242-2274;
    (334) 242-2276
Fax: (334) 242-0268
E-Mail: hhector@ache.state.al.us
URL: www.ache.state.al.us

State Department of Education
Gordon Persons Office Building
50 North Ripley St.
Montgomery, AL 36130
Tel: (334) 242-8082
URL: www.alsde.edu

ALASKA

Commission on Postsecondary Education
3030 Vintage Blvd.
Juneau, AK 99801
Tel: (907) 465-6741; (800) 441-2962
Fax: (907) 465-5316
E-Mail: custsvc@educ.state.ak.us
URL: http://www.state.ak.us/acpe

State Department of Education
Goldbelt Place
801 West 10th St., Suite 200
Juneau, AK 99801
Tel: (907) 465-2875

ARIZONA

Commission for Postsecondary Education
2020 North Central Ave., Suite 275
Phoenix, AZ 85004
Tel: (602) 229-2591
Fax: (602) 229-2599
E-Mail: toni@www.acpe.asu.edu
URL: http://www.acpe.asu.edu/

State Department of Education
1535 West Jefferson
Phoenix, AZ 85007
Tel: (602) 542-7469

ARKANSAS

Arkansas Department of Higher Education
114 East Capitol
Little Rock, AR 72201
Tel: (800) 547-8839; (501) 371-2000;
    (501) 371-2050
Fax: (501) 371-2003
E-Mail: stevef@adhe.arknet.edu or
    finaid@adhe.arknet.edu
URL: http://www.arscholarships.com/

Arkansas Department of Education
4 State Capitol Mall, Room 107A
Little Rock, AR 72201
Tel: (501) 682-4474

CALIFORNIA

California Student Aid Commission
3300 Zinfandel Dr.
P.O. Box 419026
Rancho Cordova, CA 95741
Tel: (916) 526-7590
Fax: (916) 526-8002
E-Mail: jgarcia@csac.ca.gov
URL: http://www.csac.ca.gov/

COLORADO

Colorado Commission on Higher Education
Colorado Heritage Center
1300 Broadway, 2nd Floor
Denver, CO 80203
Tel: (303) 866-2723
Fax: (303) 860-9750
E-Mail: tim.foster@state.co.us
URL: http://www.state.co.us/cche_dir/
    hecche.html

State Department of Education
201 East Colfax Ave.
Denver, CO 80203
Tel: (303) 866-6678

CONNECTICUT

Connecticut Department of Higher
    Education
61 Woodland St.
Hartford, CT 06105
Tel: (860) 947-1855
Fax: (860) 947-1310
E-Mail: dhewebmaster@commnet.edu
URL: http://www.ctdhe.org/dheweb

DELAWARE

Delaware Higher Education Commission
Carvel State Office Bldg.
820 North French St., 4th Floor
Wilmington, DE 19801
(800) 292-7935; (302) 577-3240
Fax: (302) 577-6765
E-Mail: dhec@state.de.us
URL: http://www.doe.state.de.us/high-ed/

State Department of Public Instruction
Townsend Bldg. #279 / Federal &
    Lockerman
P.O. Box 1402
Dover, DE 19903
Tel: (302) 739-5622

DISTRICT OF COLUMBIA

Department of Human Services
Office of Postsecondary Education, R&E
2100 Martin Luther King Jr. Ave., SE /
    Suite 401
Washington, DC 20020
Tel: (202) 727-3688; (202) 698-2400
Fax: (202) 727-2739
URL: http://dhs.washington.dc.us/
    Office_of_Postsecondary_Educat/office_
    of_postsecondary_educat.htm

District of Columbia Public Schools
Division of Student Services
450 Lee St., NE
Washington, DC 20019
Tel: (202) 442-4080; (202) 442-5110

FLORIDA

Florida Department of Education
Office of Student Financial Assistance
124 Collins Building
325 W. Gaines St.
Tallahassee, FL 32399-0400
Tel: (888) 827-2004; (850) 488-4095
Fax: (850) 488-3612
URL: http://www.firn.edu/doe/bin00065/
home0065.htm

GEORGIA

Georgia Student Finance Commission
2082 East Exchange Place
Tucker, GA 30084
Tel: (800) 776-6878; (770) 724-9000
Fax: (770) 724-9089
E-Mail: info@mail.gsfc.state.ga.us
URL: http://www.gsfc.org/

State Department of Education
2054 Twin Towers East
205 Butler St.
Atlanta, GA 30334
Tel: (404) 657-0183

HAWAII

Hawaii Postsecondary Education
Commission
2444 Dole St., Room 209
Honolulu, HI 96822
Tel: (808) 956-8213
Fax: (808) 956-5156
E-Mail: hern@hawaii.edu
URL: http://www.hern.hawaii.edu/hern/

Hawaii Department of Education
P.O. Box 2360
Honolulu, HI 96804
Tel: (808) 586-3230
Fax: (808) 586-3234
URL: http://doe.k12.hi.us/

IDAHO

Idaho State Board of Education
P.O. Box 83720
Boise, ID 83720
Tel: (208) 334-2270
Fax: (208) 334-2632
E-Mail: board@osbe.state.id.us
URL: http://www.sde.state.id.us/Dept/

State Department of Education
P.O. Box 83720
Boise, ID 83720
Tel: (208) 332-6946

ILLINOIS

Illinois Student Assistance Commission
1755 Lake Cook Rd.
Deerfield, IL 60015
Tel: (800) 899-4722; (847) 948-8500
Fax: (847) 831-8508
E-Mail: isac@wwa.com
URL: http://www.isac-online.org/

INDIANA

State Student Assistance Commission
150 West Market St., Suite 500
Indianapolis, IN 46204
Tel: (317) 232-2350
Fax: (317) 232-3260
E-Mail: grants@ssaci.state.in.us
URL: http://www.ai.org/ssaci/

IOWA

Iowa College Student Aid Commission
200 10th St., 4th Floor
Des Moines, IA 50309
Tel: (800) 383-4222; (515) 281-3501
Fax: (515) 242-3388
E-Mail: icsac@max.state.ia.us
URL: http://www.state.ia.us/collegeaid/

State Department of Education
Grimes State Office Building
Bureau of Instruction & Curriculum
Des Moines, IA 50319
Tel: (515) 242-6716
URL: http://www.state.ia.us/educate/

KANSAS

Kansas Board of Regents
700 S.W. Harrison, Suite 1410
Topeka, KS 66603
Tel: (785) 296-3517
Fax: (785) 296-0983
E-Mail: kim@kbor.state.ks.us or
jbirmingham@kbor.state.ks.us
URL: http://www.kansasregents.org/

State Department of Education
Kansas State Education Building
120 East Tenth St.
Topeka, KS 66612
Tel: (785) 296-4876

KENTUCKY

Kentucky Higher Education Assistance
1050 U.S. 127 South, Suite 102
Frankfort, KY 40601
Tel: (800) 928-8926; (502) 696-7200
Fax: (502) 696-7496
E-Mail: webmaster@kheaa.com
URL: http://www.kheaa.com/

State Department of Education
500 Mero St.
1919 Capital Plaza Tower
Frankfort, KY 40601
Tel: (502) 564-3421

LOUISIANA

Louisiana Office of Student Financial
Assistance
P.O. Box 91202
Baton Rouge, LA 70821
Tel: (800) 259-5626; (225) 922-1012
Fax: (225) 922-0790
E-Mail: custserv@osfa.state.la.us
URL: http://www.osfa.state.la.us/

State Department of Education
P.O. Box 94064
626 North 4th St., 12th Floor
Baton Rouge, LA 70804
Tel: (504) 342-2098
Fax: (225) 922-1089
URL: http://www.doe.state.la.us/DOE/
asps/home.asp

MAINE

Finance Authority of Maine
P.O. Box 949
Augusta, ME 04332
Tel: (800) 228-3734; (207) 623-3263
Fax: (207) 626-8208
E-Mail: info@famemaine.com
URL: http://www.famemaine.com/

Maine Department of Education
23 State House Station
Augusta, ME 04333
Tel: (207) 624-6600
URL: http://janus.state.me.us/education/
homepage.htm

MARYLAND

Maryland Higher Education Commission
Jeffrey Building, 16 Francis St.
Annapolis, MD 21401
Tel: (800) 974-0203
Fax: (410) 974-3513
URL: http://www.mhec.state.md.us/

Maryland State Department of Education
200 West Baltimore St.
Baltimore, MD 21201
Tel: (410) 767-0480; (410) 767-0488

MASSACHUSETTS

Massachusetts Higher Education Board
One Ashburton Place, Room 1401
Boston, MA 02108
Tel: (617) 994-6950
Fax: (617) 727-6397
E-Mail: bhe@bhe.mass.edu
URL: http://www.mass.edu/access/
   resources.htm

Massachusetts Department of Education
350 Main St.
Malden, MA 02148-5023
Tel: (781) 338-3000
http://www.doe.mass.edu/

Massachusetts Higher Education
   Information Center
Boston Public Library
700 Boylston St.
Boston, MA 02116
Tel: (877)-ED-AID-4U (IN MA);
   (617) 536-0200 (OUTSIDE MA)
URL: http://www.heic.org/

MICHIGAN

Michigan Higher Education Assistance
Office of Scholarships and Grants
P.O. Box 30462
Lansing, MI 48909
Tel: (517) 373-3394; (888) 447-2687
Fax: (517) 335-5984
E-Mail: oir@state.mi.us
URL: http://www.MI-StudentAid.org/

State Department of Education
P.O. Box 30008
608 West Allegan St.
Lansing, MI 48909
Tel: (517) 373-3324
http://www.mde.state.mi.us/

MINNESOTA

Minnesota Higher Education Services Office
1450 Energy Park Dr., Suite 350
St. Paul, MN 55108-5227
Tel: (800) 657-3866; (651) 642-0567
Fax: (651) 642-0675
URL: www.mheso.state.mn.us
E-Mail: info@heso.state.mn.us

Minnesota Department of Children, Families
   and Learning
Learner Options Division
1500 Highway 36 West
Roseville, MN 55113-4266
Tel: (651) 582-8259

MISSISSIPPI

Mississippi Postsecondary Education
   Financial Assistance Board
3825 Ridgewood Rd.
Jackson, MS 39211
Tel: (800) 327-2980; (601) 432-6997
Fax: (601) 432-6527
E-Mail: sfa@ihl.state.ms.us
URL: http://www.ihl.state.ms.us/

State Department of Education
Mississippi Teacher Center
P.O. Box 771
Jackson, MS 39205
Tel: (601) 359-3631

MISSOURI

Missouri Coordinating Board for Higher
   Education
3515 Amazonas Dr.
Jefferson City, MO 65109
Tel: (573) 751-2361
Fax: (573) 751-6635
URL: www.cbhe.state.mo.us

State Dept. of Elementary & Secondary
   Education
P.O. Box 480
205 Jefferson St., Sixth Floor
Jefferson City, MO 65102
Tel: (573) 751-2931; (573) 751-1191
URL: http://services.dese.state.mo.us/

MONTANA

Montana Office of Higher Education
2500 Broadway, P.O. Box 203101
Helena, MT 59620
Tel: (406) 444-6570
Fax: (406) 444-1469
URL: http://www.montana.edu/wwwoche

Montana Office of Public Instruction
P.O. Box 202501
Helena, MT 59620-2501
Tel: (406) 444-5663

NEBRASKA

Coordinating Commission for
   Postsecondary Education
P.O. Box 95005
Lincoln, NE 68509
Tel: (402) 471-2847
Fax: (402) 471-2886
E-Mail: staff@ccpe.state.ne.us
URL: http://www.ccpe.state.ne.us/

Nebraska Department of Education
P.O. Box 94987
301 Centennial Mall South
Lincoln, NE 68509
Tel: (402) 471-2784
URL: http://www.nde.state.ne.us/

NEVADA

Nevada Department of Education
700 East Fifth St.
Carson City, NV 89701
Tel: (775) 687-9200
Fax: (775) 687-9101

State Department of Education
700 East Fifth St.
Carson City, NV 89701
Tel: (775) 687-9228

NEW HAMPSHIRE

New Hampshire Postsecondary Education
   Committee
2 Industrial Park Dr.
Concord, NH 03301
Tel: (603) 271-2555
Fax: (603) 271-2696
E-Mail: jknapp@nhfa.state.nh.us
URL: http://www.state.nh.us/
   postsecondary/

State Department of Education
State Office Park South
101 Pleasant St.
Concord, NH 03301
Tel: (603) 271-6051
URL: http://www.ed.state.nh.us/

NEW JERSEY

Office of Student Financial Assistance
4 Quakerbridge Plaza, CN 540
Trenton, NJ 08625
Tel: (800) 792-8670
Fax: (609) 588-7389
URL: www.hesaa.org

State Department of Education
CN500, 100 Riverview Plaza
Trenton, NJ 08625
(609) 777-0800; (609) 984-6314

NEW MEXICO

New Mexico Commission on Higher
   Education
1068 Cerrillos Rd.
Santa Fe, NM 87501
Tel: (800) 279-9777; (505) 827-7383
E-mail: highered@che.state.nm.us
URL: http://www.nmche.org/

State Department of Education
300 Don Gaspar, Education Bldg.
Santa Fe, NM 87501
Tel: (505) 827-6648
URL: http://sde.state.nm.us/

NEW YORK

New York State Higher Education Services
  Corporation
One Commerce Plaza
Albany, NY 12255
Tel: (888) NYS-HESC; (518) 473-1574;
  (518) 474-5642
Fax: (518) 473-3749
URL: www.hesc.com

State Education Department
111 Education Building, Washington Ave.
Albany, NY 12234
Tel: (518) 474-3852; (518) 474-5313
URL: http://www.nysed.gov/

NORTH CAROLINA

North Carolina Educational Assistance
  Authority
P.O. Box 14103
Research Triangle Park, NC 27709
Tel: (919) 549-8614; (800) 700-1775
Fax: (919) 549-8481
E-Mail: information@ncseaa.edu
URL: http://www.ncseaa.edu/

North Carolina Department of Public
  Instruction
301 N. Wilmington St.
Raleigh, NC 27601
Tel: (919) 807-3300
URL: http://www.dpi.state.nc.us/

NORTH DAKOTA

North Dakota University System
North Dakota Student Financial Assistance
  Program
Department 215
600 East Boulevard Ave.
Bismarck, ND 58505-0230
Tel: (701) 328-4114
Fax: (701) 328-2961
E-Mail: ndus_office@ndus.nodak.edu
URL: http://www.nodak.edu/

State Department of Public Instruction
State Capitol Building, 9th Floor
600 East Boulevard Ave.
Bismarck, ND 58505
Tel: (701) 328-2098; (701) 328-2317

OHIO

Ohio Board of Regents
309 South Fourth St.
P.O. Box 182452
Columbus, OH 43218
Tel: (888) 833-1133; (614) 466-7420
Fax: (614) 752-5903
URL: http://www.regents.state.oh.us/sgs/

OKLAHOMA

Oklahoma State Regents for Higher
  Education
Oklahoma Tuition Aid Grant Program
500 Education Building, State Capitol
  Complex
Oklahoma City, OK 73105
Tel: (405) 524-9100
Fax: (405) 524-9230
URL: http://www.okhighered.org/

OREGON

Oregon Student Assistance Commission
1500 Valley River Dr., #100
Eugene, OR 97401
Tel: (541) 687-7400; (800) 452-8807
Fax: (541) 687-7419
E-Mail: thomas.f.turner@state.or.us
URL: http://www.osac.state.or.us/

PENNSYLVANIA

Pennsylvania Higher Education Assistance
  Agency
1200 North 7th Street
Harrisburg, PA 17102
Tel: (800) 692-7435; (717) 720-2800
URL: http://www.pheaa.org/students/
  index.shtml

RHODE ISLAND

Rhode Island Higher Education Assistance
  Authority
560 Jefferson Blvd.
Warwick, RI 02886
Tel: (800) 922-9855; (401) 736-1100
Fax: (401) 732-3541
URL: http://www.riheaa.org

State Department of Education
255 Westminster St.
Providence, RI 02903
Tel: (401) 222-4600
URL: www.ridoe.net

SOUTH CAROLINA

South Carolina Higher Education Tuition
  Grants
1310 Lady St.
P.O. Box 12159, Suite 811
Columbia, SC 29211
Tel: (803) 896-1120
Fax: (803) 734-1426
URL: http://www.state.sc.us/tuitiongrants/

South Carolina Commission on Higher
  Education
1333 Main St., Suite 200
Columbia, SC 29201
Tel: (803) 737-2260
Fax: (803) 737-2297
URL: www.che400.state.sc.us/web/
  services.htm

South Carolina Department of Education
1100 Rutledge Building
1429 Senate St.
Columbia, SC 29201
Tel: (803) 734-8815
URL: http://www.state.sc.us/sde/

SOUTH DAKOTA

Department of Education & Cultural Affairs
Office of the Secretary
700 Governors Dr.
Pierre, SD 57501
Tel: (605) 773-3134

South Dakota Board of Regents
306 East Capitol Ave., Suite 200
Pierre, SD 57501-2409
Tel: (605) 773-3455
E-Mail: info@ris.sdbor.edu
URL: http://www.ris.sdbor.edu/

TENNESSEE

Tennessee Student Assistance Corporation
Parkway Towers, Suite 1950
404 James Robertson Parkway
Nashville, TN 37243
Tel: (800) 342-1663; (615) 741-1346
Fax: (615) 741-6101
URL: www.state.tn.us/tsac/

State Department of Education
100 Cordell Hull Building
Nashville, TN 37219
Tel: (615) 741-2731
URL: http://www.state.tn.us/education/
  index.html

TEXAS

Texas Higher Education Coordinating Board
P.O. Box 12788, Capitol Station
Austin, TX 78711
Tel: (800) 242-3062; (512) 427-6101
Fax: (512) 427-6420

UTAH

Utah State Board of Regents
Three Triad Center
Suite 550
355 West North Temple
Salt Lake City, UT 84180-1205
Tel: (801) 321-7100
Fax: (801) 321-7199
E-Mail: heyring@utahsbr.edu
URL: http://www.utahsbr.edu/

Utah State Office of Education
250 East 500 South
Salt Lake City, UT 84111
Tel: (801) 538-7782
URL: http://www.usoe.k12.ut.us/

VERMONT

Vermont Student Assistance Corporation
Champlain Mill, P.O. Box 2000
Winooski, VT 05404
Tel: (800) 642-3177; (802) 655-9602
URL: www.vsac.org/

VIRGINIA

State Council of Higher Education
James Monroe Bldg., 101 North 14th St.
P.O. Box 2120
Richmond, VA 23219
Tel: (804) 786-1690; (804) 225-2877
Fax: (804) 225-2604
E-Mail: bradford@schev.edu
   or nardo@schev.edu
URL: http://www.schev.edu/

WASHINGTON

Washington State Higher Education
   Coordinating Board
917 Lakeridge Way, S.W.
P.O. Box 43430
Olympia, WA 98504
Tel: (360) 753-7800; (360) 753-7850
Fax: (360) 753-7808
E-Mail: info@hecb.wa.gov
URL: www.hecb.wa.gov

State Department of Public Instruction
Old Capitol Building FG11
Olympia, WA 98504
Tel: (360) 753-2858
URL: http://www.k12.wa.us/

WEST VIRGINIA

Higher Education Policy Commission
P.O. Box 4007
Charleston, WV 25364
Tel: (304) 558-4016; (304) 558-2101
Fax: (304) 558-0259
E-Mail: healey@scusco.wvnet.edu
   or thralls@scusco.wvnet.edu
URL: http://www.scusco.wvnet.edu

WISCONSIN

Higher Educational Aids Board
P.O. Box 7885
Madison, WI 53707
Tel: (608) 267-2206
Fax: (608) 267-2808
E-Mail: heabmail@heab.state.wi.us
URL: http://heab.state.wi.us/

State Department of Public Instruction
125 South Webster St.
P.O. Box 7841
Madison, WI 53707
Tel: (608) 266-2364; (608) 266-3706
URL: http://www.dpi.state.wi.us/

WYOMING

Wyoming Community College Commission
2020 Carey Ave., 8th Floor
Cheyenne, WY 82002
Tel: (307) 777-7763
Fax: (307) 777-6567
E-Mail: thenry@commission.wcc.edu
   or blovejoy@commission.wcc.edu
URL: http://commission.wcc.edu/

State Department of Education
Hathaway Building
2300 Capitol Ave., 2nd Floor
Cheyenne, WY 82002
Tel: (307) 777-6265; (307) 777-6984
URL: http://www.k12.wy.us/wdehome.html

ScholarshipCoach.com Keyword Master List

	Scholarship/Topic	**Keyword**
A	Angier B. Duke Memorial Scholarships	DUKE
	All-USA College Academic Team	ALLUSACOL
	American Legion Oratorical Contest	LEGIONORA
	Ayn Rand Scholarships	AYNRAND
B	Barbara Thomas Enterprises Scholarship	BTHOMAS
	Barry M. Goldwater Scholarship	BARGOLD
	Beth K. Fields Scholarship	BFIELDS
	BMI Student Composer Awards	BMICOMP
	Burger King/McLamore North American Scholarship	BURGER
C	California Institute of Technology Freshman Merit Awards	CALTECH
	Canon Envirothon	ENVIRO
	Century III Leaders	CENTURY
	Coca-Cola Scholars Program	COKE
	Collegiate Inventors Competition	COLINVENT
D	Discover Card Tribute Awards	DISCOVER
	Dollars for Scholars Program	DOLSCHOL
	Dore Schary Awards	SCHARY
	DuPont Challenge	DUPONT
	Duracell/NSTA Invention Challenge	DURACELL
E	Elie Wiesel Prize in Ethics	WIESEL
	Elks "Most Valuable Student" Scholarship	ELKS
	Emory Scholars Program	EMORY
	ESPN SportsFigures Scholarship	ESPN
	Essay Critiques	ESSAY
	Executive Women International Scholarship Program	EXECWOMEN
F	First Nationwide Network Scholarship Program	FIRSTNAT
	FTE Undergraduate Fellows	FTE
G	Georgia-Pacific Foundation Community Scholarship	GEOPAC
	Golden Key Adult Scholar Awards	GOLDKAD
	Golden Key Art Competition	GOLDKART
	Golden Key Literary Contest	GOLDKLIT
	Golden Key Performing Arts Showcase	GOLDKPERF

Scholarship/Topic	Keyword
H Harry S. Truman Scholarship Program	TRUMAN
Hearst Journalism Awards Program	HEARST
Hertz Foundation Fellowship	HERTZ
Hodson Scholarships	HODSON
Homework Helpline	HELPLINE
I Imation Computer Arts Scholarship	IMATION
J Jacob Javits Fellowship	JAVITS
Jazz Club of Sarasota Scholarship Program	JAZZSARA
Jefferson Scholars	JEFFERSON
John Lennon Scholarship	LENNON
K Karla Scherer Foundation Scholarship	SCHERER
Kemper Scholars Grant Program	KEMPER
Kodak Scholarship Program	KODAK
L Lilly for Learning Diabetes Scholarship Program	LILLY
Little Family Foundation MBA Fellowship Award	LITTLEFAM
M Matching Scholarships	MATCHMONEY
McCabe Scholarships	MCCABE
Milky Way/AAU High School All-American	MILKYWAY
Miss Active Teen Across America	ACTIVTEEN
Morehead Awards	MOREHEAD
Morris K. Udall Scholarship	UDALL
N NACA Regional Council Student Leader Scholarships	NACA
National Alliance for Excellence Scholarships	EXCEL
National Defense Science & Engineering Graduate Fellowship	NATLDEF
National History Day Contest	HISTDAY
National Honor Society Scholarship	HONOR
National "Make It Yourself With Wool" Contest	WOOL
O Optimist International Essay Contest	OPTESSAY
Optimist International Oratorical Contest	OPTORA
Orville Redenbachers Second Start Scholarship	ORVILLE

	Scholarship/Topic	*Keyword*
P	Parke-Davis Epilepsy Scholarship Award	PDAVIS
	Perspectives from Parents	PARENTS
	Portland Trailblazers Scholarship	BLAZERS
	President's Student Service Scholarships	PRESSERV
	Prudential Spirit of Community Awards	PRUDENT
R	Rice University Merit Scholarships	RICE
	Robert C. Byrd Honors Scholarship	BYRD
	Rotary Foundation Ambassadorial Scholarships	ROTARY
S	Scholarship Coach National Tour	TOUR
	Scholarship Coach Search Profile Worksheet	PROFSHEET
	The Scholarship Scouting Report	SCOUTREP
	Scholarship Search Case Studies	CASESTUDY
	Scholarship Database Updates	DATABASE
	Scholastic Art & Writing Awards	SCHOLART
	State Farm Exceptional Student Fellowship	STATEFARM
	"Stuck at Prom" Scholarship Contest	PROM
T	Talbots Women's Scholarship Fund	TALBOTS
	Tall Clubs International Scholarship	TALL
	Target All-Around Scholarship	TARGET
	ThinkQuest Internet Challenge	TQUEST
	Toshiba/NSTA ExploraVision Awards	EXPLORA
	Tylenol Scholarship	TYLENOL
U	University of Chicago College Honor Scholarships	UCHICAGO
	U.S. Senate Youth Program	SENATE
	U.S. Student Fulbright Grants	FULBRIGHT
V	Voice of Democracy Program	VOICE
W	Washington Crossing Foundation Scholarship	WASHCROSS
	Washington University in St. Louis Scholarships	WASHU
	"Will to Win" Asthma Athlete Scholarship	ASTHMA
Y	Young American Creative Patriotic Art Awards	PATRIART
	Young Naturalist Awards	YOUNGNAT

Index

A

AAU High-School All-American
   scholarship, 201–202
ABC/Capital Cities, 76
academic record
   alternative achievement, 234
   demonstrating achievement, 228–229
   nudging up your GPA, 229–233
   quality of, 233
Academic Research Information System,
   134
Academic Scholarship and Fellowship
   Programs (Washington University in
   St. Louis), 164
academic scholarships, 162
accredited institutions, 85
action steps. See academic records;
   interviews; recommendation letters;
   searching for scholarships
Activist application theme, 190
activities, targeted awards based on, 79
activities lists, 311–314, 321
ACT scores, 83
addenda to transcripts, 316–317
additional materials for applications,
   319–320, 322
administrators of scholarships, 72–73,
   87, 346–347
admirable persons essays, 279
adult students, 65–66, 328
   application themes of, 180
   Lifetime Learning tax credit, 45–46
   strategies for, 160
Advanced Placement (AP), 349–351
advisers, school, 248
age requirements, 27
Air Force National Guard, 53
Alabama, 69
All-USA College Academic Team
   Program, 66
alternative academic achievement, 234
American Association for Nude
   Recreation, 71
American Online (AOL), 132
AMIDEAST, 167
Angier B. Duke Memorial Scholarships
   (Duke University), 163
Annual Survey of Financial Aid Programs,
   129–130
AOL, 132
applicants, 41, 74–79
application components, 88
   auditions, 82
   awards/honors, 83
   essays/short answer questions, 80
   extracurricular activity lists, 80–81
   focus of, 79–80
   grade transcripts, 81
   interviews, 82
   letters of recommendation, 81–82
   sample work/project submissions, 80
   test results, 83
application judges. See judges; judging
   criteria
applications. See also content strategies;
   essays; paperwork; winning
   applications

activity lists, 311–314, 321
additional materials, 319–320, 322
awards/honors lists, 314–315, 322
blank spaces in, 307–309, 321
mailing, 113, 320–321, 322
multiple, 81
myths about, 27–28
paperwork, 321
prioritizing multiple, 240
requesting, 113–114
rereading/reviewing before interviews,
   332
reviewing, 98, 103
stat sheet part, 310–311, 321
transcripts, 322
trimming the fat from, 309
unsuccessful/successful, 176–177, 195
application themes
   about, 178–179
   Activists, 190
   of adult students, 180
   among recommendation letters, 289
   Athlete, 194
   balance, 196
   Brainiac, 189
   Creative Talent, 187
   credibility, 180, 196
   Do-Gooder, 186
   employing your theme, 181–184, 196
   Entrepreneur, 191
   examples of winning, 185–194
   Leader, 192
   painting your self-portrait, 177–180,
      195
   primary and secondary, 179–180, 196
   Scientist, 193
   staying balanced, 184
   Survivor, 188
   thematic variety, 195
Army National Guard, 53
arriving for interviews, 333
art scholarships, 162
Arts Recognition and Talent Search, 82
Ask the Coach
   about Ask the Coach, 13
   adult returning students, 160
   applying for difficult-to-win
      scholarships, 242
   athletic scholarships and merit awards,
      51–52
   college versus high school students,
      judging of, 223
   databases for minority students, 139
   deadlines, 84
   demonstrating need, 34
   distance learning scholarships, 67
   effect of merit scholarships on
      financial aid packages, 43–44
   eligibility of homeschoolers, 62
   graduate students, databases for, 134
   international students, 167–168
   Internet resources for Canadian
      students, 144–145
   long-distance (telephone) interviews,
      337
   merit, meaning of, 35
   motivating your children, 99

paying others to find scholarships,
   130–131
prepaid-tuition/college-savings plans,
   46–47
recommendation letters, using for
   college applications, 290–291
school-specific scholarships for
   incoming freshmen, 163–164
students with disabilities, 155–156
study abroad scholarships, 147–148
taxes on scholarship money, 86
time investment for winning
   scholarships, 249
transcripts for homeschoolers,
   317–318
U.S. agency scholarship funding, 68–69
word limits in essays, 259
younger students' preparation, 227
Association of Universities and Colleges
   of Canada Online, 144
"Associations Unlimited," 166
asthma, scholarship for people with, 155
Athlete application theme, 194
athletes, 26, 161
athletic scholarships, 48–50, 51–52, 162
auditions, 82
availability of funds, 55, 87
awards/honors, 83, 314–315, 322
Ayn Rand Institute, 246

B

balance in application themes, 184, 196
Barbara Thomas Enterprises Scholarship,
   66
Beth K. Fields Scholarship, 160
Better Business Bureau (BBB), 85
blank spaces in applications, 307–309,
   321
body language during interviews, 335
Brainiac application theme, 189
browsing systems in databases, 121–122
Bureau of Educational and Cultural
   Affairs, 168
Burger King/McLamore North American
   Scholarship, 79
bursaries, 144
Business and Professional Women's
   Foundation, Career Advancement
   Scholarship Program, 78
business skills application theme, 191
Byrd scholarships, 153–154

C

California Institute of Technology
   (Caltech), 72, 163
campaigning for scholarships
   applying for many scholarships,
      239–240, 251
   attitude, 252
   learning by example, 248–249, 252
   leveraging school work/class time,
      246–248, 251–252
   multiple applications, 242–243, 251
   personal inventory lists, 244–246, 251
   recycling essays, 243–244, 251
   smaller, local scholarships, 241–242,
      251

campaigning for scholarships (*continued*)
    sticking with it, 250–251
campus jobs, 118
Canadian students, 144–145
Capital Cities, 76
Career Advancement Scholarship
    Program, 78
career aspirations essays, 278
career exploration programs, 75–76
career goals, targeted awards based on,
    76–77
Carson, Will, 289
CASHE/Wiredscholar database, 128–129
Cassidy, Dan, 132
Century III Leaders program, 82, 203
Chambers of Commerce, 151
chapter summaries, 56–58, 87–88,
    103–104, 169–171, 195–196,
    215–216, 233–234, 251–252,
    283–284, 303–304, 321–322,
    338–339
character traits, 207, 209, 213
character witnesses, recommendation
    letters from, 287
church-affiliated colleges, 150
Citizens' Scholarship Foundation of
    America (CSFA), 73
civic organizations, 71
class work, 246
club participation, 223
Coach's Locker Room, 15. *See also* Ask
    the Coach; Scholarship Coach
Coca-Cola Scholars Program, 154,
    281–282, 346–347
college admissions advantage, 42–43, 57
College Aid Sources for Higher
    Education (CASHE) database,
    128–129
College Board
    Advanced Placement (AP) testing, 350
    *Annual Survey of Financial Aid
        Programs*, 129–130
    ExPAN database, 129–130, 161–162
    loan statistics, 37
    tuition statistics, 30
college goals, targeted awards based on,
    76–77
College Honor Scholarships (University
    of Chicago), 163
College-Level Examination Program
    (CLEP), 352
CollegeLink, 141–142
CollegeNet, 141–142
CollegeQuest database, 131–132
College Quickfinder, 162
college-savings plan, 46–47
college-specific financial aid
    applications, 34
college-sponsored scholarships, 72
college students, undergraduate, 62–64
college versus high school students,
    judging of, 223
Commission for Adult Learners (Penn
    State University), 160
community groups, 150–151
community service programs, 54, 153
company programs, 154

competitors for awards, 205–207
components of applications. *See*
    application components
consulting other essays, 271–272
content strategies, 233–234
contests
    administrators of, 73
    essay, 246
    "Make It Yourself with Wool," 34
    "Stuck at Prom," 35
    Voice of Democracy, 205
    for younger students, 60
continuing education, 160
Cornell University Graduate Fellowship
    Notebook, 134
Cornwell, Casey, 210
corporate sponsors, 70–71, 76, 168, 241
Cost of Attendance (COA), 34
costs. *See* fees
cover letters, 293–296
creating opportunities, 225–227
Creative Talent application theme, 187
creativity, 187
credential management programs, 62
credentials, analyzing your, 219–220
credibility, 180, 196
criteria. *See* judging criteria
CSS Profile, 34
cultivating relationships with
    recommenders, 291–292, 303

D

databases. *See also* websites
    about, 119–121
    browsing systems in, 121–122
    CASHE/Wiredscholar, 128–129
    CD-ROM databases, 122–123
    College Aid Sources for Higher
        Education (CASHE), 128–129
    College Board/ExPAN, 129–130
    CollegeQuest, 131–132
    essential techniques for, 142–143
    exploring a variety of, 126
    FastAid/National Scholarship
        Research Service, 132
    Fastweb, 133
    fees for using, 121
    FreSch, 134–135
    for graduate students, 134
    Internet, 121–122
    keywords in, 137
    licensed, 124–125
    matching systems in, 121–122,
        142–143
    for minority students, 139
    New York University, Grants in
        Graduate Studies, 134
    print directories, 123
    questionnaires for, 121, 132, 133
    rated alphabetical listing of, 128–142
    rating system for, 126–128
    Reference Service Press (RSP),
        135–136
    reviews and profiles of, 126–128
    Scholaraid/Student Advantage,
        136–137
    Scholarship Experts, 137–138

Scholarship Resource Network (SRN),
    138
Scholarships 101, 139–140
searching source, 125
source, 124–125, 125
SRN Express, 138
strengths and weaknesses of, 145–146
tools for, 169
types of, 123–125
Wintergreen/Orchard House (WOH),
    141–142
deadlines, 84, 114, 143, 298
debt, effects of on future, 37–38
defining yourself. *See* application themes
definitions
    grants, 31
    loan, 31
    scholarships, 31
    subsidized, 31
    unsubsidized, 31
DeLaite, Alexandra, 180
demonstrating achievement, 228–229
demonstrating need, 24, 34
Department of Defense, 53
dependents, veterans' benefits for, 53
Descendants of the Signers of the
    Declaration of Independence
    Scholarship, 76
diabetes, scholarship for people with, 155
Direct Stafford Loans, 31, 68
disbursement of scholarship awards,
    345–346
discouragement, 250–251, 252
Discover Card Tribute Awards, 3, 183,
    203
distance learning scholarships, 67
distributions of awards, need-based, 38
Do-Gooder application theme, 186
Dollars for Scholars, 151–152
dollar value of scholarships, 153
drama scholarships, 162
dressing for interviews, 333
Duke University, 72, 163
Duracell/NSTA Invention Challenge, 80

E

Eisenhower, Dwight D., 209
eligibility
    expanding your, 76
    of homeschoolers, 62
    HOPE Scholarship, 45
Eli Lilly sponsorship, 155
Elks' "Most Valuable Student"
    scholarship, 36
Emory Scholars Program (Emory
    University), 163
Emory University, 72
employer benefits, 154–155
employing your application theme,
    181–184, 196
employment, targeted awards based on,
    79
employment/activities/hobbies, 79
Encyclopedia of Associations, 165–166
Entrepreneur application theme, 191
entrepreneurialism, 221
entry fees, 84–85, 88

essay contests, 246. *See also* contests
essays, 203, 243–244
  advice for specific topics, 278–280, 283
  effective organization, 257–258
  finding your voice, 266–270, 283
  help from parents with, 96–97
  honing, 273–277, 283
  keeping things personal, 256–257
  making each sentence count, 259–260
  organization of essay, 282
  personal details, 282
  short answer questions, 80, 283
  show, don't tell principle, 254–256, 282
  spanning topics/recycling essays, 261–266, 283
  tips for revising, 276–277
  unique and memorable, 260–261, 282
  writer's block, 270–273, 283
ethnicity, targeted awards based on, 77–78
examples
  asking for, 199
  great recommendation letters, 299–302
  sample recommendation cover letter, 295–296
  winning application themes, 185–194
  winning essays, 267–270, 273–276
ExPAN database, 129–130, 161–162
expanding on strong points, 220–222
Expected Family Contribution (EFC), 34, 43
exploring a variety of databases, 126
extension schools, 160
extracurricular activity lists, 80–81, 223

F

family affiliation, targeted awards based on, 76
family income, 36
famous people, recommendation letters from, 302
FastAid/National Scholarship Research Service database, 132
Fastweb database, 133
Federal Trade Commission (FTC), 85
Federal Work-Study (FWS) program, 47–48
fees
  entry, 84–85
  for scholarship search companies, 130–131
  using databases, 121
fellowships, 64–65
filling blank space in forms, 308
financial aid offices, 117
financial aid sources
  Americorps, 54
  athletic scholarships, 48–50
  effect of merit scholarships on, 43–44
  military scholarships, 52–54
  summary of, 58
  tax credits, 44–47
  work-study, 47–48
financial burden, considering for future, 37–38

First Cavalry Division Association Scholarship, 76
529 investment plans, 46–47
flexibility in collecting payment, 346
Florida, 69
focusing on a few awards, 29–30
follow-up, 97, 113–114
Foundation Directory, 166
Foundation Grants to Individuals, 166
Franklin, Benjamin, 211
fraternal lodges, sponsorship by, 71, 78
Free Application for Federal Student Aid (FAFSA), 34
  when to file, 36
  and work-study programs, 47
free writing, 271
FreSch database, 134–135
Freshman Merit Awards (Caltech), 163
"front-loading," 38
full portability, 85
"full-ride" athletic scholarships, 50
funding. *See* programs; scholarships by name; sources of funding
Future Farmers of America, 206

G

Geise, Mattias, 335
gender, targeted awards based on, 78–79
geographic region, targeted awards based on, 75
Georgia HOPE Scholarship, 69
Georgia-Pacific Corporation, 241
GI Bill, 53
goals, describing your future, 181–182
Golden Key Adult Scholar Awards, 66
government funding, 33, 67–69, 153–154, 357–362
GPAs (grade point averages), 153, 189
  being resourceful, 233
  focusing on most important material, 231
  grade cutoffs, 234
  improving, 229–233
  myths about, 25–26
  procuring course overview materials, 232–233
  putting yourself in teacher's shoes, 231–232
  raising, 248
  requirements on maintaining, 346–347
grade point averages. *See* GPAs (grade point averages)
grade transcripts, 81
GraduateAid, 144
Graduate Awards Database (Simon Fraser University), 145
graduate students, 64–65, 117
  application themes of, 179
  databases for, 134
  essays by, 263
  interviews for, 327
graduate studies funding, 68
grandparents, 98
grants
  definition of, 31
  versus loans, 55

  Pell Grant, 33, 68
  summary of, 56
Grants in Graduate Studies database, 134
Gray, Jennifer, 240
greatest achievement essays, 278–279
Grinnell College, 48
grooming for interviews, 333
growth experiences essays, 280
Guerilla Tactics
  about, 14
  addressing weak areas in your record, 224
  appending school transcripts, 317
  exploring a variety of databases, 126
  filling blank space in forms, 308
  getting electronic copies of recommendation letters, 297
  highlighting personal qualities, 214
  interviewing local bank managers, 152
  making homework count, 247
  obtaining numerous recommendation letters, 290–291
  revising/editing essays, 277
  searching source databases, 125
  supplementary materials, placing with interviewers, 332
  tailoring your materials, 204
  typing names of scholarships into search engines, 159
  using the Internet to scout other schools, 149
  working in your school's scholarship center, 118

H

handshakes, 334
Harry S. Truman Scholarship, 64
Harvard University, 4, 72, 117, 350
Hertz Foundation Fellowship, 64
Hicks, George, 204
HigherEd Net, 129
highlighting personal qualities, 214
high school students, 60–61, 220–222
  advanced placement courses, 351
  versus college, judging of, 223
  government funding, 153–154
  homeschoolers, 62, 317–318
hobbies, targeted awards based on, 79
Hodson Scholarships (Johns Hopkins University), 163
Holley, Heidi, 205
homeschoolers, 62, 317–318
homework, 247
Hong, Donna, 351
honing your essays, 273–277
honors/awards, 83, 314–315, 322
HOPE Scholarship, 44–45, 69

I

Illinois Student Assistance Commission, HigherEd Net, 129
income, family, 36
individual achievement, 39
Intel Science Talent Search, 73, 80
International Baccalaureate (IB) exams, 349

International Education Financial Aid, 167
International Institute of Education, 147
International Maritime Organization, 168
international students, finding scholarships for, 167–168
International Study and Travel Center Study Abroad Scholarships, 147
International Telecommunications Union, 167
Internet. *See also* websites
  researching interviewers, 325–326
  resources for Canadian students, 144–145
  using to scout other schools, 149
interviewers
  finding common ground with, 335
  placing supplementary materials with, 332
  questions to ask the, 330
  researching, 325–326
interviewing local bank managers, 152
interviews, 82
  anecdotes, 326–327
  anticipating questions, 327–328
  avoiding annoying habits during, 335–336
  day of, tips for, 332–333, 338
  key points, 326
  monologues during, 334–335
  practicing, 330–331
  preparing for, 324–332, 338
  questions to ask the interviewer, 330
  responses, preparing, 329–330
  reviewing written application before, 332
  samples of your work, preparing, 331
  by telephone, 337, 339
  tips for behavior during, 334–336, 338
  wrapping up, 336
IRS publications, 970, "Tax Benefits for Higher Education," 46
issue-oriented essays, 279–280
Ivy League institutions, 72, 163

J

Jacob Javits Fellowship, 65
jobs on campus, 118
Johns Hopkins University, 41, 43, 163
judges, 73–74, 87
  catching interest of, 260–261
  panels of, 335
judging criteria, 74, 201–202
  addressing the, 213–215
  character, 212–213
  civic duty, 211
  competition, 215
  hard work, 208
  individual initiative, 209–210
  overcoming obstacles, 208
  overview of, 207
  passion/enthusiasm, 210
  perseverance, 209
  preparing key points for interviews, 326
  purpose, 211–212
  responsibility, 210–211
  teamwork, 208–209
  universal criteria, 216

K

Kaplan, Gary and Patana, 101-102
Kennedy, John F., 211
Kentucky, 69
keywords
  about, 15–16
  in databases, 137
  ScholarshipCoach.com, 15–16, 58, 88–90, 104, 171–172, 196, 216, 234, 252, 284, 304, 322, 339, 363–366
Kuo, Tom, 221

L

Leadership skills application theme, 192
League of Red Cross Societies, 167–168
letters of recommendation. *See* recommendation letters
letter-writing for scholarship information, 113
leverage, 38–39, 55, 57
leveraging school work/class time, 246–248, 251–252
licensed databases, 124–125
Lifetime Learning tax credit, 44, 45–46
Lilly for Learning Diabetes Scholarship Program, 155
Little Family Foundation MBA Fellowship Award, 64
loans
  deferments of through Americorps, 54
  definition of, 31
  Direct Stafford Loan, 31
  versus grants/scholarships, 55
  numbers of, 37
  replacing with scholarships/grants, 32
  subsidized/unsubsidized, 31
  summary of, 56
local businesses, 151
local-level sponsorship, 71
long-distance (telephone) interviews, 337
Louisiana, 69
low-income families, 24–25

M

MacDowell-Boyer, Grace, 66
Mach25 browsing system, 141
mailing applications, 113, 320–321, 322
"Make It Yourself with Wool" contest, 34
making your points during interviews, 335–336
Maryland, 69
Massachusetts Institute of Technology, 163
matching scholarships, 161
matching systems in databases, 121–122, 142–143
MBA Fellowship Award (Little Family Foundation), 64
McCabe Scholarships (Swarthmore College), 164
McLamore North American Scholarship, 76

medical conditions, 155–156, 226
mentors, 193
merit, 33–36, 56–57
merit-based awards, 164. *See also* need-based awards
  athletic scholarships, 51–52
  effects on need-based awards, 43–44
  hidden benefits of, 39–43
  importance of, 55
  leverage offered by, 39
  myths about, 25–26
  spending your, 85–86
  state-funded, 69
  state government funded, 69
  who provides, 35
Merit Scholarships (Rice University), 164
merit within need, 40–42
metaphors, 261–266
Michigan, 69
military scholarships, 52–54, 69, 76
Milky Way/AAU High-School All-American scholarship, 201–202
minority students, 26, 77–78, 139, 161, 162
Montgomery GI Bill, 53
Moss, William, 256
"Most Valuable Student" scholarship (Elks), 36
multinational corporations, 168. *See also* corporate sponsors
multiple applications, 81, 261–266
music scholarships, 162
myths about scholarships
  age requirements, 27
  applying for scholarships, 27–28
  focusing on a few awards, 29–30
  low-income families, 24–25
  merit scholarships, 25–26
  minority students, 26
  past actions/choices, 28–29

N

National Association of Press Women, 78
National Association of Secondary School Principals (NASSP), 73
National Association of State Student Grant and Aid programs, 69
National Collegiate Athletic Association (NCAA), 48–49, 51
National Defense Science and Engineering Graduate Fellowship, 65
National Guard programs, 53
National Honor Society (NHS) Scholarship, 71, 73, 75
National Scholarship Research Service database, 132
National Science Teachers Association (NSTA), 73
need, 33–36, 56–57
need-based awards. *See also* merit-based awards
  effects of merit awards on, 43–44, 57
  government, 40–41
  limitations of, 36–38, 57
  Pell Grant, 33, 68
"need-gapping," 37

New Mexico, 69
New York University, Grants in Graduate Studies database, 134
nomination statements, 298
nontraditional students, 65–66, 317–318. *See also* adult students
North Atlantic Regional Schools, 62
North Dakota Division of Independent Study, 62
nudging up your GPA, 229–233
nursing scholarships, ROTC, 52

O

official transcripts, 315–316
older students. *See* adult students
Oregon, 70
organizational membership, targeted awards based on, 75–76
Organization of American States, 167
organization of essays, 257–258
Orville Redenbacher's Second Start Scholarship, 66
overcoming obstacles application theme, 188

P

painting your self-portrait, 177–180, 195
paperwork, 321
    attaching additional sheets to application, 307
    copies of, 306
    organization of, 97, 103
    saving drafts/revisions, 309–310
    tracking details of awards, 347–348
    transcripts, 315–319
    typing your application, 306–307
parents
    being a sounding board, 97–98, 103
    employer benefits, 154–155
    follow-up by, 97
    giving support/encouragement, 100, 104
    motivating your child, 99, 103
    organizing, 97, 103
    research assistance, 96–97, 103
    reviewing the application, 98, 103
    role of, 101–102
    scholarship searching, 93–95, 103
    strategizing, 95–96, 103
    tracking details of awards, 348
    ways to help with strategies, 95–96, 103
partially portable scholarships, 85, 88–90
past achievement, 79
past actions/choices, 28–29
paying others to find scholarships, 130–131
payment plans, 345–346
Pell Grant, 33, 68
Penn State University, 155, 160
people with disabilities, 79, 155–156
perseverance, 250–251
personal information, 131, 256–257, 314
personal qualities, 52, 213–215, 282
Petrovic, Michelle, 226
political convictions, 190

portable merit scholarships, 85, 88–90
positioning strategies, 198, 215. *See also* judging criteria
practicing for interviews, 333
"preferential packaging," 40–42, 44, 57
prepaid-tuition/college-savings plans, 46–47
preparation of younger students, 227
preparing for interviews, 325–326. *See also* interviews
primary and secondary websites, 157–158
primary application themes, 179–180, 196
primary Websites, 157–158
Principal's Leadership Award, 73
principles of scholarship campaigns. *See* campaigning for scholarships
principles of searching. *See* databases; searching for scholarships
printed directories, 131
prioritizing multiple applications, 240
prison inmates and scholarships, 29
private colleges, 168
private-sector scholarship programs, 70
programs. *See also* scholarship programs; scholarships by name
    All-USA College Academic Team Program, 66
    Annual Survey of Financial Aid Programs, 129–130
    Business and Professional Women's Foundation, Career Advancement Scholarship Program, 78
    career exploration programs, 75–76
    Century III Leaders program, 82
    Coca-Cola Scholars Program, 154, 281–282, 346–347
    College-Level Examination Program (CLEP), 352
    community service programs, 54, 153
    company programs, 154
    credential management programs, 62
    Emory Scholars Program, 163
    employer programs, 154
    Federal Work-Study (FWS) program, 47–48
    Free Application for Federal Student Aid (FAFSA) and work-study programs, 47
    Lilly for Learning Diabetes Scholarship Program, 155
    for merit-based financial aid, 55
    National Association of State Student Grant and Aid programs, 69
    National Guard programs, 53
    private-sector scholarship programs, 70
    public officers' programs, 70
    Robert C. Byrd Honors Scholarship program, 68, 153
    special government funding for high school students, 153–154
    U.S. Senate Youth Program Scholarship, 327
    Washington University in St. Louis, Academic Scholarship and Fellowship Programs, 164

proofreading, 98
providers of scholarships. *See* programs; scholarships by name
Prudential Spirit of Community Awards, 73
PSAT scores, 83
public officers' programs, 70

Q

qualities of great recommendation letters, 299–302
quality of academic record, 233
questionnaires, 121, 132, 133
questions
    anticipating interview, 327–328
    to ask, 200–201, 230
    essays/short answer, 80, 283
questions during application process. *See also* essays
    anticipating interview questions, 327–328
    short answer, 281–282
    typical interview, 328–329

R

race, targeted awards based on, 77–78
ranking your activities, 312–313
rating system for databases, 126–128
recommendation letters, 81–82, 183
    accumulating numerous, 289–290, 303
    action steps for great, 287–288
    asking for modifications to, 303
    from character witnesses, 287
    communicating with writers of, 293–294, 303
    cultivating relationships with recommenders, 291–292, 303
    from famous people, 302
    getting copies of, 297, 303
    list of potential writers, 288, 303
    minimizing work for writers of, 296–299
    obtaining numerous, 290–291
    qualities of great, 299–302
    recognizing outstanding, 304
    sources for, 288
    themes among, 289
    using for college applications, 290–291
recording yourself, 272
recycling essays, 261–266
Reference Service Press (RSP) database, 135–136
religious affiliation scholarships, 162
religious denomination, targeted awards based on, 77–78
requesting applications, 113–114
research assistance from parents, 96–97, 103
Reserve Officers' Training Corps (ROTC), 52–53, 162
returning students. *See* adult students
rewriting essays, 273–277
Rice University, 72, 164
Richmond, Aileen, 241

Robert C. Byrd Honors Scholarship program, 68, 153
role of parents, 101–102
ROTC nursing scholarships, 52

S

Sallie Mae funding, 129
sample work/project submissions, 80, 331
SAT scores, 83
saving drafts/revisions, 309–310
savings, family, 37
Scholaraid/Student Advantage database, 136–137
Scholarship Coach. *See also* Ask the Coach
  background of, 2–9, 18
  Search Profile Worksheet, 115, 154, 165, 355–356
ScholarshipCoach.com
  about, 15–16, 115–116, 128
  keywords, 15–16, 58, 88–90, 104, 171–172, 196, 216, 234, 252, 284, 304, 322, 339, 363–366
Scholarship Experts database, 137–138
scholarship programs. *See also* programs; scholarships by name
  attention to details, 201–202
  collecting, 199–200
  competition, 215
  customizing your materials, 204–205
  gauging the focus of the award, 200–201
  positioning strategies, 215
  unusual programs, 202–203
Scholarship Resource Network (SRN) database, 138
scholarships. *See also* contests; scholarships by name; searching for scholarships; sources of funding
  for adult/nontraditional students, 66
  for college graduates, 63–64
  definition of, 31
  for graduate students, 64–65
  versus loans, 55
  paying others to find, 130–131
  providers of, 87
  range of available, 60–61
  summary of, 56
  for younger students, 61
Scholarships 101 database, 139–140
scholarships by name. *See also* keywords; programs; scholarships
  Angier B. Duke Memorial Scholarships, 163
  Barbara Thomas Enterprises Scholarship, 66
  Beth K. Fields Scholarship, 160
  Burger King/McLamore North American Scholarship, 79
  Business and Professional Women's Foundation, Career Advancement Scholarship Program, 78
  Citizens' Scholarship Foundation of America (CSFA), 73
  Descendants of the Signers of the Declaration of Independence Scholarship, 76

First Cavalry Division Association Scholarship, 76
Georgia HOPE Scholarship, 69
Harry S Truman Scholarship, 64
Hodson Scholarships, 163
HOPE Scholarship, 44–45, 45, 69
International Study and Travel Center Study Abroad Scholarships, 147
Lilly for Learning Diabetes Scholarship Program, 155
Merit Scholarships, 164
National Honor Society Scholarship, 73
National Scholarship Research Service, 132
Orville Redenbacher's Second Start Scholarship, 66
Robert C. Byrd Honors Scholarship program, 68, 153
ScholarshipsCanada, 144
Swarthmore College, McCabe Scholarships, 164
Talbots Women's Scholarship Fund, 66
University of Chicago College Honor Scholarships, 163
University of Louisville, Beth K. Fields Scholarship, 160
U.S. Senate Youth Program Scholarship, 327
Washington University in St. Louis, Academic Scholarship and Fellowship Programs, 164
"Will to Win" Asthma Athlete Scholarship, 155
ScholarshipsCanada, 144
Scholarship Scouting Report, The (Kaplan), 61, 116
  about, 17
Scholastic Art and Writing Awards, 80
school-specific scholarships, 86, 88–90, 163–164, 171
Science Service, 73
Scientist application theme, 193
search engines, 156–159
searching databases. *See* databases
searching for scholarships. *See also* databases; programs; scholarships by name; websites
  assembling search tools, 115–116
  canvassing your community, 149–152, 170
  casting wide with narrow focus, 110–111
  for future years, 111–112
  getting organized, 112–114
  government sources, 152–154, 170
  "know thyself," 109–110
  other schools' resources, 148–149, 170
  by parents, 93–95, 103
  personal/family affiliations, 154–155, 170
  related organizations and foundations, 165–167, 171
  researching, 108–109
  uncovering school-specific awards, 161–164
  using effective Internet search techniques, 156–159

younger students, 111
  your school's resources, 116–119
secondary application themes, 179–180
secondary Websites, 157–158
Second Start Scholarship (Orville Redenbacher), 66
Selected Reserve, 53–54
self-addressed stamped envelopes, 113
self-portrait. *See* application themes
short answer questions, 80, 281–282
SilverPlatter Information, 135
Simon Fraser University Graduate Awards Database, 145
Soros Foundation, 168
source databases, 124–125
sources of funding. *See also* contests; financial aid; loans; scholarships by name
  colleges/universities/technical/trade schools, 72
  federal government, 67–69, 153–154
  GI Bill, 53
  local businesses, 151
  for merit-based financial aid programs, 55
  private sponsors, 70–71
  Sallie Mae, 129
  special interest associations/foundations, 71
  state governments, 69–70
special interest associations/foundations, 71
specialized awards, 65
spell-checking, 277
spending your merit scholarships, 85–86, 88
SRN Express database, 138
standardized testing
  Advanced Placement (AP), 349–351
  College-Level Examination Program (CLEP), 352
  PSAT scores, 83
  test scores in transcripts, 318–319
Stanford University, 163
state agencies, 69, 357–362
state residence scholarships, 162
stat sheet part of applications, 310–311, 321
strategies
  for adult students, 160
  content, 233–234
  creating opportunities, 225–227
  expanding on strong points, 220–222
  positioning, 198, 215
  shoring up weak areas, 223–224
  time juggling, 222
strategizing by parents, 95–96, 103
stress, avoiding, 333
"Stuck at Prom" scholarship contest, 35
student activity organizations, 71
Student Advantage database, 136–137
Student Awards Scholarship Search, 145
students with disabilities, 79, 155–156
study abroad scholarships, 147–148
submission guidelines, college applications, 290–291

subsidized loans, 31
successful applications, 176–177, 195. *See also* winning applications
supplementary materials, placing with interviewers, 332
support/encouragement from parents, 100, 104
Survivor application theme, 188
Swarthmore College, McCabe Scholarships, 164

T

Talbots Women's Scholarship Fund, 66
Tall Clubs International scholarship, 29
targeted scholarship awards, 87, 205–207
    applicants, 74–75
    college and career goals, 76–77
    employment/activities/hobbies, 79
    family affiliation, 76
    gender-based, 78–79
    geographic region, 75
    organizational membership, 75–76
    people with disabilities, 79, 155–156
    race/ethnicity/religious denomination, 77–78
"Tax Benefits for Higher Education" (IRS publication 970), 46
tax credits, 44–47
taxes, 86, 88
telephone interviews, 337
test results, 83
test scores in transcripts, 318–319
Texas, 69
themes, application. *See* application themes
themes among recommendation letters, 289
time investment for winning scholarships, 249
time juggling, 222
time off from college, 349
tracking details of awards, 347–348, 348
transcripts, 315–319, 322
transferring to another school, 352
tuition reduction, 349
Twain, Mark, 233
typing names of scholarships into search engines, 159
typing your application, 306–307

U

undergraduate college students, 62–64
"underrepresented" students, 68
United Nations, 167
University of Chicago, 72, 163
University of Louisville, Beth K. Fields Scholarship, 160
University of Nebraska, 50
University of North Carolina at Chapel Hill, Morehead Awards, 164
University of Texas at Austin, 72

University of Virginia, Jefferson Scholars, 164
University of Waterloo Scholarship Information File, 145
unsubsidized loans, 31
unsuccessful applications, 176–177, 195
U.S. agency scholarship funding, 68–69
U.S. citizens, 167
U.S. Department of Education, 68
U.S. Department of Veteran Affairs, 53
U.S. News & World Report, 140
U.S. Senate Youth Program Scholarship, 327
U.S. State Department, 168
using recommendation letters for college applications, 290–291

V

variety in application themes, 195
Vermont, 70
veterans associations, 71, 76
veterans' benefits, dependents, 53
Villanova University, 50
visiting other schools, 170
voice, finding your, 266–270
Voice of Democracy contest, 205

W

Washington, Booker T., 188
Washington Crossing Foundation, 77, 301
Washington (state), 69
Washington University in St. Louis, Academic Scholarship and Fellowship Programs, 164
weak areas, shoring up your, 223–224
web-based search engines, 156–159, 170–171. *See also* databases; searching for scholarships
websites
    about keywords for, 15–16
    Academic Research Information System, 134
    for access to Reference Service Press (RSP) database, 136
    Better Business Bureau (BBB), 85
    Canadian students, resources for, 144–145
    CASHE/Wiredscholar database, 128
    College Board/ExPAN database, 129, 161–162
    CollegeLink, 141–142
    CollegeNet, 141–142
    CollegeQuest database, 131
    Cornell University Graduate Fellowship Notebook, 134
    FastAid/National Scholarship Research Service database, 132
    Fastweb, 133
    Federal Trade Commission (FTC), 85
    for finding associations/organizations/groups, 166–167

FreSch database, 134
graduate students, resources for, 134
Grants in Graduate Studies database, 134
International Education Financial Aid, 167
international students, resources for, 167
IRS, 46
minority students, resources for, 139
North Atlantic Regional Schools, 62
North Dakota Division of Independent Study, 62
primary and secondary, 157–158
Scholaraid/Student Advantage database, 136
ScholarshipCoach.com, about, 5–16, 115–116, 128
Scholarship Experts database, 137
Scholarship Resource Network (SRN) database, 138
Scholarships 101 database, 139
search engines, 156–159
study abroad, resources for, 147–148
U.S. News & World Report, 140
Wintergreen/Orchard House (WOH) database, 141–142
Weiss, David, 181
Western Sunbathing Association, 71
William Randolph Hearst Foundation, 70
"Will to Win" Asthma Athlete Scholarship, 155
winning applications, 195. *See also* successful applications
    asking for examples of, 199
    excerpt, 205
    sources of samples of, 249
winning essays, examples of, 267–270
Wintergreen/Orchard House (WOH) database, 141–142
Wiredscholar database, 128–129
Wooden, John, 230
word limits for essays, 259
word usage in applications, 311–312
working in your school's scholarship center, 118
work-study programs, 47–48
World Council of Churches, 168
World Health Organization (WHO), 168
writing ability, 254
writing essays. *See* essays

Y

younger students, 220–222, 234
    contests for, 60
    preparation of, 227
    scholarships for, 61
    searching for scholarships, 111
youth-oriented organizations, 75

Z

zooming in on topics, 272–273

Other Great Scholarship Resources!

Multi CD Set

Audiobook: How to Go to College Almost for Free
This must-have audiobook features additional material—including anecdotes, examples, interviews, and insights—not found in the standard print edition of *How to Go to College Almost for Free*. Produced in a lively workshop-style format that highlights the entertaining speaking style of Ben Kaplan, it is the perfect complement to the print edition and ideal to listen to in your car, by your computer, between classes, while jogging, or as part of a group learning environment.

Special Report

The Scholarship Coach™ Guide to Online Searching
If you don't have a lot of time to waste searching for scholarships online, then this special report is the turbo boost you need. The electronic report, which is available for immediate Internet download, goes beyond the material covered in *How to Go to College Almost for Free* by profiling a series of prototypical students as they go step-by-step through an online scholarship search. These illuminating case studies reveal exactly where to go and what to do. Key information is documented for each scholarship unearthed in the case studies to save you time and energy. The report also features important scholarship website listings for students with specific academic and extracurricular interests.

Essay Critiques

The Scholarship Coach™ Guide to Essay Contests
Jump inside the scholarship judging process to observe how and why certain essays won the college cash and others didn't. This downloadable electronic report features interviews with scholarship essay judges and official judging critiques of actual essays submitted to the annual Scholarship Coach National Tour Awards scholarship program. With this important guide by your side, you'll be able to craft better essays in less time—essays that result in high marks from the decision makers who evaluate them.

Learning Tools

The Scholarship Coach™ Ultimate Course Guide
Schools across the nation have shared Ben Kaplan's proven scholarship methodology with their students. Now with this superb course guide to *How to Go to College Almost for Free,* you'll have all the essential teaching materials at your fingertips—including lesson plans, exercises, and assignments—to teach others how to find and win scholarships, or to conduct your own self-administered scholarship course. This creative course guide is quite simply the essential teaching tool that every high school, college, educator, guidance counselor, and proactive parent should put to use.

Preview & order these special products at ScholarshipCoach.com

SCHOLARSHIP COACH.com
Your personal adviser for winning college cash

ABOUT THE AUTHOR

BEN KAPLAN won more than two dozen merit-based scholarships—accumulating nearly $90,000 in scholarship funds for use at any college. In 1999, he graduated from Harvard University magna cum laude with a degree in economics, completing his degree in six academic semesters. Virtually the entire cost of his college education had been covered by his scholarship winnings.

In addition to *How to Go to College Almost for Free*, Kaplan is the author of *The Scholarship Scouting Report*, an insider's guide to the nation's top scholarship opportunities. Kaplan has also written numerous articles on winning scholarships, including columns for the *New York Times* and *U.S. News & World Report*, which have been syndicated in publications nationwide. He has been featured on hundreds of television and radio programs, including appearances on *The Oprah Winfrey Show*, National Public Radio, NBC, and CNN.

Known as "The Scholarship Coach," Kaplan has advised many thousands of students and parents on college scholarships, financial aid, and personal growth. He has served as the resident scholarship adviser at some of the Internet's most popular scholarship search websites, and is the founder of ScholarshipCoach.com, the leading online scholarship advice portal. His annual Scholarship Coach National Tour brings unique college scholarship and financial aid workshops to students, parents, and guidance counselors across the nation.

In 1996, Kaplan attended both the Democratic and Republican National Conventions and wrote a series of political commentaries from the youth perspective for *The Oregonian* and the *Boston Globe* newspapers. He also co-authored the book and lyrics for the Hasty Pudding Theatricals' 151st annual musical "I Get No Kick from Campaign."

Prior to college, Kaplan attended South Eugene High School in Eugene, Oregon, where he played varsity tennis, served as student body president and editor of his school newspaper, and founded the "Homework Helpline" telephone tutoring service. Among other awards and honors, he was selected the "Top Student Leader in America" by the National Association of Secondary School Principals.

Kaplan currently resides in Oregon and can be contacted via e-mail at Ben@ScholarshipCoach.com. For more information, visit BenKaplan.com.